WEDLOCK –

THE FIRST HERO OF BRISTOL CITY

D.P. HURLEY

ADDITIONAL RESEARCH
AND EDITING BY

DAVID WOODS
(OFFICIAL HISTORIAN,
BRISTOL CITY FC)

BRISTOL CITY OFFICIAL PROGRAMME

WEDLOCK, The Wonderful.

We tender no apologies for devoting the columns of this programme to our popular captain, for has not the day been set apart with the object of affording his many admirers an opportunity of showing in some tangible form their appreciation of his services to the game of Association football. Bristolians claim him as their own despite the many calls made by the Mother Country upon his services, calls that have brought him every honour that the football world can bestow.

William Wedlock was born within sight of the Bristol City football ground. It has

ing in their ranks. Wedlock has great recollections of the time when he first donned the Red and White. Leinster Payne allowed Ashton Gate to play a trial match on the second rope-race, and the game was played on that part of the ground where now is laid the excellent green of the Bristol Bowling Club. So well did "Fatty" show that he was included in the side against Millwall (Southern League) away and Queen's Park Rangers (Western League) also in London.

The following season next-time he moved to Aberdare. Why such a football genius should have been allowed to leave his native home must remain a mystery. Possibly the fact that the great football genius Hugh Wilson, occupied the centre-half position, had more than a little to do with what must be a matter of general regret.

Aberdare boasted his services for four years, and whilst with the Welshmen he scored no less than twenty goals in one season from the centre-half position, and assisted them in carrying off the South Wales

For my Dad, who first showed me that the 'Red' road was the right road to follow…

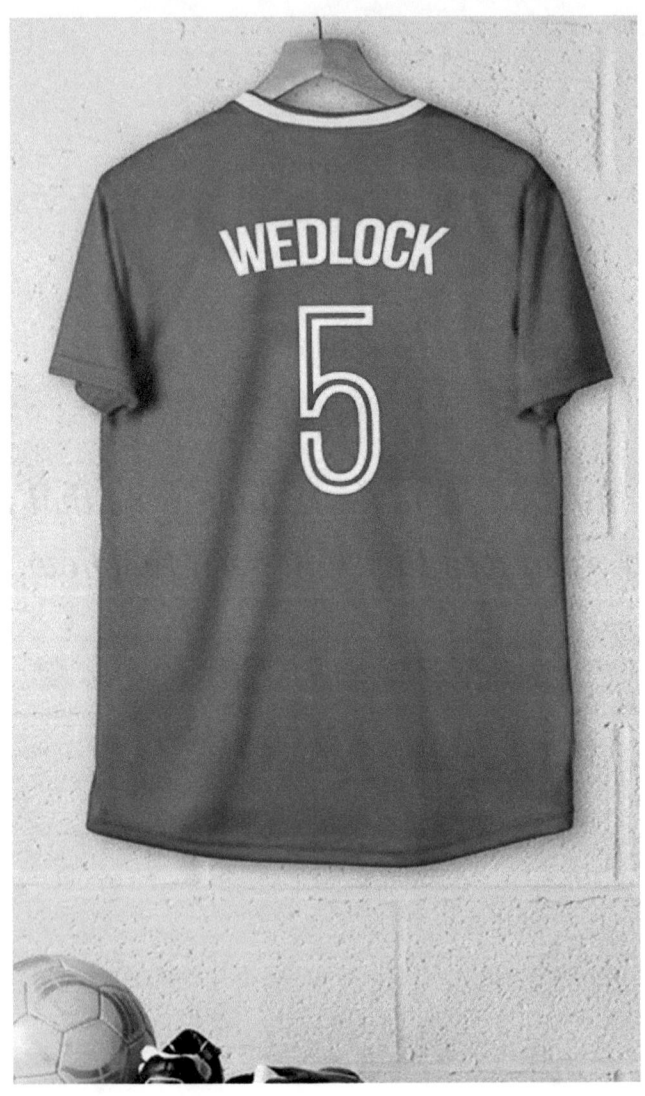

"I would rather have a team of genuine tryers to lead on the field any day, than a side of brilliant stars, not all of whom were workers in the real sense of the word. It is the flyers who sometimes win matches, but they more often lose them. To every young player going into the game I would say – cut the fancy work and never forget that speed isn't everything"

(William J Wedlock, November 1924)

First published in 2019 by

Darren Hurley @ Passage House Books

c/o Billy Wedlock Online,
go to billywedlockonline.co.uk

© Darren Hurley 2019

The right of Darren Hurley to be identified as the Author of the Work has been asserted by him in accordance with the Copyright, Designs and Patents Act 1988.

ISBN 978-0-9566263-2-5

British Library Cataloguing-in-Publication Data
A catalogue record for this book is available from the British Library
All rights reserved. Except for the purpose of a review, no part of this book may be reproduced, stored in a retrieval system, or transmitted, in any form or by any means, electronic, mechanical, photocopying, recording or otherwise, without the prior permission of the publishers.

This book was printed in Peterborough, Cambs, England

and was distributed by Lulu.com

www.lulu.com

DAVID WOODS WOULD LIKE TO POINT OUT THAT THE COVER PHOTO OF BILLY WEDLOCK ON THE FIELD OF PLAY IS HISTORICALLY INACCURATE, BECAUSE THIS IS A REPRESENTATION OF THE 1909 FA CUP FINAL, WHEN OF COURSE, BRISTOL CITY FAMOUSLY WORE BLUE.

Cover Design by the Author.

CONTENTS

Introduction..IX

Foreword (By Richard Latham)..............XXI

1. *1909 and all that*..1

2. *Bedminster beginnings*............................21

3. *In demand*..41

4. *He who Dares*..61

5. *Two sides of the Severn*............................81

6. *Up, up and away*.....................................105

7. *The rise of the Babes' –*
   an unforgettable journey!......................127

8. *On his way to the Palace*........................151

9. *Against the tide and on the slide*..........179

10. *The darkest hour*...................................201

11. *England expects*.....................................225

12. *A Bridge too far*.....................................251

13. *A Red Sky at Night*...............................277

    'Triers', tributes and testimonials....305

WITH HIS INTERNATIONAL TEAM-MATES AS THE ENGLAND SQUAD PREPARES TO FACE SCOTLAND AT HAMPDEN PARK ON APRIL 4TH 1908. WEDLOCK IS SEATED ON THE LEFT OF THE FRONT ROW.

Introduction (by the Author)

"What about Fatty?"

Back in the year 2005, I was the fascinated reader of a brand new publication called '*Atyeo – The Hero Next Door*' – I won't go into too much detail regarding the subject, as, for loyal followers of Bristol City (at least, those of a 'certain generation') – this will need little explanation. It was of course, a book telling the life story of the late, great John Atyeo, by a country mile the greatest and most famous Bristol City idol of the post-war era (of that, there is *no doubt*). When I eventually finished it, I put the book down and thought "*Wow! Great! Brilliant! Now then.....what about WEDLOCK?*"

To me, this now became the last remaining piece of the Bristol City jigsaw. That is to say, of the *historical* jigsaw. I thought to myself – *"Who's going to do it? And when?"* Nearly 15 years later, it so happened that I found myself *still waiting...*

To my everlasting surprise, no-one had ever got around to *'tackling it'*. In a way, it is perhaps easy to understand why. The passage of time has not been easy on William Wedlock. We have had *reminders* of course – the pub...the stand...the '*Wedlock Wall*'. Occasional pub anecdotes, whispered legendary tales of yesteryear...

But not a *book*. Not a comprehensive *life story*, as such...

Yes, time has not ran smoothly for Wedlock. In 2005, there remained a sizable band of 'senior' City fans *still around* who had actually seen John Atyeo *play*. Their accounts were *first-hand*. This couldn't be said with regards

WEDLOCK – THE FIRST HERO OF BRISTOL CITY

the case of Billy Wedlock. And today, there is practically no-one still alive who can claim to have seen *'Fatty'* in his element, on the field of play – that's even if they had bore witness to the dying embers of his professional career.
A problem? Maybe. Football fans sometimes are 'capable' of reminiscing only *so far* back...

Yet here's the strange thing – had Billy Wedlock known that a book was being written about him, I believe he would have been frankly embarrassed. For when it came to talking of his own accomplishments, he was famously the man of few words, always changing the subject onto something else. He could chat about the achievements of *the team* of course, and would be happy to talk about the game of football all day long – but so rarely about *himself*. I get the feeling that Billy simply believed he was merely an honest guy just doing his job – albeit a job he thoroughly enjoyed, representing a club he genuinely *loved*...

But I am one of those who felt that there *had* to be a book about Wedlock. At least at some point in time. *Eventually.* There are now new generations of supporters growing up, walking up and down *'Wedlock Way'* every other Saturday, and not noticing – or even *knowing*...

Other groups of supporters are aware of the fact that there *used to be* a pub opposite the ground, called **'Wedlock's'** – but aren't sure *why*, or what the history or true significance of the building was. Before the re-build of the Ashton Gate stadium began in 2014, everyone was aware that the old *'East End'* of the ground was by then known as the *'Wedlock*

INTRODUCTION – BY THE AUTHOR

Stand' – but how many knew *why*? (I remember viewing a Bristol City internet chat-room forum, and one supporter was bemoaning the fact that the '*East End*' was no longer known as the '*East End*'...and continuing his rant, proceeded to claim that company sponsorships, meaning the *'Wedlock'* Stand, ought to keep their sponsors' deals to themselves!
Now this alone is one good reason why there had to be a book on Billy!)

But there was actually a double-incentive for writing this book. Aside from my longstanding interest in Wedlock, I had also harboured a long-term fascination with the '*Glory Years*' Bristol City teams of 1906 – 1911. Now this had been running a long while indeed...
Even as a young child, I remember being told by my grandfather that Bristol City, for an all-too-brief period, had at one time been one of the leading clubs in the land. They had apparently been First Division runners-up and had reached the FA Cup Final. This all seemed highly unlikely, and not a little far-fetched to me! But later on, I got a rather dog-eared copy of Peter Godsiff's '*History of Bristol City*', and there it was in black and white – all true! And I started to read far-off stories of Willis Rippon, Fred Staniforth, '*Cocky*' Bennett and Billy Wedlock – I was hooked!
All those years on, the chance to write about Wedlock, coupled with the prospect of further exploration of City's legendary Edwardian team, presented a temptation simply too good to miss! Proverbially-speaking, it was one of those classic cases of '*Two birds with one stone*'!

WEDLOCK – THE FIRST HERO OF BRISTOL CITY

Having finally decided to take on the onerous task of what looked on paper to appear a somewhat formidable project, I soon came to realise that the extensive research required was to prove, unsurprisingly, a draining and exhausting experience. Yes, even in the WWW era of the *information superhighway*, the searching was long, tiring and laborious. But (forgive the *cliché*) – it was also ultimately *rewarding*. There were so many surprises along the way...

* The fact that Wedlock, despite being a centre-half, was not really a *defender* at all...(Well! I really did *not* know that!)

* The fact that Wedlock had a long-running England international 'rivalry' with one Charlie Roberts, of Manchester United. (Back in the day, if you were a football journalist, you had to take sides, and you were either one, or the other – a Wedlock man or a Roberts man). However, rather like the Blur / Oasis rock feud of the 1990's, it soon became apparent that this 'duel' had actually been a storm whipped up by the media more than anything else, and any genuine bad feeling between the two players in question was almost certainly non-existent. Wedlock himself *confimed* this fact when he once said *"Charlie was a lovely player and a lovely fellow"*.

* The fact that Wedlock was also an outstanding *cricketer*, and at one time used to spend twelve months of the year playing on the hallowed turf at Ashton Gate - winter for football, summer for cricket. (Again - something that was *new* to me!)

* The fact that Wedlock *did not* spend practically the whole of season 1900/01 playing for Bristol City's Reserve team – before his move to Aberdare. (*Really?* That's not what I had heard!) Or *did he*? We shall explore that later in the book...

INTRODUCTION – BY THE AUTHOR

* The fact that Wedlock *did not* retire from professional football in 1921, to then immediately take up residence in *'The Star Inn'* public house (He had already been there for a long time before that...)

All of these revelations, and many others, took this story into different directions, involving twists and turns I had never been expecting to take.

Yet if there were surprises, there were also rumours *confirmed*. I never knew a massive amount about Fatty Wedlock at the start, but from what I *did* know, the legends all spoke of Billy's tendency for *sporting* behaviour, his desire to 'play the game' *fair*, to accept the decisions of the referee, to help others, and – in general – rumours abounded of a jolly decent, likable all-round guy. Yet the further I got into the research, the sooner I began to realise that the rumours, far from being exaggerated, had - if *anything* – been considerably *understated*...

With hindsight, it soon became my opinion that even if you had taken away Billy's entire sporting career, relieved him of his club captaincy, took Bristol City FC off the map, and stripped him of his 26 England caps – you would still be left with Wedlock, the *human being*, Wedlock the model of manners, Wedlock the humble, Wedlock the modest, Wedlock the conscientious *thinker-of-others* –

'Wedlock the Wonderful'...

By the end of the research, my perception of Billy had *changed* considerably. I had *expected* a decent player and a 'nice character'. But what I *found* was a *great* player and a magnificent man, an infectious personality, an almost-pristine persona and a hugely likable character of great integrity. This man was *good to the bone*. He had humanity and humility from his soul to his fingertips. And it began to dawn on me that, even without having seen him play, William Wedlock was fast-becoming my favourite player, the footballing hero I never even knew I had...

Yet for every revelation *unearthed*, for every new surprise *unveiled*, there was to be *one thing* left undiscovered – because generally, for every rule, there is an exception...

...Wedlock's most famous and iconic nickname. '*Fatty*'.

So why '*Fatty*' Wedlock exactly? Yes, many people may have heard that when he stopped playing professionally, Billy piled on the pounds somewhat. But the '*Fatty*' tag had been hanging around for a long, long time before that...

He had been known by this less-than-flattering sobriquet from at least as far back as his Aberdare days, when he had been in his early 20's. Yet all photos available from the prime of his sporting career appear to show Wedlock being as slim and trim as they come. So WHY '*Fatty*'?

My research into this specific area ultimately, drew a blank. Well. A *relative* blank. There were snippets and little clues, but not much more. My *personal* feeling is this – that Wedlock the *footballer* knew he had a potential problem with the pounds and ounces, and he was – *candidly* speaking – a 'fat man' simply waiting to happen. Henceforth, Wedlock then set a personal 'target weight' between the months of August and May (the football season), during which time he made

INTRODUCTION – BY THE AUTHOR

absolutely certain not to go through the self-imposed threshold. This situation of course, would have led to regular trips to the Ashton Gate scales, and with professional footballers being what *they are*, and understanding the dressing room banter that goes hand-in-hand with the nature of the sport, it is not difficult to imagine how good-natured teasing and giggling at Billy's expense may well have escalated into full-blown *'Fatty-dom'!* Having said all this, it should be re-stated – that the 'Fatty' tag had *definitely* followed him from Aberdare, and accounts of the era *seem* to suggest that he was slightly 'plumper' when playing in south Wales than would be the case when he was turning out – *professionally* - for Bristol City. At Aberdare in fact, the local media rarely referred to Billy using his Christian name, always preferring – with much regularity – *'Fatty Wedlock'*.
In September 1904, one of the leading Welsh newspapers wrote of Billy *"though short of stature, he possesses the girth of a Hercules, while his love of work is such as to impel him to be all over the field. It is no unhappy sobriquet that of the 'Ubiquitous Fatty', which has been conferred upon him by his host of admirers!"*

The 40-plus year era of Billy's time at the *Star Inn* pub (AKA *'Wedlock's'*) does not form a large part of the book. Whilst there may be a fair amount of older fans out there who can recount many a legendary story concerning Wedlock behind the bar, I felt that these were potentially the stories that everyone *already knew* – the England caps on show in a mahogany case, displayed on the wall behind the bar, etc.

WEDLOCK – THE FIRST HERO OF BRISTOL CITY

These were the legends that were *already* familiar with many – I felt it was my remit to showcase the earlier stories, the ones that people were not so familiar with...

Despite a lot of work on my own, there has been help along the way. A number of organisations and individuals are much deserving of my gratitude. I would like to thank some of them now. The **British Archive Newspaper website** – which probably accounted for about 80% of the sum total of research, and, without whom, I wouldn't have been able to get through Chapter One, let alone write an entire book!
(They won't be reading, but - Thankyou!)
The **Bristol Record Office,** for general help, and for the use of photographs.
Peter Godsiff and his book '*Bristol City – The Complete History of the Club*' – which was the original inspiration from my childhood, and which even today remains an indispensable source of research – and a cracking read! Thanks Peter!
David Woods. Your help has been completely *invaluable*. Without your numerous Bristol City publications over the years, I wouldn't have been able to even get started. Statistically-speaking, these were and *are* essential reading, and crucial for fact-checking. Chief among these books was '*Bristol City – A Complete Record 1894 – 1987*' and '*The Bristol Babe*', published in 1994. Covering the years 1894 to 2007, David's series of '*Desert Island*' books was also simply indispensable for match-checking, and these are highly recommended to all Bristol City fans out there. Mr Woods has

INTRODUCTION – BY THE AUTHOR

also kindly provided a good deal of photographs for this project, including a number of the 'Cup Final images'.
David, thanks for agreeing to be a part of this project, for all your valuable time used up on editing, fact-checking, proof-reading - and for general (*massive!*) help. Thankyou!
Thanks also go to my old friend **Damian Stone** for his vital contributions which were gratefully received at the eleventh hour.
Love and thanks to **S, L & J Davies**, in the '*Wedlock Engine-room*', for their long hours of help and patience!
Thanks also to **Clive Burlton** of *Bristol Books*, and to **Harrison Wedlock** for his vital snippets of information.
Last but certainly not least, **Richard Latham,** for so much help and advice, for giving up his own valuable time, and for agreeing to be associated with this project. Thankyou Richard!

Finally, this, ultimately – is a book for families. That is to say, it is a book for the Wedlock family, and a book for the wider Bristol City 'family'. I hope the reader enjoys the reading part just as much as I enjoyed (*cough!*) the writing part!

Whether this book proves to be a *success*, and whether I have done the great man *justice*, I don't know - that is for others to decide. We shall see, but I do know *one thing* for sure – I tried my best. Yes. I *tried*. And this is the whole irony really. Because if there's one thing that Billy Wedlock appreciated, almost more than anything else, it was certainly that *very* thing – a '*trier*'...

DARREN HURLEY – AUGUST 2019

"...I believe above all that he values the fact that he has been able to do so much for his beloved Bristol City..."

W. WEDLOCK.

"Fatty" Wedlock.

A Jack-in-the-box, a non-stopper, a nuisance to eleven men on some field every Saturday, and a very present help in time of trouble to ten others. You can sum up the captain of Bristol City after that fashion. Like Bobs, he's little, but a terror. One of the most keenly anticipated meetings of last season was the encounter in the Cup Final between Wedlock and the man whose place he had taken in England's team—Charlie Roberts. Five feet eleven and a half versus five feet four and a half, if you please. "Fatty" did his level best, and was game to the last, but it has to be confessed that that time the believers in the old proverb "A good big un's better than a good little 'un," were justified. The comparison was too close to give Wedlock a proper chance. I call Wedlock a man of the moment because he appears to have just come back to form. He has been good all the season, yet not quite himself. On Saturday he "arrived," and Blackburn Rovers had the narrowest squeak imaginable of being defeated at Bristol. Let's hope, as Bristol City's followers most fervently do, that Wedlock will keep it up and, what is more, succeed in imbuing his comrades with his own unquenchable spirit. Wedlock is a born centre-half. He must be where there's always work to do. A Bedminster lad, he joined the City from Aberdare in 1905. Two years later he became England's centre-half. Since then England has used no other. Wedlock is a good cricketer as well as footballer, and there is some talk of his playing for Gloucestershire one day.

WEDLOCK
BRISTOL CITY

FOREWORD

"Everyone associated with Bristol City for any length of time knows the name of Billy Wedlock, the club's most capped England player, not least because of the pub and later the stand at Ashton Gate that were named after him. We smile at the fact that, despite being nicknamed 'Fatty' and standing just 5ft 4ins tall, he somehow forged an outstanding career as a centre-half, and picture a tiny figure in bagging pants springing like a Jack-in-the-Box to win headers against towering forwards, who could almost fit him in their pockets...

It wasn't quite like that, as Darren Hurley's fascinating study reveals. Wedlock was, in fact, a centre half-back in the days of 2-3-5 formations and in no way an outright defender. Indeed, winning the ball in the air was just one of his roles, along with sharp tackling, turning defence into attack and linking up with his forwards like a box-to-box midfielder in the modern game.

We are talking about more than a century ago, before the Great War, when football managers wore bowler hats above their suits, waistcoats and watch chains, and players enjoying a team night out often sported bow ties. A hugely different world and a very different game, which it is all too easy to belittle from the small amount of grainy film footage available. Anyone tempted to do so will find from this book that Wedlock and his contemporaries were every bit as important to the fans as their more glamorous counterparts today...

WEDLOCK – THE FIRST HERO OF BRISTOL CITY

...When Billy earned one of his 26 England caps against Scotland at Hampden Park, the attendance was 121,452.

A Bedminster boy, written off by many as too small to play football professionally, Wedlock had risen from humble beginnings in amateur football to be the pride of club and country, representing his beloved Bristol City in the top flight of English football and leading them to the 1909 FA Cup Final. Darren Hurley writes with the enthusiasm of a fan and knowledge that only comes from diligent research about the life, on and off the pitch, of a man renowned as much for his sense of fair play as his outstanding ability.

I quickly realised that, despite having chronicled City's fortunes for 40 years as a reporter, I knew precious little about Wedlock the man or the footballer. I commend this book to supporters everywhere as an appropriate celebration of a player worthy of mention in the same breath as John Atyeo when it comes to the very greatest to have donned a Robins shirt".

RICHARD LATHAM

"It has been said of Queen Mary that she protested the word *Calais* was written on her heart.
I fully believe *Bristol City* is written on the heart of Wedlock"

"Ours is a team of *triers* to a man. We will work very hard…"

XXIV

1] 1909 and all that....

It was the greatest of days, it was the worst of days, it was the dual of destiny, it was the dual of dubiety, it was the Final of fate, it was the Final of fear, it was the season of sublimity, it was the season of sobriety, it was the Spring of hope, it was the Spring of despair, they had *everything* before them, they had *nothing* before them, they were destined for glory, they were fated for defeat. *This* was the hour that dreams would be made of – yet this was the hour that dreams would be shattered...

And *this* was the day that Billy Wedlock had been *born* for... Bristol City versus Manchester United in the English Cup Final, at the Crystal Palace, in London, the capital of the world! Wedlock, 5 feet 4 inches tall, 10 stone 7 lbs in weight, the unlikeliest footballing hero, leading *his* team, his Bristol team, into the biggest match of all, in London, against their great Northern rivals.
At 28 years of age, Wedlock was at the peak of his powers. Surely now, his time had finally come. His career was in its prime, *this* is what it had all been gearing towards, his whole life had been hurtling headlong to this one date with destiny...
Yet the road to *'The Palace'* had been a long one. It had been an emotional one. Including replays, it had taken the City *nine matches* to reach the final. In contrast, it had taken United only five.
Back in January, Southampton had been the visitors to Ashton Gate in the very first round. 20,000 Bristolians had packed the ground to see the Saints rolled over. But the Saints would not roll over. The Saints proved to be stubborn. *Very stubborn.*

WEDLOCK – THE FIRST HERO OF BRISTOL CITY

Star striker Willis Rippon had netted for City in the first half, but it was 1-1 at the break. Andrew Burton had then found himself with a glorious chance to win it for City with only two minutes remaining of the second half, but his penalty was superbly saved by Lock. Burton would not get another chance from the spot when City were *again* awarded a penalty in the replay, the following week. Willis Rippon was selected *instead*, he scored it, and City led 1-0 at half-time. Hardy finished off the Saints' in the second half, and City had won 2-0 to secure their *first-ever* victory at The Dell. Bury had then come to Ashton Gate for round two – 24,000 Bristolians had scented blood. But - another draw. 2-2. Another replay. Gilligan then scored the only goal and City had won 1-0. In the third round, it was the turn of Norwich City to visit Ashton Gate. It had been the Robins versus the Canaries. There had been 24,009 people in attendance, 24,009 natives baying for blood...
Bang! Andrew Burton had struck for Bristol - 1-0 to the Red side at half-time!
Bang! Willis Rippon had doubled the lead, 2-0 to Bristol City at the final whistle. Wedlock's boys had made it through to the quarters. Wedlock's boys were in the last eight.
On March 6th, 4,500 hardy souls had braved the blizzards at Glossop – but to no avail. 0-0. There had to be yet another replay. So 16,000 came for the re-match at Ashton Gate. 16,000 locals came to roar Wedlock's boys to victory. Gilligan had popped up with the only goal in the second-half, and City were in the semis. Derby County had then awaited the Bristol *'Babes'* at Stamford Bridge, London, the home of Chelsea FC. A neutral ground for a crucial fixture. 33,878 had been in attendance. What a match!

1909 AND ALL THAT...

What drama!
They could have written books about this one! There could have been a Shakespearean drama concerning this one! City had been a goal down with only seconds left on the clock. And then – HANDBALL! Penalty to City!! The last kick of the game. It had been a *'score or die'* situation. A one-kick shoot-out. Wedlock and his City boys could barely look, as Willis Rippon, the coolest head in the stadium, stepped up...
GOAL!! A goal for City, an equaliser for City!! And the final whistle was immediately blown. Another replay...
Birmingham FC would play host for the re-match. St Andrews was the venue, 27,600 was the attendance, with many, perhaps *thousands*, from Bristol...
...*Déjà vu* - once again, Rippon would prove to be the City penalty hero, this time netting a spot-kick to give City the lead just before half-time. Derby though, grabbed a second-half equaliser, and the game had appeared to be in the balance. But Fred Staniforth was working his magic out on the right-wing. In the second half, he had teased and tormented the defenders of Derby County with his speed, dribbling and general clever play. He had weaved and dribbled, and had teased and tormented. He had ran and had passed, and had crossed and had shot. He had led the defenders of Derby County on a merry dance, and by the close of the game they were practically begging for mercy. Staniforth and his City team mates pummelled the Derby boys into submission, and when Fred's decisive low cross came over in the second half, Andrew Burton allowed the ball to run through his legs, he knew that Bob Hardy was approaching behind him, in a better position to score. Hardy made no mistake, though sprinting at such high pace that

WEDLOCK – THE FIRST HERO OF BRISTOL CITY

both man and ball ended up tangled in the back of the net.
The final whistle had brought scenes of delirium, City had won 2-1 and were in the final, in their *first* final - where an old foe awaited...
Manchester...Manchester...
Manchester United was that foe.
Manchester United was that enemy.
It had all started back in the autumn of 1905, on September 2nd - at Bank Street, Clayton, the home of the Red Devils.
The home of Manchester United.
Charlie Roberts was the captain of Manchester United, Charlie Roberts, six feet tall, as thin as a rake, a classic looking centre-half.
Billy Wedlock was the captain of Bristol City, and Billy Wedlock was *not* a classic looking centre-half, Billy Wedlock, of Bedminster, was short and stout. *Not* six feet tall, *not* as thin as a rake. Charlie Roberts had then been at Manchester United for a year, whereas Billy Wedlock, as far as Bristol City was concerned, had just arrived.
September 2nd 1905, where it had all began. At Bank Street, Clayton, Manchester – the home of Manchester United. The first match of the season, the 1905/06 season, in Division Two, of the English Football League. At Bank Street. With 25,000 people in attendance. And Bristol City went two goals down half-time. And Wedlock's boys were shell-shocked. Wedlock's boys did not know what had hit them. And it was 5-1 to United at the final whistle. 5-1! At Bank Street. 5-1 to Manchester United! In the opening game of the season. On Billy Wedlock's debut. In Billy Wedlock's first match for Bristol City. A farce. A humiliation. 5-1. *5-1!*
But Billy Wedlock would not forget this. And the Bristol City team

1909 AND ALL THAT...

would not forget. And Harry Thickett, the new Bristol City manager, would not forget. 5-1. *5-1!*
And when Charlie Roberts brought his Manchester United team to Ashton Gate, for the return match at the end of December, Bristol City could not gain revenge for their hiding. A draw. 1-1. A draw, but *not* revenge. Despite the recent record-equalling run of 14 straight wins which had propelled Wedlock's boys to the top of the league. A record which had been set during the previous season by – *Manchester United.* A draw, but not revenge. Not revenge for the 5-1 autumn humiliation that had been dumped unceremoniously onto Billy Wedlock's debut...at Bank Street, Clayton, in Manchester, in front of 25,000 onlookers.
But come the end of the season, and Bristol City would have the last laugh - *champions.* Runaway Champions of Division Two. Promotion gained to Division One for the first time in their history – with Charlie Roberts, and Manchester United, also promoted – but in *second place.* And the following season, it was *Bristol* who had gone from strength to strength. And Wedlock's outstanding performances for City had gained the attention of the England international selectors. And henceforth, Billy Wedlock made his international debut in February 1907, when England beat the Irish by a goal to nil, at Goodison Park, the home of Everton FC.
And Billy Wedlock had played for England again. And *again.* And *again*. Billy Wedlock was playing for England. Billy Wedlock, of Bedminster, was playing *regularly* for England. But Charlie Roberts, of Manchester United, was *not* playing for England. Roberts had played three times for England in 1905. But Roberts was not playing for England anymore. The reason he was not playing for England anymore, was that Billy Wedlock was playing

WEDLOCK – THE FIRST HERO OF BRISTOL CITY

for England. And Billy Wedlock, of Bedminster, was a centre-half. And Charlie Roberts, of Manchester United, was a centre-half. And they could not *both* play as centre-half. Not at the *same time*. And the England selectors preferred Billy Wedlock as their centre-half. Billy Wedlock, of Bristol City. Billy Wedlock, of Bedminster. And not Charlie Roberts, of Manchester United. Not Charlie Roberts, of Darlington, County Durham. And Wedlock *justified* his international selection. His performances for Bristol City, in Division One, were outstanding. And Bristol City would finish up in second place in season 1906/07. At the end of their first-ever campaign in the top flight. And they very nearly finished at the top of the table, which would have landed them the League Championship. They would have become Champions of England. *Nearly*. Very nearly. But Newcastle United had just too much in the tank for the West Countrymen. And *Newcastle* finished as Champions. And Bristol City finished as runners-up. But Manchester United were *nowhere*. Nowhere. They had finished in *eighth*. That was well behind Bristol City. Well behind Wedlock's boys.

The following season however, would see roles reversed. In 1907/08, it was *Bristol City* who would finish nowhere. They would finish in tenth. In no-man's land. But Charlie Roberts and his Manchester United boys were riding high at the top of the table. They finished the season as *Champions*. It was their first-ever League Championship victory. And Billy Wedlock, Billy Wedlock and his Bristol boys finished *nowhere*.

But then Billy Wedlock was playing for England. And Charlie Roberts was *not* playing for England. Billy Wedlock, of Bedminster, and of Bristol City, was playing for England.

1909 AND ALL THAT...

And Charlie Roberts, of Darlington, County Durham, and of Manchester United, was *not* playing for England. Charlie Roberts was not favoured by the Football Association. Charlie Roberts wanted to help set up a Union for professional footballers. Charlie Roberts provoked the wrath of the FA by daring to wear his shorts above his knees! But Billy Wedlock did not particularly care about the length of *his* shorts. The FA preferred Billy Wedlock. Charlie Roberts was tall and thin. Billy Wedlock was short and stout. But Billy Wedlock could out-jump *any man*. He was the '*India Rubber Man*'. The FA liked Wedlock. They *preferred* Wedlock. Wedlock was not a troublemaker. And he could out-jump *any man*. But then Roberts was a *Champion*. He had been an English Football League Champion at the end of 1907/08. As the captain of Manchester United. And Wedlock had *not* been a champion. Wedlock had only been a *runner-up*, at the end of 1906/07. As the captain of Bristol City.

But the following season, 1908/09 – the season after Manchester United had become Champions of England – would be a little different again. And Bristol City would gain a scrap of consolation for their recent slide down the table - for their run of indifferent form against their Lancastrian rivals. And when Wedlock's boys went to Bank Street, Clayton, in Manchester – the home of Charlie Roberts' Manchester boys – Andrew Burton scored a goal after 35 minutes for the visitors. And Manchester United could not reply. And Charlie Roberts' boys were finally defeated. On Good Friday. Defeated by Bristol City. By Billy Wedlock and his Bristol boys. By a score of 1-0. Not a victory by five goals to one – but a victory all the same. At last. Their first top-flight victory over Manchester United. In front of 18,000 spectators. On April 9th 1909. Their first

WEDLOCK – THE FIRST HERO OF BRISTOL CITY

victory over Roberts' Manchester boys since that infamous humiliation three and a half years earlier. September 2nd 1905. Wedlock's debut. 5-1. Humbled, humiliated. *5-1.* City manager Harry Thickett had not forgotten. Bristol City's players had not forgotten. And Billy Wedlock, Billy Wedlock of Bedminster, had not forgotten. Billy Wedlock and his Bristol boys had *never* forgotten. And three days later, on Easter Monday, April 12th, Charlie Roberts had brought his United troops to Ashton Gate for the return fixture, only twelve days before the English FA Cup Final, at the Palace, in London – the capital of the world. And 20,000 football fans had packed into Ashton Gate to see the encounter, knowing they would be watching the Cup Finalists in-waiting...
But to the huge disappointment of the big crowd, *this* game finished goal-less. And onlookers could see no indication of how the big game in London might go. And Bristol City would finish in eighth position in the Football League table. In Division One. A respectable eighth. But Manchester United would only finish in *thirteenth* place. Lower than Bristol City. There would only be a single point between the two clubs. But Bristol City, Wedlock's boys, finished in eighth place, and Manchester United, Roberts' boys, finished in thirteenth. *Nowhere.* But then Manchester United had been crowned English Champions only twelve months earlier - when *Bristol City* had finished nowhere. And for that reason, many people regarded *them* (United) as being the slight favourites for the English FA Cup Final. At the Palace. At the Crystal Palace, in London, the capital of the world.
But not *everyone* made them favourites.
Billy Wedlock, of Bedminster, did not make them favourites. Billy Wedlock regarded his *Bristol boys* as the favourites. Billy Wedlock

1909 AND ALL THAT…

believed that his Bristol City team would win. In his *head*. Because Billy Wedlock would not always tell you what he was thinking. He was a man of few words. He refused to make rash predictions. The weekend before the Cup Final, Wedlock had spent a day or two in south Wales, meeting up with old friends. He had been hero-worshipped in Aberdare, when playing football for *them*, previous to his days with Bristol City. In fact, it was always said of Wedlock, that *"never has a player been more idolised in the Aberdare district".* And when, on that same weekend, he took in a rugby match, played between Maesteg and Mountain Ash, Billy was recognised by the crowd, and they had given him an almighty reception. And having next been approached by a newspaper reporter, from the **South Wales Daily News**, and asked about how he expected Bristol City to do in the Final, he had refused to be drawn into predictions. Wedlock had been coy, Wedlock had been guarded, but Wedlock had been *honest* – *"Ours is a team of triers to a man. We will work very hard, as you might guess, and many critics will be confused on finding that our attack is skilful, as our defence is generally admitted to be".*
And so it finally came to the big day. April 24th 1909.
The Crystal Palace, in London - capital of the world. And special train after special train had departed Temple Meads, carrying Bristol football fans, along Brunel's railway, and into London, the capital of the world. And an estimated army of 6,000 Bristolians travelled to the Palace, from Bristol, to see Billy Wedlock and his Bristol boys win the Cup. And an even greater number travelled from Lancashire, to see Charlie Roberts and his Manchester boys win the Cup. It was Roberts versus Wedlock. It was the Manchester men opposing the Bristol *'Babes'*. It was the gritty

northerners against the southern softies.
And – *for one day only* – it would be the Whites against the Blues. Because both teams usually wore red, so there would have been a clash. And for this reason, on *this* day, on this *special* day only - *neither* of them wore red. So Manchester wore white jerseys emblazoned with a large red 'V'. With a Lancastrian red rose emblem on their left breast. And Bristol wore Royal Blue jerseys, with the *Bristol Coat of Arms* on their left breast.
And the scene was set... And Mr Thickett, of Coronation Road, Southville, came out to survey that scene. Mr Harry Thickett, the manager of Bristol City, came out to stand on the side of the pitch. To survey the scene. And he saw people on the terraces. And he saw people in the grandstand. And he saw people congregating on the large grass banks. The large grass banks, sloping away, behind both the goals, and on the sides of the pitch. And he saw people climbing the trees, in order to obtain a better view of the field. And he saw people standing on wooden fences. And standing on other people's shoulders. To get a better view.
And he saw the Bristol City supporters. And he heard them. And he saw the Manchester United supporters. And he heard *them*. And he noticed the other spectators. And there were a vast number of them. They were the local folk, the Londoners.
And Thickett saw – *and heard* – that the local folk, the Londoners, were cheering for *his* team – for Bristol City. Because they were cheering for the *'Hope of the South'*. They did not want the northerners to win. They did not want the norm. They wanted Bristol City to win. They wanted Billy Wedlock, from Bedminster, and his Bristol boys to win. And Thickett knew this was a *good* thing. At least, it certainly wasn't a *bad* thing. It perhaps gave

1909 AND ALL THAT...

Bristol City a very slender advantage. And Bristol City needed *any* advantage they could take. Because Bristol City were not at full-strength. Willis Rippon, the star striker in their ranks, could not play. Willis Rippon had suffered a knee injury on Easter Tuesday, against Blackburn Rovers, at Ashton Gate. The day after the Cup Final 'dress rehearsal' against Manchester United. The day after the goalless draw with Charlie Roberts' boys, in the league. Rippon was not available for selection. Rippon needed an operation. He could not play. And neither could Reuben Marr, one of Billy Wedlock's partners in the City back line. It was a double-blow for City. A double-blow for Wedlock's boys. All week, the Press had gathered outside the City training camp at Portishead, waiting for any snippets, waiting for any news on Rippon or Marr. But the rumours were not good. And the rumours, on this occasion, were proved to be reliable. Neither Rippon or Marr could play.
And so it came to be, that most of London, most of the 'neutrals' in the crowd, wanted Bristol City to win. Because Bristol City *were* indeed the *'Hope of the South'*.
And as Wedlock quietly sat in the changing room, and then stood up, and prepared to change into his playing gear, he *may* have had a few reflections to himself. He *might* well have thought *back* for a moment or two, musing on the old days...
And perhaps, *if* he did so, he would have remembered the Melrose Bible Class, and its football team, where, for Wedlock, it had all begun, all those years ago...
And perhaps he thought of Masonic Rovers, and of his old Arlington team-mates, Marsh and Harding, who, like Wedlock, had been on trial at Bristol City as young amateurs, the best part of a

WEDLOCK – THE FIRST HERO OF BRISTOL CITY

decade ago...
Perhaps he remembered Jack Hughes, his old Aberdare team-mate who had once *unsuccessfully* recommended the young Wedlock to Liverpool...
And maybe Wedlock spared a thought for his friend Frank Bacon, the City director who had battled so hard to bring Billy back home to Bristol from his south Wales exile...
And finally, perhaps Wedlock thought of his late father, Thomas, who had died only seven and a half weeks previously, but who, during his lifetime, had seen Billy become captain of his team, Bristol City, had seen Billy win 11 caps for his country, had seen Billy become a Second Division Champion, and an English League runner-up – but who would *not* live to see his son play in the FA Cup Final in London...
And having mused upon these melancholic themes, Wedlock, now being changed into his gear, began to concentrate on the job in hand, and began to focus fully on the task that lay ahead...
And outside, the supporters of Bristol City were waiting, they were waiting *patiently* for their team to make its entrance onto the field, and they were singing, and chanting, and *counting down the minutes...*
...and just for *once*, on this *one*, single, *rare* occasion – it seemed as if the make-up of this City team, and more specifically, of *who* it was representing, was somehow slightly *different.* It was not, for once, Harry Clay, from Nottinghamshire. Or Archie Annan and Pat Hanlin, of Scotland, and Billy Wedlock, Joe Cottle and Arthur Spear, of Bristol, and Fred Staniforth, of South Yorkshire, and Bob Hardy, of South Bank, Middlesbrough, or Andrew Burton, of Scotland, and so on, and so on....

1909 AND ALL THAT...

Instead, it was Harry Clay, of *Breach Road - off Luckwell Lane*, Archie Annan, Pat Hanlin and Billy Wedlock, of *Chessel Street*, Joe Cottle and Arthur Spear, of *East Street*, Fred Staniforth, of *Luckwell Lane*, Bob Hardy, of *Beauley Road*, and Andrew Burton, of *Ashton Road, and so on...*

Because this was not merely a collection of untouchable football stars, whose origins were spread across the length and breadth of the United Kingdom. It was a group of skilled tradesmen, who, *wonder-of-wonders*, actually *lived* amongst the communities they served. Yes, some of them were hero-worshipped. Yes, some of them were placed on pedestals. But they were also *respected* as being *working-men*, and accepted by the folks of Bedminster, Southville and Ashton as being 'one of their own'.

And before long, *this* City team – led by Wedlock - jogged out onto the field of play, and there was a deafening roar, the like of which Billy had never heard before. This was the biggest crowd that Billy Wedlock and his Bristol boys had ever played in front of. Never before had a Bristol City team performed in front of such a great number of spectators. And never *again* would they perform in front of such a great number of spectators. Not for the greater part of a century. And with the City out onto the field, Billy Wedlock looked around, and surveyed the scene. And very shortly *United* came out, led by Charlie Roberts, of Darlington, County Durham.

The hour had arrived.

Those boys, those heroes! Billy Wedlock, and his Bristol boys! Harry Clay...Archie Annan...Joe Cottle (of Bedminster) - and Pat Hanlin. Billy Wedlock and Arthur Spear (both of Bedminster)... Fred Staniforth, Bob Hardy, Sammy Gilligan, Andy Burton and Frank Hilton.

WEDLOCK – THE FIRST HERO OF BRISTOL CITY

But no Willis Rippon. And no Reuben Marr.
The captains, Wedlock and Roberts, faced off, at the centre of the pitch. And the referee, Mr Mason, called for a shake of hands.
And he asked for a good, clean game. And he declared *"May the best team win"*. And then the coin was flipped, which spun, and landed in Wedlock's half of the field, in the mud...
And so Wedlock bent over to have a look, and his frowning expression was a notable feature as the camera snapped.
On which side had the coin landed? The opening battle had been *lost,* first blood to the men from Manchester, they would play with the wind for the duration of the first half. Billy Wedlock and Bristol City, Billy Wedlock, Bedminster's favourite son, and his Bristol boys would be against the wind, the London wind, in the first half.
And Sammy Gilligan, late of Palmyra Road, Bedminster, kicked off for Bristol City, at just before 3:30pm - and the match got under

1909 AND ALL THAT...

way. Bristol City against Manchester United, and Bristol City against the wind, the London wind. And Roberts wasted little time in tripping Wedlock, who fell to the ground. Wedlock was floored, by his great northern rival, Roberts. And Wedlock was not best pleased. Yet Wedlock, Billy Wedlock of Bedminster, picked himself up from the floor, and got on with the game.
Bristol City's worries, however, were to get bigger than *this*...
After 22 minutes of play, Harold Halse of Manchester United hit a thunderbolt of a shot towards the Bristol City goal. It struck the City crossbar with such force, that the frame of the goal appeared to shake quite violently. And the City 'keeper Harry Clay was helpless, he was stranded. And as the ball rebounded back into play, Wedlock watched on in horror.

"Wedlock watched on in horror"

WEDLOCK – THE FIRST HERO OF BRISTOL CITY

The ball fell to the United inside left Sandy Turnbull, who could not miss...

The net was empty. And Wedlock watched on in terror, he watched on in dread. And Turnbull fired the ball into the roof of the City net.

And there was a great roar of approval from the crowd, and Wedlock's boys were a goal down. And so Bristol City huffed and they puffed, and they tried to get back into the game. But their tight passing game was not working, whilst their longer, higher balls were inevitably swallowed up by the wind, the London wind. And the Manchester United back line was strong, and it kept Bristol City at bay. And Meredith, of Manchester, the star man, the outside-right, the friend of Roberts – caused City a succession of problems with his attacking play. And when the whistle sounded for half-time, Roberts' boys still held the lead. 1-0 to Manchester United at the break. Yet Wedlock's boys hoped that with the wind at their backs in the second half, the deficit could be overturned. And in the second period, United went down to ten men, through injury. *Temporarily*. And Bristol City appeared to get stronger. And they huffed and they puffed for an equaliser. And they scrapped and they scraped. They toiled and they laboured. But an equaliser could not be found. And before long United's injury problem was solved, and they went back to eleven men.

But then Sammy Gilligan galloped through for City, he ran clear of the United defence, he was one-on-one with the 'keeper Harry Moger. But Moger dived at Gilligan's feet, and smothered the ball, Gilligan could not take it round the goalkeeper, and he could not slip it into an empty net.

And the clock ticked down....

1909 AND ALL THAT...

And Wedlock snapped into tackle after tackle, he tried to push the ball forwards, and tried to get it out to the flanks, as he attempted to rally his forwards into a degree of urgency...

And Wedlock looked around his team for some 'cool heads' in front of goal – but there were none to be found.

And Frank Hilton missed a clear chance for City, the chance of the game. But he could not score. It had needed a good, clean, hard shot – he *should* have buried it – but he could not score. The ball went flying *wide*.

Spear is the dark-shirted City player in the centre.
Hilton (right) awaits the ball on the touchline

And City harried and hurried, but they could not find a way past Roberts. They could not find a way past Charlie Roberts, and they could not find a way past his half-back partners, Dick Duckworth, or Alex Bell. And Wedlock's boys found that this particular half-back trio was rather akin to that of a brick wall. And United held the City back, and Wedlock's boys could not score. And *still* the

WEDLOCK – THE FIRST HERO OF BRISTOL CITY

clock ticked down...
And Roberts' boys continued to frustrate City, they began to commit fouls, they bullied City off of the ball. They threw themselves down onto the floor, as if they had been magically up-ended by an invisible opponent. But the referee, Mr Mason, did not give the appearance of being a man who had noticed any of these antics. And Charlie Roberts' boys were wily, and streetwise. And they found ways to waste time, and to run down the clock. And the clock *did* tick down.
And Bristol City could not find a way through. Wedlock's boys could not find the answer. Manchester United had been too strong. Roberts' boys had been too powerful. They had been too clever. It had not been an outstanding game. But they – *United* - had been the better side. And the whistle for full-time was soon blown. And Roberts' boys had done it. And Wedlock's boys, Wedlock's Bristol boys, had been defeated.
And the players of Bristol City felt great disappointment. 1-0. 1-0 to the men from Manchester. But the Bristol boys had given it their *all,* as Wedlock had correctly predicted. They had given everything. *Everything.* And their drenched royal blue shirts were saturated with Bristol sweat, their socks rolled around their ankles. And beads of perspiration trickled down their faces, as tears of despair rolled down their cheeks. Had the City taken their chances in the second-half, then Wedlock's boys would have won. 2-1, or maybe 3-1. Yes, Reuben Marr had been missed, but Rippon had been *desperately* missed. Wedlock's boys had possessed no cool heads in the forward line, they had no cutting-edge.
And so Manchester United had won the Cup for the first time in its history. It meant that *Charlie Roberts and his team* went up into

1909 AND ALL THAT...

the grandstand, to pick up the Cup. The English FA Cup.
And Charlie Roberts collected the trophy from Lord Charles Beresford, of the Royal Navy. And Roberts waved the trophy above his head, in great delight. But Roberts also found time to pay tribute to Bristol City and their gallant efforts. To Billy Wedlock and his Bristol boys. And Roberts called for *"Three Cheers"* for his defeated opponents. *"Three Cheers"* for Billy Wedlock - for Billy Wedlock, from Bedminster, and his Bristol boys. Because they had been noble and worthy opponents, and they had taken their defeat like true sportsmen.

And that evening, Wedlock's boys had to accompany their conquerors for a night out in London town, as an arrangement had been made for both teams to attend the theatre together on Cup Final eventide. And Wedlock's disappointed troops had to simply 'grin and bear it', for as Billy would later recall - *"They (United) naturally had their chests out – but we felt proud too, for we had all done our best, and it had been a very close game"*.

And the 6,000 Bristol City supporters came home on their trains that night, greatly disappointed, because the team was not bringing the Cup back with them. And Wedlock's dream had died. The biggest match of his club career had ended in defeat.

And Bristol City had climbed towards the top of the mountain, they had nearly reached the summit. But when Bristol City looked down from the top of the mountain, they perceived a feeling of giddiness, and did not like the view. It was a long way down. And Bristol City felt queasy, and dizzy. And Manchester United had climbed towards the top of the mountain, and then they reached the summit. And then Manchester United *climbed onto* the summit. And they looked down. And they decided that they

WEDLOCK – THE FIRST HERO OF BRISTOL CITY

liked the view that came into sight. It *was* a long way down...
But they were on *the top*. And there was no need to come down. Not just yet. And although Billy Wedlock's career would go on – for he was not finished yet – Bristol City would *not* go on.
And Wedlock would continue to perform at the highest level for another two years, he would still play for England for another *five*. His career was not over, not by a long way. He still had *years* in front of him. But Bristol City could no longer *compete*, not with the leading teams in the country, not in the First Division. And two years later, in 1911, Manchester United would be crowned as Champions of England for the second time. But Bristol City would finish second from the bottom of the table.
And Bristol City were on their way down.
But Manchester United were on their way to *immortality*...

"The winning goal"
Wedlock recalls *"He was unmarked and could not miss with our goal open before him"*

2] Bedminster beginnings

'The Nursery' – looking towards North Street Green

Charlie Roberts probably had a fair bit more in common with his rival Billy Wedlock than many people would have realised. And the predictable stereotype that is to contrast 'gritty northerners' with 'southern softies' is a cliché that doesn't really work so accurately in this case. For although Charlie Roberts was indeed from the north of England, and probably, it can be guessed, had something of the 'gritty' about him – Wedlock was certainly no softy. And although Roberts' radicalism and left-wing views stemmed from his Durham background, which was steeped in the rise of the trade union movement – and although Roberts came from a mining family – the surprising fact of the matter is, that Wedlock had come from a mining family too...

WEDLOCK – THE FIRST HERO OF BRISTOL CITY

William John Wedlock was born on October 28th 1880, at No 10 York Buildings, just a whisker off the main road that is North Street, Bedminster. He was the son of Thomas and Sarah Wedlock, who, before she married Thomas, had been known as Sarah Cox.

Billy was one of ten children, for there had been five boys and five girls. And Billy was the eighth of the ten, also being the fourth out of the five boys. Starting with the birth of the first child, in 1864, Billy's brothers and sisters were Henry William, Sarah Ann, Walter Parkman, Louisa Elizabeth, Thomas James, Eliza Mary, Lydia, Mary Louise and Frederick.

The Wedlocks' area of Bedminster in the 1880's was thick with the labouring classes of south Bristol. There were coal miners, furnace tenders, painters, builders, brick-makers, bricklayers, iron workers, factory hands and rag-and-bone men.

North Street was a harsh world in those days. It was not quite the busy, carefree suburban hub that we see today. The air was of dust and soot. The ethos was grime, muck and toil. And of *survival*. North Street has now moved on. North Street is different. And any Wedlock fans of the modern era, looking to pay pilgrimage to their long-gone hero of the early 20th century by visiting his place of birth, would be hard-pressed to do so.

York Buildings in the 1880's was a ragged collection of about a dozen humble dwellings, basically bolted onto the bottom of the slope which is *now* known as '*The Nursery*', but was *then* called '*Mount Pleasant Terrace*'. These houses would have backed onto the area which today contains the patch of grass known as '*North Street Green*'. They linked the bottom end of *The Nursery*

(Mount Pleasant Terrace) to the top of Luckwell Lane (*now* Luckwell Road).

The bottom of The Nursery, as seen in modern times

Several of these dwellings were sold on in the 1880's, and by the turn of the century they had been completed submerged into the main flow of *The Nursery*, becoming re-numbered according, before later still, being totally demolished - leaving the open space and bare patch of grass that we see today. The main run of dwellings on *that flank* of *The Nursery* are still fully intact – but tellingly, the house numbers only run from 20 upwards... Billy Wedlock's younger sister Mary Louise was *also* born in the house at York Buildings, this information being confirmed through her christening record on December 7th 1882 (at the church of Ashton Gate St Francis). And Billy's youngest brother Frederick – christened on January 8th 1886 – *also* appears to have started life at that dwelling – though his baptismal record actually states

'*No 10, The Nursery*', which is almost certainly the *same address*, but under a slightly different name.

From the air...
the bottom of The Nursery, leading out to North Street - with the modern-day 'North Street Green', showing centre-left of this picture

Essentially, the long and the short of it is, that the three youngest Wedlock siblings spent their very earliest years being cared for at - literally - *The Nursery*, but then, around about the time that young Billy had reached his tenth birthday, the Wedlock family crossed North Street, and began living at No 2, Ashton Place. Ashton Place, as with the case of York Buildings and Mount Pleasant Terrace, was basically a sub-division of North Street... It was a run of a dozen or so dwellings, set in between Upper Sydney Street (*then Sidney Road*) and Myrtle Street (*Myrtle Road*). The houses would later lose their '*Ashton Place*' status, through being swallowed up into the great North Street re-numbering scheme of 1900. Henceforth, the address known as

BEDMINSTER BEGINNINGS

No 2, Ashton Place would eventually morph into the rather more anonymous - sounding '*172 North Street'*.

The new Wedlock dwelling was set roughly half way between two public houses, the '*Hen and Chicken*' and the '*Masonic Arms*'. The house was to stay in the family for a good number of years after the passing of Billy's parents, as his sister Louisa (who continued living there, even after her wedding) took ownership as Mrs Louisa Edworthy, following the death of her mother.

Sadly, all that marks the rough spot of the Wedlock homestead today is a rather bland and predictable '*Tesco Express'*. Readers of a certain age will no doubt recall the *'Cashmans'* DIY store, which was also on this site.

Billy was christened at the church of Ashton Gate St Francis, as '*William John Wedlock',* on December 1st 1880. However, a rather strange fact complicates matters somewhat, because he actually wasn't the *only* Billy Wedlock christened at this venue on that particular day. The other one was his cousin, '*William Thomas Wedlock',* who was a little over eighteen months senior to our Billy. It is practically certain that the two Billy Wedlocks had been named after their coal miner grandfather, in other words, William, the father of Thomas.

The information concerning Billy Wedlock's grandfather William is rather sketchy, however, what *is known* is that he was born and raised in Bedminster, almost certainly during the first decade of the nineteenth century, that he was married to Sarah Parkman, and that he was a lifelong collier. He also lived to a very good age. The family lived in the North Street area of Bedminster, they had a fairly sizable amount of children, producing in fact a relatively even spread of boys and girls, and these included

WEDLOCK – THE FIRST HERO OF BRISTOL CITY

Thomas James Wedlock (Billy's father) – born in 1838, and Walter Parkman Wedlock (Willliam Thomas's father) – born in 1848. Like his father, Thomas Wedlock would work at the nearby colliery, first as a miner, then later into the 1870's as a coke burner, a coke burner being a man who loaded and emptied the sealed coal ovens. In his declining years, Thomas would find alternative employment as a watchman at the local *Electric Light Works*. He married Sarah Cox, of Long Ashton, in the summer of 1863, when he was approaching the age of 25 years.

The Wedlock family were of good, honest, solid working-class stock. To say that they were *'Bedminster through and through'* would be something of a massive understatement. The Wedlocks' were workers and grafters. They were sweaters and toilers. Billy's brothers all went into tough, gruelling manual work, unsurprising perhaps, given their grim surroundings. Henry William became a forge labourer and a brick maker. Walter Parkman was an iron worker at *Ashton Vale Rolling Mills*, before moving away with his family in the mid - 1890's to do similar work in Stalybridge, Lancashire. Thomas James (*Junior*) was a coal hewer down the mines. Frederick was a machinist at the nearby tobacco factory. One or two of the sisters also found work at the tobacco factory.

And then there was young Billy. But Billy was *different*.

Billy would become a tanner, a stonemason, and – *eventually* – a professional footballer.

So how exactly did he manage to make the long transition from Bedminster obscurity to the Cup Final at the Crystal Palace, London – the capital of the world? How did it become possible for this tiny, fair-haired young boy to emerge from such incredibly

BEDMINSTER BEGINNINGS

humble beginnings and yet go on to become perhaps the *greatest,* arguably the most *famous* footballer in the history of Bristol City?

These questions are not easily answered. But it became clear from a young age that Billy, and his three elder brothers, all possessed an unusual aptitude for sport. That is to say, for sporting activities in general, and for football and cricket *in particular*. As far as football was concerned, despite his small frame, Billy always played as a centre-half. Or to put it into terms more suitable for the era, as a *centre half-back*. Yes, he was small. Yes, he was slight. But as Billy would explain years later, at the end of his career – the art of winning the ball in the air was all in the jump. And perhaps more scientifically, it was in the *timing* of the jump. When asked about it, Wedlock replied simply, though perhaps, rather *un*-scientifically - *"All a matter of timing. I made sure to get up in the air before the big bloke I was marking."*

Wedlock attended the Ashton Gate School, just off Greenway Bush Lane, yet although he *may* have began kicking his first ball in this playground, for years there was actually no organised sport played here, and oddly it was at his *Sunday School,* via the 'Melrose Bible Class', where he really began to develop his lifelong love of the game of football. Billy is believed to have helped form a team with his classmates, they began to play matches after Sunday lessons, Melrose FC was soon 'born', and from then on, Billy never looked back...

But an edition of the **Athletic News** dated February 24th 1908 revealed some surprising sporting secrets about Wedlock, including the eye-opening revelation that all three of Billy's elder brothers had each previously played as forwards with local club Masonic Rovers. Allegedly inspired by their exploits, young Billy soon followed them into the team, though certainly *not* playing as a forward. So why *exactly* did Wedlock first choose the position of centre-half? As Billy would later reveal, it was all rather simple – *"Because there was always plenty to do.....centre-halves in those days were attacking players..."*

The Masonic Arms, North Street, Bedminster

Masonic Rovers were connected with the nearby hotel and public house of the same name, they used the former sports field on the Chessels for their activities and from there ran both football and cricket teams. *At least one* of Billy's brothers played for the cricket XI too, the eldest – Henry. In fact he was still playing for them as recently as the summer of 1894, by which time he had reached his 30th birthday.

As far as football was concerned, a love of the *Association code* would have been quite an unusual thing at the time, as, to a large extent, Bristol was firmly a *rugby* city, with 'soccer' still being in its relative infancy. Nevertheless, football and cricket were clearly the preferred avenues for the Wedlock brothers.

Years later, the masters of Ashton Gate School would have reason to feel a good deal of pride, as it would one day be able to claim to have produced a number of professional footballers. Wedlock was the first, but at three or four years Billy's junior, there later appeared Billy Pocock, who began playing at Bedminster St Francis, later going to Reading of the Southern League, before joining the army and then having to experience his career becoming *totally* disrupted by the First World War. He eventually came home to his native City, joining Bristol City FC relatively late in his career, in 1919, at a time when Wedlock too, was beginning to wind down his professional career. Later still, there came goalkeeper Ted Davis, Bedminster-born, who went on to star for Clapton Orient, Huddersfield Town and Blackburn Rovers.

Outside his activities at Ashton Gate School, Wedlock's first team of any real note seems to have been the previously-mentioned Masonic Rovers FC, but this would have *followed,* of course, his original stint as a junior for Melrose FC, the Sunday School outfit who had ran football and cricket teams and who were administered from No 1, Coronation Road by a Mr Jonathan W Shillam.

But it was really at his third club, the up-and-coming Arlington Rovers, where Billy seriously began to get himself noticed...

WEDLOCK – THE FIRST HERO OF BRISTOL CITY

From an organisational point of view, Arlington Rovers AFC in 1897 was practically run from Ashton Place, North Street, just a few doors down from where the Wedlock family lived. So it was perhaps always inevitable that one day Billy was going to play for them. Their history appears to date back to the year 1894, and after four complete campaigns of playing sporadic 'friendly fixtures', the Rovers finally made it into Division One of the East Bristol and District League – for the start of season 1898/99. Wedlock would join at the age of 16 around the summer of 1897, staying for four seasons – and soon helping them to win two Gloucestershire County Junior Cups and two Bristol and District League titles. His arrival seemed to trigger a vast improvement in Arlington's fortunes, as they appeared to make the transition from being a *good* team to an *outstanding* one over the course of eighteen months. When League debutants Arlington won their first-ever Division One title at the end of 1898/99, which was Billy's second term, the team remained *unbeaten* over the course of the 18-match season.

Wedlock's uncanny knack of being able to win the ball in the air despite his lack of inches has already been mentioned, yet his strengths on the field of play amounted to much more than this – even as a teenager, Wedlock seemed to have *everything*.

Yes, he could jump – yes, he could head the ball. But he could also tackle. And he could tackle *hard*. Firm but fair. And *always fair*. He could tackle and he could pass. He could run with the best of them. He could run and he could chase and he could hassle and he could harry. He could absorb the knocks and take the 'rough stuff'. You could kick him, trip him, pull him, push him, or you could wrestle him to the floor. Wedlock would still get up with a smile on his face, bearing no malice or ill-will towards his frustrated opponent. And absolutely *no retaliation!*

He could push himself forward well into advanced attacking positions, and assist his forward line in their endeavours, and yet still be able to sprint back in order to defend from an opposition breakaway. And he could certainly shoot. Yes, Wedlock possessed a *rasping* shot, with either foot.

But crucially, he was also an organiser-in-chief, and could read games like a book. The manager on the touchline may have selected the team, the manager on the touchline may have been shouting out the odd instruction. But on the field of play, there was only *one manager* – Wedlock. He could sit back in his centre half-back position, and he could simply *read* the match. He could assess what was going on. What was going right, and what was going wrong, the strengths and weaknesses - of the opposition, and of his *own* side. And he could organise his team-mates accordingly...Wedlock was a reader of games. And he was a natural *leader of men.*

Even as a youngster, it appears that Billy took his fledgling football career *very seriously.* On Christmas morning 1899, where was Billy to be found? At home in North Street, sat in front of the fireplace unwrapping his Christmas presents with the rest of the Wedlock family? No. On the cold Yuletide morning of 1899, Wedlock was turning out for Arlington Rovers against Beaufort, in the Final of the Gloucestershire Junior Cup, on the Bell Hill ground of the recently wound-up St George club. Rovers won easily, by three goals to nil, and it was reported that in the first half, Wedlock hit the upright, with a tremendous shot from long range. Rovers were later presented with the trophy, cheered on

WEDLOCK – THE FIRST HERO OF BRISTOL CITY

by about 700 spectators. It was the first time that Arlington had reached the Final in the history of the competition, and they had won it to boot! But there would be more successes to follow...

On Good Friday, April 13th 1900, Wedlock played for Arlington Rovers against St Philips in the *Bristol and District League Vase* Final – at *'Bedminster Park'* (Greville Smyth Park, Ashton Gate). There were about 1,000 spectators in attendance, and their *"enthusiasm was very great, and their language at times, painfully strong"*. St Philips won the toss, and inexplicably, decided to make their opponents play with the wind in the first half. Wedlock and Arlington Rovers never looked back – gale-assisted, they cruised into a 3-0 half-time lead, and held that score right through until the end of the game, despite St Philips gaining a second-half penalty – which hit the post.

Arlington Rovers were starting to getting noticed. An edition of the **Bristol Magpie** dated May 3rd proudly bragged:-

"I would like to call their attention to a very good performance by a local Junior team. Arlington Rovers is in the favourable position of having won everything they entered for, they started with the 'Gloster Junior Cup' on Xmas Day, on Good Friday they won the 'Bristol and District Challenge Vase', on Easter Monday they sent a team to Warminster to compete in the six a-side tournament got up by the club of that name, and after playing five times, won the Cup and gold badges, and wound up by taking top place in the Bristol and District League, beating such clubs as St. Francis, St. Philip's, Beaufort, Clevedon, etc., they only lost two matches and these were played away with scratch teams, this is a record for one season's work that any club would be proud of and it is to be hoped they will stick together and aim at bigger things next

BEDMINSTER BEGINNINGS

season..."
That may have been so, but Wedlock had other things on his mind at this time, some rather pressing matters...
Billy's girlfriend Rosina was with child, his young bride-to-be being in the early stages of pregnancy. There was another little Wedlock on the way. The wedding was arranged, and henceforth, Billy Wedlock married Rosina Lilly at the church of Bedminster St John's, on May 20th 1900.
Rosina Maria Lilly had been born in Bedminster during the spring of 1882, making her about eighteen months younger than Billy. And although it may seem that 18 years was quite a young age for a bride, especially during the Victorian era, it was by no means unheard of.
She was the daughter of George Henry Lilly, a sawyer from Bristol and Maria Bray, from Devon. Rosina was one of nine children and the family at one time lived in Bartley Street, Bedminster, just behind the existing '*Barley Mow*' pub in East Street, and next door to the long-demolished '*Bartley Arms*'.
In the late 1880's however, the Lilly family had relocated to Kingston-on-Thames in Surrey, first leaving their children with Maria's parents in Bristol, and then gradually taking them one by one with them to Surrey, as they began to settle into their new surroundings. By the early 1890's, all but two of their children had still to be moved to Kingston, Rosina and her brother George, who at this time were living with their Bray grandparents in Coronation Court, Bedminster. George however, eventually made it to the Home Counties, leaving only Rosina, who for some strange reason, never ended up going. No doubt this would end up becoming something of a relief for young Billy Wedlock, who

had clearly fallen in love with the young lady in question. The spring of 1900 saw Wedlock in lodgings at 55 Mill Lane, Bedminster, along with his bride-to-be, Rosina Lilly, who was more commonly known as simply *'Rose'*. St John's Church was literally a stone's throw away, just past Little Paradise and over yonder, so there was never any doubt where the wedding was going to take place. A tradition on these happy occasions was generally for a brother or sister of both the bride and groom to act as official witnesses for the day, and to place their mark or signature onto the marriage documents, in order to confirm their blessing and presence, and to say that, in-effect, all things were good and in order. On this occasion however, the two witnesses were *both* siblings of Wedlock, his brother Thomas and his sister Eliza. Suffice to say, it appeared by now that all of Rosina's family had long since departed for Surrey, and there were now no other Lilly's remaining in Bristol. This however, was the beginning of fifteen and a half years of happy marriage...

Yet at precisely the *same* time, it happened to be that these teenaged lovers were not the *only* two bodies being joined together in holy matrimony...

...A little under six weeks earlier, just up the road at Bedminster Temperance Hall, the two south Bristol football clubs of Bedminster and Bristol City had been revealing the details of their *own* perfect union. As with the partnership of Lilly and Wedlock, these two entities had essentially decided they would be better off as *one*, and as such, they might as well do something about it. Plans of a grand amalgamation were henceforth announced at a big meeting on April 10th, at the aforementioned Temperance Hall, Bedminster. So while Billy and Rosina were busy tying the

BEDMINSTER BEGINNINGS

knot at St John's Church on that very special Sunday in May, so the grand union between two local soccer clubs was also being eased through its course...

Bristol City FC of course, was later to form a simply enormous part of Billy Wedlock's life, and as we have now come up-to-date with the account of *his* Bedminster beginnings, so must we now turn to Bristol City in order to do the same.....

Bristol City's origins had dated back to the spring of 1894, their birth as *'Bristol South End'* being announced via a meeting at the *'General Eliot'* Public House in East Street, Bedminster. They had quickly built up a keen rivalry with already-established neighbours Bedminster FC, the latter of whom became outraged when they accused the former of poaching their players.

But Warmley were the top dogs as far as local soccer was concerned, with Bedminster, St George and Clifton *(Association)* not too far behind, whilst Eastville Rovers (later to become Bristol Rovers) were very much the poor relations at this time. All these clubs - including Bedminster FC - competed in the Western League. But it was *Bedminster's* very place in the League that the newly-formed Bristol South End coveted for *themselves*.

The mere *presence* of the new upstarts called Bristol South End got on Bedminster's nerves, and they took every opportunity to vote down the former's applications to join the League. For a while, the relationship between the two clubs was bitter, childish and petulant. Bedminster even refused to play friendly matches against their deadly rivals. The bad feeling did not improve when Bristol South End finally grabbed their own Western League spot for season 1896/97, meaning derby matches between the two clubs. In short, it took nigh on three years for the dust to settle and the insults to stop.

Quite what the young Billy Wedlock might have thought of all these shenanigans is unknown, but it is interesting to speculate on where he may have stood on all the various little debates and arguments. As has already been alluded to, Billy's fledgling football career had been a busy one, but, had he actually managed to find the time to *watch* the game of football in the local area, one can imagine it's much more likely, geographically, that he would have been a *Bedminster* fan rather than a Bristol City one.

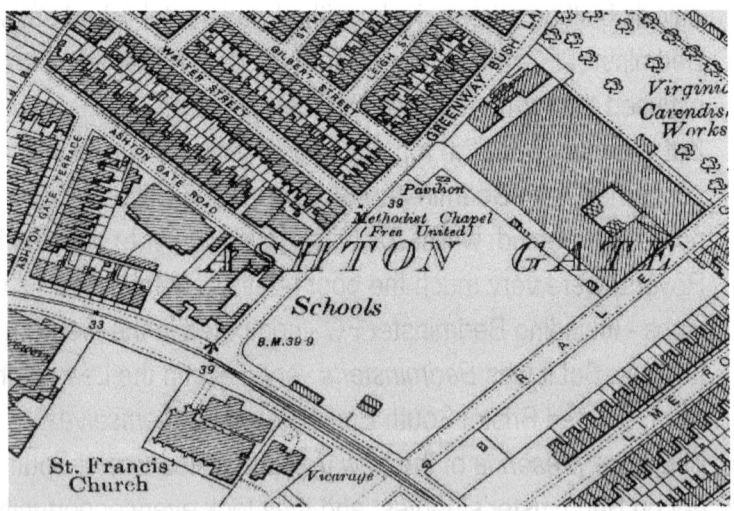

Wedlock's world in the early 1890's – his church, school and Bedminster Football & Cricket ground, all together in a neat triangle. The sports pitch is directly opposite the church, it's the square with the word 'Schools' in it. His school can be seen in Ashton Gate Road

Bedminster had played their home games at Greenway Bush Lane when Billy had been in his early teens, just yards away from

BEDMINSTER BEGINNINGS

his Ashton Gate school. Additionally, the traditional Wedlock family church - Ashton Gate St Francis - on one side of North Street, actually *overlooked* Bedminster's cricket and football pitch, from across the road. (*Aldi*'s supermarket and car park today occupies this site). Even in 1896, as Bedminster moved operations to land owned by the Smyth family, on the Ashton Gate site (later to become the permanent home of *Bristol City FC*) - they were still very much in Wedlock's neck of the woods. Bristol South End meanwhile, had been based all the way over at St John's Lane since *its* formation in 1894...

In April 1897, the rapidly–improving new club (South End) voted to adopt professionalism and additionally managed to negotiate entry into the much more prestigious Southern League. (Bedminster FC though, would join them in the same Division just a year later). As if in celebration, Bristol South End's name was then updated to the much more ambitious-sounding '*Bristol City FC*'. 31 year-old Nottingham-born Sam Hollis would become the club's first-ever professional football manager, having previously been team trainer at Woolwich Arsenal. Despite their change of name and elevation into the more advanced Southern League, Bristol City would retain a keen interest in Western League affairs, fielding a first-choice XI in the 'Professional' section of that Division in season 97/98, with 14 regular matches being slotted in handily amongst their higher-priority Southern League fixtures. A similar system would be adopted on occasional seasons between 1898 and 1901, for there were six Western League engagements in 1899/1900 and sixteen in 1900/01.

As far as the 'priority' matches were concerned, City finished the 1897/98 season as runners-up in the Southern League (over the course of 22 matches). In 1898/99, they again finished in second place (over 25 matches) and in 1899/1900 they finished a disappointing 9th (32 matches).

The first Southern League 'derby' match between Bristol City and Bedminster FC took place on December 17th 1898 at St John's Lane, City winning by 5-2 in front of over 10,000 fans. The return game at Bedminster's Ashton Gate was on March 4th 1899, Bedminster winning 1-0 in front of 7,000.

But the big shock came just two weeks later when City manager Sam Hollis walked out, due to what he perceived to be boardroom interference. It wasn't just his sudden departure that caused such a *furore,* it was *who* he jumped straight into the arms of, in order to become their new manager – Bedminster FC! His place was taken by Sunderland's Scottish supremo Bob Campbell.

By the end of the 1899/1900 Southern League campaign, Bristol City and Bedminster had swept away virtually all the local competition from across the city. Even Warmley had disbanded in January 1899, with Bristol St George following them at the end of the season. Only Eastville Rovers (by this time morphing into *Bristol Rovers*) – who had *themselves* attained a Southern League place in 1899/1900 - were left...

Yet the footballing powers-that-be in south Bristol were still not satisfied. They did not merely want two 'good' teams from south Bristol punching above their weight but never achieving anything of note. They no longer wanted petty rivalries and squabbles.

In short, they believed that south Bristol would no longer be able to support two clubs. They dreamed of one day entering the national *Football League*. The only true chance of success in

BEDMINSTER BEGINNINGS

south Bristol was to be if there were just *one club* to unite behind. They wanted the trivial rivalries put aside – they wanted a full-blown *merger*. In the event, to the delight of some, and to the misery of others, the two rival clubs were formally merged at the end of the 1899/1900 season. The big irony was that if Warmley had similarly decided to merge with *their* rivals Bristol St George, then they too would have probably survived. But it was not to be... Bristol City *themselves* did rather well out of the merger, for it was *Bedminster* who had done all the chasing, and *Bedminster* who had looked at the situation with Warmley and St George, and had feared a repeat performance in the south of the city.

As such, Bristol City would hold all the cards, keeping their full name, their club colours, their manager (Bob Campbell), chairman (William P Kingston) and stadium at *St John's Lane*. The *latter* was to the dismay of some however, as numerous fans rated Ashton Gate as the superior headquarters. To keep everyone happy, it was announced that for the upcoming Southern League campaign of 1900/01, home matches would be played *alternately* between St John's Lane and Ashton Gate. The big loser here was Sam Hollis, who twice now in little over a year had lost his job as a football manager, both times due in some way to the actions of Bristol City directors. The irony meanwhile, was the fact that the name of *'Bedminster FC'* was about to disappear from the professional footballing map, even though the majority of its players would be playing under the *'Bristol City'* banner in the coming season.

The whole affair was rather a curious one. But *these* were the general circumstances involving Bristol City that would meet Billy Wedlock upon his eventual arrival at the club.

WEDLOCK – THE FIRST HERO OF BRISTOL CITY

Wedlock himself would always be renowned as a humble chap who was modest about his achievements. He was known to be a man of few words and not the kind of guy to be shouting things from the rooftops. He just got on with things. When he had been at school, he got on with it. When he played football, or cricket, or other sports, he got on with *that*. When he was at work, he rolled up his sleeves and prepared for a day of sweat and toil – a fair day's work for a fair day's pay. He simply *got on* with things.

The early stages of Wedlock's south Bristol life were fundamentally and inextricably *rooted* in Bedminster, as had been those of Bristol City. But *there*, the similarity ended...

Bristol City at the time was not like that. Bristol City *wanted* to be shouting from the rooftops. It *wanted* to tell everyone about its lofty ambitions and intentions. It *wanted* to let everyone know that it could be the '*Best in the West*', if not, then of further afield. The '*Bristol Babe*' was almost like a petulant child, demanding attention from the adults of the English Football League. Bristol City was highly ambitious and had aspirations of great things. Billy Wedlock meanwhile didn't have a clue what the future held, and just took things as they came...

Perhaps these contrasting personalities did not make for, on the surface of it, a natural partnership. They were not necessarily the most logical of bedfellows. They were not of the same mindset. But now, the time of reckoning had arrived and for the first time, the worlds of Wedlock and Bristol City were about to collide...

3] In demand

In the summer of 1900, the newly-married Billy Wedlock went off to play cricket – as he would appear to do *every* close-term – waited for the new football season, and looked forward to the birth of his first child, which was due in the autumn. He was supporting his wife by working at the local tannery, and no doubt, was not expecting a long career in professional football at this particular stage in his life. However, things were about to get a little complicated...

During the busy football season of 1900/01, Wedlock would end up representing no fewer than *three* teams – Arlington, the County of Gloucestershire, and, briefly - Bristol City's First Team. It would prove to be his most hectic sporting schedule to date, and only when it's considered that he was also holding down a full-time job at the tannery, plus looking after his new wife who was expecting a child, can it be appreciated how *full-to-bursting* Wedlock's diary must have been. Flexibility was the order of the day – but Wedlock would later become known as the '*India Rubber Man*' and those types of gentlemen are generally nothing if not flexible. As has been mentioned, the exploits of Arlington Rovers AFC during season 1899/90 had been *noticed*. In fact, they had been *more* than noticed....

In August 1900, the **Bristol Mercury** announced that Bristol City FC – during a series of practice matches – had given trials to *all* of the young players representing Arlington Rovers and Bedminster St Francis Football Clubs. And it was also announced that the Bristol City directors had decided *not* to run a reserve team for the season ahead, the practice of paying two sets of professional teams having proved to be not very cost-effective. Hitherto, that during the course of the trials being given to both Arlington Rovers and Bedminster St. Francis, *"the City Management Committee were offering to adopt the better eleven and give them no end of advantages in the shape of opportunities of shining in higher spheres, of training, and use of the ground. In the practice matches these young players were divided up along with the City professionals, and with very Interesting results".* In the event, City were true to their word – they went through the entire 1900/01 season without using a reserve team to back up its First XI. At least, that is to say – they didn't make use of an 'official' reserve team, and certainly not a *professional* one. What there *was* to be was a very cheaply-run reserve XI *of sorts.* This second-string side would essentially be made up of a specially-selected bunch of keen, young local amateurs like Wedlock, who as it happened, would only be too willing to play for nothing if it meant the *slightest* chance of a professional contract at the end of the season. The typical line-up of the City *'Reserve team'* that season was this:-

GOALKEEPER:- A Clapp, BACKS:- W Smith, A Marsh,
HALF-BACKS:- W Tucker, W Wedlock, Mason,
FORWARDS:- L Grant, H Stevens, J McLean, C Harding,
C Hillier.

It was basically the all-conquering Arlington Rovers line-up from the previous season! Although there appear to be no existing accounts confirming a clear *result* of the aforementioned junior trials, in the end it was *Arlington Rovers* and not Bedminster St Francis who took part in an all-important trial match against

IN DEMAND

Bristol City's first-team at Ashton Gate on August 28th 1900 – City winning 4-0 in front of 4,000 spectators. It was Wedlock's *Rovers* then, who became the main beneficiaries of this golden opportunity. And though the Rovers would essentially retain their individual status, competing in the Bristol and District League as normal (though under the watchful eye of City's board of directors), the Reds' certainly kept their promise. Arlington got full use of the training facilities, whilst the City ground at St John's Lane would play host to several of the Rovers key games in the Bristol and District League campaign.

The young Rovers lads – including Wedlock - were all put through their paces in training closely scrutinised by the City officials, this turned out to be a good situation for *everyone*, as all parties seemed to gain. Wedlock's training sessions for Arlington effectively doubled-up as his training sessions for Bristol City, as was the case for all ten of his team-mates, whilst Arlington Rovers AFC became, in-effect, City's junior wing for the season. To all intents and purposes, and to put a modern spin on things, they were basically the City 'Academy team'. The cost-cutting Bristol City directors had done away with an expensively-run *professional* Second XI, and cleverly replaced it with an in-house nursery team – for *nothing.*

As a public-relations exercise, City could also claim to have ticked a few boxes, having gone out into the community that surrounded them, seeking out young footballing talent, taking it on board, and offering to develop it, to nurture it. It appeared that *everyone* was a winner.

So Billy Wedlock himself, having clearly impressed the City management team during the original trial matches, found himself

WEDLOCK – THE FIRST HERO OF BRISTOL CITY

sat down in an office, signing a piece of paper to say that he was now an amateur footballer for, and henceforth, 'on the books of', Bristol City, his local professional club, on the understanding however, that City could let him go pretty much any time they felt like it. Bristol City had nothing to lose. But then it could also be argued that Wedlock didn't particularly have a great deal to lose either. To all intents and purposes, Wedlock – and his team-mates for that matter - would be placed on trial for the rest of the season. In between all the rigorous training sessions however, Billy would continue his full-time job as a tanner, and would still be playing for Arlington in the Bristol and District League – watched over closely, of course, by the City officials.

A very busy young footballer indeed. But training with full-time professionals for the first time meant that Wedlock would be rubbing shoulders with the likes of Billy Jones, who in many ways was the first real *'big name'* Bristol City player, and who would go on to win a single England international cap that season, against Ireland on March 9th 1901 - City's only international footballer thus far...

Yet whilst the City *'reserve team'* could be said to have been assembled wholly from up-and-coming youngsters, it could also be argued that the first-team had been well and truly swamped with the rump of the 1899/1900 *Bedminster* side, and aside from Billy Jones and one or two other exceptions, the First XI was barely recognisable from the Bristol City team of the previous term. This was of course the result of the recent amalgamation between the two south Bristol clubs, and Bedminster had, after all, finished *above* Bristol City in the table from the previous season. The City manager, Campbell, had spent the club's money on numerous expensive signings at the beginning of the term, many of whom now found themselves being shipped out and replaced by, what appeared to be, the just-as-good, if not *superior* players of their former rivals. Once again, *'the City'* had 'poached' the best of Bedminster for their own ends...

And so this is how Billy Wedlock was to begin life at Bristol City. He was strictly an *amateur* of course, and as such, could only train with the squad whenever his job permitted. Yet it is inevitable that when Wedlock *was* mixing it on the training field with many of the big, burly Bristol City professionals, he *must* have attracted a few looks of amusement as the City staff gazed on in wonder at this keen, but 'vertically-challenged' amateur. There may even have been a number of chuckles at his expense. One can imagine the odd light-hearted comment being thrown in his direction, perhaps *"So you want to be the next John McLean then?"* – a reference to the Scots-born former Liverpool man who had been the *established* City centre-half since 1898.

Wedlock though, would have taken all the jests in good heart. However, if there *had* been some sniggering, there was also *encouragement.* One player who *definitely* gave Wedlock some tips and helpful advice was City's legendary Scottish left-half Hugh Wilson, a vastly experienced professional who had previously won three League Championships with Sunderland. Hugh had been transferred to Bedminster in May 1899, subsequently coming to City a year later as part of the amalgamation process. And Wilson had remembered Wedlock from the previous season (99/00), at Ashton Gate, when an eager young Billy, his boots always at the ready, would regularly turn up at Bedminster's training sessions to try and help out in any way he could, such as making up the numbers in practice matches for example. And Billy, in his later years, would never forget his bits of valuable advice, Wedlock being very much the type of guy not to overlook the ones who had helped to put him where he was. But while many of the City players looked on in amazement, as the pint-sized amateur called Wedlock attempted to show some of the 'old dogs' a new trick or two, what they may *not* have known, is that elsewhere in the north of England there had been *another* player, just like our Billy – in fact, a *Wedlock-alike* – who had gone *before*...

Former Sunderland legend Hugh Wilson, now of Bristol City

IN DEMAND

Johnny Holt was a five feet five inch centre-half who had been a major star at Everton for a decade, between 1888 and 1898 – also winning a single cap for England in the process. The Lancashire-born pocket dynamo had played in all but *one match* when the Blues had won their first-ever English League Championship trophy in season 1890/91. Despite his obvious lack of inches, he had been regarded by many as one of the greatest centre-half-backs in England. He had bundles of energy and could out-jump *any man* on the field of play, whatever their height. The only aspect of his game which was *not* shared with Wedlock was his tendency for unsporting behaviour and gamesmanship. He had a fiery temperament and enjoyed committing the odd sly foul when the referee's back was turned. His game was occasionally crafty and he developed sneaky methods of outwitting his opponents which bordered on the outright *cheating*. For this, he became known to all at Anfield and Goodison Park by the nickname *'little Everton devil'*.

Johnny Holt

WEDLOCK – THE FIRST HERO OF BRISTOL CITY

Wedlock of course, would *never* resort to Holt's methods of gamesmanship, not during the whole length of his career. But, in *every other* respect, they were alike. The footballing gods who looked down on Bristol City must have used Johnny Holt as the very *template* when they made Wedlock. It was only much later on that – *eventually* - one or two individuals began to notice this great similarity. Years later, when Wedlock's talents were becoming more widely recognised, when Wedlock was performing *elsewhere*, and was being headhunted by potential suitors, the then-current Bristol City player Walter 'Cocky' Bennett, on seeing Billy play, is alleged to have exclaimed *"A second Johnny Holt!"* So there *had* been a precedent for the small centre-half in professional football, Wedlock was *not* the first. Although his career was now coming rapidly to an end due to his advancing years, Holt had been a major star at Everton in the Football League. It simply appeared that no-one at Bristol City around this time seemed to recognise the fact.

Both Holt and Wedlock of course, ultimately made their names in their mutual position, both as famous *centre-halves*. In Billy's case, it had not quite happened – *yet*. But it needs to be stressed that the specific role of centre-half in this particular era, was certainly not the same as that in which we see *today*. Wedlock and his like were not modern-day *stopper* centre-halves, ie, they weren't out-and-out *defenders* as such. For this was not the age of the 4-4-2 formation, nor of the 4-3-3 set-up for that matter. It was very much the era of the 2-3-5 formation, and *every team* played in this manner. Henceforth, the requirements of the centre-half placed him very much in the heart of *midfield*, where he was expected to win the ball – either in the air or on the floor –

and then set the play moving with a ready supply of passes, and general distribution, to his front men. In other words, he was expected to both defend *and* attack, so he became very much – in effect – a *midfield playmaker*.

Meanwhile, City - who had effectively attained complete supervision and control of Arlington Rovers' Bristol and District League campaign, had good reason to claim early success, as Wedlock's young team enjoyed a sensational start to the new season, routing Crews Hole United by *fourteen* goals to nil in their first game, on September 15th.

What seems likely, however, is that from a fairly early stage City wanted Wedlock to be playing higher grade football than the standard the Bristol and District League could offer. It also seems clear that one or two in the Boardroom must have been enjoying considerable influence with the powers-that-be who were running the Gloucestershire Football Association.

In short, City wanted Wedlock to be given a run-out for the County side, and they ended up *getting* what they wanted. Henceforth, on September 19th 1900, it was confirmed in the **Western Daily Press** that Billy Wedlock (of Arlington Rovers FC) had been selected to play for the Gloucestershire Football Association, against its Devon counterpart, in Plymouth, on October 17th.

But good things often come in twos – and the very next day, on September 20th, Wedlock became a father for the very first time. His daughter, Rosina Ellen Wedlock, was christened at Ashton Gate St Francis on October 12th 1900. The baptismal record confirmed that Wedlock and his wife were living at his parents' house at the time of the christening – namely, *'Ashton Place'* (172 North Street), Bedminster.

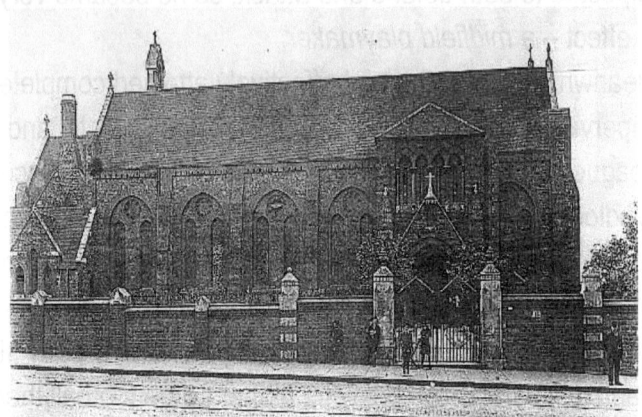

The regular Wedlock family church – 'Ashton Gate St Francis'

This may not have been ideal preparation for a busy Billy during the run-up to his big appearance for the GFA at Plymouth, but in the event, Gloucestershire beat Devon by four goals to two, in the bright south-west sunshine. Acting as one of the linesmen that day – and no doubt running a very close eye over Billy and several of his Gloucestershire team-mates – was none other than Bob Campbell, General Secretary and Team Manager of Bristol City FC. In fact, the Gloucestershire team might as well have been called simply 'Bristol', as suspiciously, the entire XI was made up of Bristolians!

On Saturday November 24th, Wedlock again represented the Gloucestershire FA, this time turning out against their Somerset counterparts at Yeovil. The match finished in a 1-1 draw.

Yet Billy did not neglect his bread-and-butter duties with Arlington Rovers, who, after their exploits from the previous season, had quickly picked up from where they had left off, clicking into gear in the Bristol & District League and leading the table, once again, by Christmas time.

On Saturday December 22nd 1900, Wedlock played for Arlington against Bedminster St Francis, in the semi-final of the Gloucestershire Junior Cup, at St John's Lane, home of Bristol City. St Francis clearly had a score to settle, having lost out to Arlington in the trial sessions held by Bristol City in the summer. But in the event, Rovers won 2-0, clinching their place in the Final for the second successive season, which this year, would be held on Boxing Day. Arlington's opponents in that Final would be Bristol St Philips, and, as had been the case for the semi, it would be played at St John's Lane. But the event proved to be something of an anti-climax, with Wedlock's Rovers retaining their title in a rather one-sided affair which ended 3-0 to Arlington. All of Wedlock's various successes, both with Arlington Rovers, and with the Gloucestershire FA, would have been noted by Bristol City with a great deal of interest. And privately, Billy himself must have felt that a fair degree of progress had been made.

What happened next, however, could not have been imagined by Wedlock in his wildest dreams...

As Bristol City's first team made their preparations for the journey to Queens Park Rangers in a Western League fixture, it became apparent that their recent spate of injuries had suddenly spiralled into a crisis. As previously mentioned, City's priority competition at this time was the Southern League, but in 1900/01, they also had a sizeable chunk of 16 Western League engagements to fulfil, this made up approximately one-third of their busy 'League'

WEDLOCK – THE FIRST HERO OF BRISTOL CITY

programme. Both the Southern League *and* Western League campaigns were classed as *'First-team matches',* and when combined this total came in at an arduous 46 matches (*excluding* cup ties) – a *lot* of football for a cost-cutting club which had recently scrapped its professional reserve team!

That risky decision meant that City had been walking a tightrope as far as injuries were concerned, on a week-to-week basis. It appeared the directors had finally been punished for their gamble, City's luck had ran out and as players and officials prepared for the journey to London, it became clear that the club could barely make up the numbers. Emergency measures having been called for, a number of untried 'reserves' were drafted into the squad at the last minute, and amongst the final names to be submitted onto the team-sheet that day, one in particular caused a fair number of raised eyebrows and more than a few expressions of *"Who?"*

That name – *'W. Wedlock'.*

So on Monday February 18th 1901, in front of a rather sparse crowd of less than 2,000 – Billy Wedlock made his first-ever appearance in Bristol City's first-team colours. That match was at Kensal Rise, London - away at QPR in the Western League.

This was a surprising debut that had in no way been coming, *but* for the sudden injury crisis.

How would he do? Was he up to it? Yes, he had played for the 'Reserves'- *in a way* – yes, he had *trained* with the professionals - but this was *something else.*

In the event, no-one need have worried. Not only did Wedlock, at centre half-back, keep a 'clean sheet' in his first match, but City won by two goals to nil, with both goals being scored by their

IN DEMAND

Scottish striker Billy Fulton.

The Sporting Life reported that *"Wedlock, who usually plays with the Arlington Rovers, made a very creditable appearance at centre half in his first match of any real importance..."*
– furthermore - QPR were *"...unable to make much headway against the Bristol half-backs, who were all in good form, especially their novice, Wedlock".* A later edition of the ***Athletic News*** made the additional observation:- *"It is to be hoped they* (Bristol City) *will not find themselves in such dire straits again for players, but if they do they now know they have a most capable centre half-back to fall back upon in Wedlock, of Arlington Rovers. He is only a little chap, but is wonderfully clever".*

> QUEEN'S PARK RANGERS v. BRISTOL CITY.
> This League match was played yesterday at Kensal Rise on a very heavy and holding ground in the presence of rather less than 2,000 spectators. In consequence of recent mishaps to different members of their team the visitors were not too well represented, and gave places in their team to some of their reserves, one of whom Wedlock, who usually plays with the Arlington Rovers, made a very creditable appearance at centre half in his first match

How 'The Sporting Life' began its report on
Wedlock's first-ever match in Bristol City's colours

Seemingly as a reward, the following Saturday (February 23rd) saw Wedlock picked for City's first team *again*, in an exhibition match at home to Leicester Fosse (of the Football League) – at St John's Lane, Bedminster. City won 1-0 courtesy of a first-half penalty by Bob Davies. So, two games - two 'clean sheets'.

But it didn't end there. Wedlock's next match for the first team came on March 9th, away at Millwall, at Eastferry Road, this time

WEDLOCK – THE FIRST HERO OF BRISTOL CITY

in the Southern League. It was Billy's third outing overall for the first-team, though only his second match 'proper' - the Leicester Fosse game being classed as, in-effect, a friendly. (The contest in London would take place on the same day that the aforementioned City star Billy Jones was making Bristol footballing history, by starring for England against Ireland in the Home international Championships at The Dell – becoming the Reds' first-ever international player in doing so).

As far as the Southern League was concerned, City had walloped Millwall 7-1 in the corresponding home fixture, so they were expected to win again. However, although Wedlock was noted to have played well, City were surprisingly thrashed 4-0, the **Athletic News** confirming that *"the backs tackled and kicked well. Wedlock, a youngster who played centre half, was the best of the three"*. **The Sportsman** newspaper further commented that *"Wedlock, who appeared as centre half-back, created a most favourable impression; he is a mere youngster, and should develop into a very useful player"*. Prophetic words indeed...

Up until this point, Wedlock had been the only Arlington player required to step up to the plate and provide emergency cover for Bristol City in their hour of need. Then, inside forward C. Harding became the second, when on April 9th yet another spate of injuries meant a vacancy in the first team for the Western League fixture at home to Queens Park Rangers at St John's Lane. City fought back from a 2-1 half-time deficit to force a draw.

Days later, full-back A. Marsh became the third and final Arlington player to receive the big call-up, when on Saturday April 13th City faced Reading at Elm Park, a match that finished in a 2-2 draw. By all accounts, Marsh, although nervous, gave a very creditable performance and was rewarded with an immediate second appearance, at home to Millwall at Ashton Gate the following weekend, another Western League clash that City lost 1-0.

Bristol City's injury woes are highlighted once again, as the 'Western Daily Press' announces the arrival of Arlington Rovers' Harding into the team

By the time the season concluded, Arlington players had contributed a total of *six* first-team games to the Bristol City cause. Wedlock had played three times, once in the Western League, once in the Southern League and once in a 'friendly'. Marsh played twice, both times in the Western League. Harding played just the once, in the Western League. No Arlington player would ever find himself on the field with *another* Arlington player at the same time. Interestingly, City used *one other* amateur player from the Bristol & District League that season, Brooks, of Bedminster St Francis, who was given a run-out in a friendly at

WEDLOCK – THE FIRST HERO OF BRISTOL CITY

Aberdare in March, proving that back in the summer, City must have taken a shine to one or two of the St Francis boys too. Brooks, however, never played for the City again.
And finally, the football season *did* come to its end.
At the conclusion Bristol City were disappointed to finish as runners-up in the Southern League, for the third time in four years. But, all things considered, even allowing for a very early exit from the English FA Cup, it had *still* been a good year.
And now, Bristol City – forever considering financial costs, forever checking their bank balance, forever fretting over their 'bottom line', had a number of key decisions to make.
Players. *Who* to retain, *who* to offload. *Who* to sign, and *who* to get rid of. *Which* of the trialists had been up to scratch?
And *which* of them had not?
And so Bristol City took another good long look at Wedlock. They looked and they frowned. They frowned and they scratched their head. They just couldn't quite work him out. They could not make up their mind. They had seen flashes of brilliance from him on the field of play. Yet somehow, he just didn't *look like* a footballer.
He did not fit their description of how a footballer *should* look.
So Bristol City had another think. And then they looked a*gain*. They looked at his height, and they looked at his waistline. And they looked at his age. '*20 years old'*. Billy Wedlock had no more growing to do. This man had reached his maximum height.
And they looked at him again. They looked him up and down. They noted his height. They noted his weight. He *was* the wrong shape. And again, they frowned. And they scratched their head. Again. It did not take too much imagination to work out their train of thought. It ran something like this – *"Bristol City Football Club*

IN DEMAND

*are going places. Bristol City Football Club are going up.
In the summer, we shall be applying for election to the Football League..."* (They were to be *successful* in this endeavour).
*"If successful, then next season we shall be competing in Division Two, of the Football League. The boy Wedlock. He's good. He can play. He's a decent footballer. He can hold his own at THIS level of football. In the Southern League. In the Western League. But next season - when we are in Division Two, of the Football League...IF we are to be in Division Two, of the Football League...well...five feet four inch centre-backs cannot be expected to be able to compete in the air against six feet two inch centre-forwards.
Can they?
The Football League surely does not play host to other five feet four inch centre-backs.
Do they?
Not in the Football League? Not in Division Two of the Football League?"*
And Bristol City *again* looked at Billy Wedlock. And they frowned, once more. And they scratched their head. Again.
But a decision *had* to be made - at some point in time. And a player could not be kept 'on trial' forever. So either way, a decision *had* to be made. Perhaps just two words summed up *exactly* what they were thinking;
"Too Small".
But Wedlock was not naive. And Wedlock was not stupid.
Billy Wedlock knew the score. He was nobody's fool. He knew what they were thinking, and although nothing was yet set in stone, he could foresee the writing on the wall. And Wedlock

knew that City already had plenty of decent half-backs on their books. And that money at the club was tight. He knew that Bristol City would be cutting costs. That Bristol City's wage bill was already too high.

Billy Wedlock knew all of these things. And Billy Wedlock could see that if next season, Bristol City *were* to be competing in Division Two of the Football League, then *his* chances of playing in the first team were going to be limited. He would be playing for the reserve team (pending its *reinstatement*). And Billy Wedlock did not want to be playing for the reserve team. Not for Bristol City, not for *any* club. Billy Wedlock wanted – and *needed* – to be playing for the *first team*. At *his* age. At *his* time of life. At *this* stage in his career. Because deep in his heart, Billy *knew* that he was good. He *knew* that he was better than *this*. He *knew* that he had it in him, to be playing professionally, to be playing to a very decent standard of football. He *knew* it.

He needed to be playing for the *first team*. Somewhere.

For *somebody*. Not languishing in a reserve team, not at Bristol City, not *anywhere*.

And meanwhile, Bristol City took *another* look at Billy Wedlock. And they shrugged. And they frowned, once again. And they scratched their head. Again...

It was a dilemma - for *both* sides. It was a dilemma, and nobody knew what to do. And it is perhaps not so much of a coincidence that the word *'Wedlock'* rhymes with *'Deadlock'*, because this is precisely what it was. But a decision *had* to be made.

And then finally, a decision *was* made. One of the two parties made a decision, with the alleged verdict from Bristol City stating *"You'll never make it – you're not good enough".*

IN DEMAND

And thus it came to be, that at the end of the season, Billy Wedlock upped and left. He packed away his boots, and he left Bristol City. Billy Wedlock had found an alternative option, he had received an offer from elsewhere. So Billy Wedlock neatly packed away his things, and he left Bristol City behind.

His days at Bristol City were over. He had finished his time at Bristol City, and he had finished his time with Arlington Rovers, bringing the curtain down on a four-year stint with that amateur outfit. He had also finished his time with the Gloucestershire FA, playing his final game for the county at Eastville Stadium (then known as Stapleton Road), the Bristol Rovers ground, on Saturday April 13th 1901, in a contest against their Devon counterparts, which Gloucestershire won 1-0.

And that summer, Billy and his family were to leave the city of Bristol *altogether.* The city they had been born in, the city in which they had grown up, the only city they had ever known.

And Bristol City frowned once more. And Bristol City scratched its head. And with a slight degree of regret, with a slight degree of reluctance, Bristol City shrugged its shoulders. Bristol City was slightly disappointed, though not devastated, to have let its young starlet slip through its fingers.

But Billy Wedlock was not devastated either.

Billy Wedlock just *got on* with things.

Billy Wedlock was looking ahead.

Billy Wedlock was looking to the future, with hope in his heart. Billy Wedlock was starting again, with a new club, and a clean slate.

And so Billy Wedlock packed his bags, and he took his wife, and he took his child - Rosina Ellen, his little baby daughter.

WEDLOCK – THE FIRST HERO OF BRISTOL CITY

And the little family, when they had packed everything that they could possibly take, then left the city of Bristol, and they crossed the River Severn, and they ended up in south Wales, in the county of Glamorganshire. Wedlock was to start afresh. Wedlock had found a new football club. A club who *wanted him.*
In the following campaign, season 1901/02, Wedlock would be playing regular first-team football in the Welsh League. Wedlock would be playing for Aberdare. One day, in the not-so-distant future, William J Wedlock would become, without doubt, the finest centre-back in the country.
And yet Bristol City had just let him go...

In the meantime, what would become of Arlington Rovers AFC? The harsh truth is relatively clear. Despite the best efforts of their professional backers, Arlington failed to retain their Bristol & District League title in 1900/01, finishing in only third place behind champions Staple Hill and runners-up Bedminster St Francis. Perhaps the sheer weight of expectation, plus the distraction and pressure of trying to impress Bristol City FC had been burdens too great to bear. City would appear to have cut ties with their 'nursery side' *completely* by the end of 1901. And although the Rovers would continue to enjoy a small degree of success for another year or so afterwards, they later sank into relative obscurity. Wedlock's final match as an amateur in Bristol appears to have been the 1-0 defeat at Bedminster St Francis on April 27th 1901 – an occasion which signalled the loss of Arlington's league title to Staple Hill... The players Marsh and Harding would never again play a first-team game for Bristol City...

4] He who 'Dares

Ynys Meadow, home of Aberdare FC

So began the Wedlock family's new life in South Wales. For the first time, Billy was to play football on a *professional* basis, at least, in part. He was actually to turn *semi*-professional, as Wedlock, ever adaptable, was to be a man with *two* trades. By day, Wedlock was to work in the building trade, having secured a full-time position as a stonemason. On occasional week-nights, he would be engaged in training sessions with his new Aberdare team-mates, then, on Saturday - for Billy, the *biggest* day of the week - he would be made available for team selection. If he *played*, he was paid – if he didn't, he wasn't. But in theory, for the first time in his sporting career, Wedlock would actually be *earning money* through playing the game he loved. From his 'day job' as a stonemason, Billy would be taking home a fairly decent 'working-man's wage', supplemented, it was

WEDLOCK – THE FIRST HERO OF BRISTOL CITY

to be assumed, by week-to-week *'Saturday bonuses'* earned through his football appearances for Aberdare. As he settled down into new digs with his wife and young child, Billy must have known that, if he played his cards right, the potential was there for him to be earning a half-decent amount of money at the end of the working week. But for pure *footballing* reasons, it was also a chance to shine, a chance to start again. This was a brand new team, an ambitious club who, as Wedlock well knew, actually *wanted* him. It was an opportunity to get his football career firmly back on track. In his heart of hearts, perhaps Wedlock may have known that he had *needed* a change. He had outgrown Arlington Rovers, and was going nowhere at Bristol City, at least, not as long as John McLean remained in the team at centre-half.

Like Bristol City, Aberdare was a fairly young club, it being about eight years old at the point of Wedlock's arrival. Formed in the year 1893, the team was originally and formally known as *Aberdare Town*, eventually switching to the name *Aberdare Athletic AFC* in 1920. From day one, their home ground had been the *Athletic Ground*, also referred to as *Aberdare Stadium* but popularly known to most fans as *Ynys Meadow*. Average crowds were relatively small, but very passionate nonetheless. The stadium had a small grandstand, and there was a cycle track running around the outside of the pitch. Curiously, Bristol City had actually *played there* in a friendly match against Aberdare earlier that year, on Monday March 4th 1901, when a near full-strength City side had cruised home by four goals to nil, in front of around 1,000 spectators. Wedlock certainly didn't play for Bristol that day, although this *had* been the game in which City had given a run-out to Bedminster St Francis youngster Brooks – a trial which ultimately came to nothing.

*'The Aberdare footballer'. **NOT** Wedlock, but a good example of how one of his team-mates may have looked at the time*

The standard of football on offer for the Welsh fans was quite high, with Aberdare playing in Division One of the South Wales League, or – to give it its full title *'The South Wales & Monmouthshire League'*. This competition had been running since the league was first established back in 1891. Aberdare's playing colours were yellow and black striped shirts, with white shorts and black stockings. The team had finished as runners-up in the South Wales League title race during the previous season, and had high hopes of going one place better *this term*. In theory, everything seemed geared up to future success.

However, unfortunately for young Billy Wedlock, he had walked into a football club that had, just at that time, run into a series of behind-the-scenes problems that were beginning to *seriously* mount up - something he couldn't have known about when he had signed the contract. By a twist of fate, as Wedlock had departed Bristol City, so Aberdare's star striker Steve Jones had gone in the opposite direction. This was seen as a major blow for the Welsh side, and left the fans wondering where on earth the goals were going to come from in the upcoming season.

In addition to this, Aberdare's Welsh international centre-half W P Jones had *also* left the club, having secured a summer transfer to Southern League Kettering. It could be argued that this might not have been seen as *such* a severe blow, as Wedlock had certainly been signed as cover for Aberdare's half-backs, if not, then as a *direct replacement* for W P Jones *himself.*

These *playing* matters, however, were merely the tip of the iceberg as compared to Aberdare's off-the-field issues. The **South Wales Daily News,** of Monday September 16th 1901, went as far as to say *"Up to the present time, as far as the general supporters of the team are concerned, the Aberdare Soccer Club is in comatose state..."* - the newspaper went on to explain the gist of the matter, namely, that a disagreement had broken out between the club directors and other local parties as to the ownership of the stadium, *Ynys Meadow,* and more specifically, of *how* it should be used. One side of the argument suggested that the Football Club *alone* could not justify or afford the sole use of the stadium, but the directors of Aberdare appeared to disagree. Negotiations between all interested parties had dragged on, but had failed to produce a conclusive result, the directors subsequently adopting a 'bunker mentality' by hiding themselves away, with the newspaper complaining that supporters had been kept in the dark every step of the way. Matters appeared to have reached a bizarre new level of intrigue when it was claimed that the club directors "*have not seen fit to publish their fixtures yet. The crux of the whole thing is - they have decided to form a limited liability company, and, provided they were enabled to obtain the grounds - which are in every way adapted for the purpose - an athletic syndicate would accrue and govern the Football Club. The negotiations, however, have not been successful so far, and it is thought that the old conditions will be reverted to, and the ground used for matches only. Seeing that the season has now practically begun, together with the fact that a great counter-attraction will be afforded the Aberdare public by the Aberaman Club, the apparent dilatoriness of the Committee must be detrimental to their already diminished exchequer".*

The paper went on to join the mourning of Aberdare's loss of Messrs W. P. and Steve Jones, its parting shot ruefully conveying the fact that the latter of the two had "*scored twice for Bristol on Saturday*". Given all these problems, a thought of *"Have I done*

WEDLOCK – THE FIRST HERO OF BRISTOL CITY

the right thing in coming here?" must surely have crossed Wedlock's mind soon after his arrival in south Wales during the summer of 1901.

After a delayed start to the season, Aberdare *finally* got their league campaign underway on Saturday October 19th 1901, at home to Rogerstone, yet even at *this* late stage, due to the ongoing debates concerning their stadium issues at *Ynys Meadow*, the club was forced to 'host' the fixture at the nearby Blaengwawr Athletic Ground, home ground of rivals and neighbours Aberaman. To make matters worse, the game kicked off half an hour later than scheduled when the visitors failed to arrive at the makeshift venue in time. These were hardly ideal circumstances for Billy Wedlock on the day of his Welsh League debut for Aberdare. But when the first half eventually began, Aberdare rushed into a 2-0 lead, with Wedlock scoring the second goal, described by the **South Wales Daily News** thus:- *"Greenaway sent in a nice centre* (corner) *and Wedlock judging his kick scored a second goal".* The visitors though, grabbed two goals before the break and it was 2-2 at half-time. In the second half, *"Jones re-started for the visitors, and Wedlock immediately obtaining possession, got through the centre, where he beat Jones and Williams before giving up to Hugh Williams"...*

Later on, after Aberdare had fallen 3-2 behind, the report excitedly continued:- *"the home lot now tried all they knew to equalise the score, and Wedlock was once more conspicuous with a clever dribble and a timely pass to Hugh Williams".*

A dramatic finish ensued, resulting in a late, late equaliser for Aberdare - a very exciting match thus ended in a 3-3 draw, with Wedlock playing a stormer and also scoring a goal! It hadn't turned out to be too bad a debut for Billy after all...

The season began to make progress, with Wedlock quickly settling into his new team, slotting neatly into his accustomed centre-back position. So steady were his early performances that he was to become an automatic fixture in the Aberdare line-up, for the complete duration of his stay in south Wales in fact.

It quickly began to look as if he had played with the Glamorganshire men his *whole life*, though it helped, one would imagine, having five other natives of Bristol being in the squad with him, including striker Dicky Osborne, who – like Wedlock – had previously experienced a spell at Bristol City.

As the season slowly unfolded, so Aberdare's problems seemed to ease a little, and this in turn would see the team appearing to play with a bit more freedom. Semi-professionalism however, clearly meant occasional lapses of basic organisation, and in a friendly match at Porth on November 16th, Aberdare had only ten players present to pick from at the time of the kick-off. The resultant re-shuffle saw Billy tried out as a *striker*, with the team sacrificing its centre-half position and playing with only two half-backs. The tactics didn't work however, Aberdare losing 1-0.

Generally speaking though, Aberdare appeared to be making some progress. On Friday December 27th 1901, the team played Leominster at home, and despite a goal-less first-half, in the second period Aberdare went goal crazy, Wedlock scoring twice as the hosts won 5-0.

Despite the late start to the season, the South Wales League, fixture-wise, was not a particularly busy one. In reality, it was more of a mini or *'super league'*, there being only *seven* teams participating in the First Division in season 1901/02 – meaning just 12 matches. Aside from the league campaign, the diary was generally filled up via the entering of various cup competitions, and the staging of exhibition games and friendly matches. As far as the friendlies and exhibitions were concerned, then for Aberdare, the situation clearly demanded that the more 'high-profile' opposition the club could attract, the better it would become for the good of the finances, due to greater publicity and enhanced gate receipts. In short, there were plenty of opportunities for friendlies, with clubs sometimes going two or three weeks without a league fixture.

On Monday December 30th 1901 came yet another one of these exhibition games, which no doubt was to prove a very special match for Wedlock *personally*. The visitors to *Ynys Meadow* that day were none other than a Bristol amateur outfit called *Arlington Rovers*, of all teams! There seems little doubt that this particular contest must have been arranged *almost totally* for the benefit and satisfaction of Billy himself, and one can imagine that the young Bristolian must have felt pretty keen on getting his old mates over the Severn so that he could gain an opportunity to show them how he had moved on, and how he was now playing for a *superior* outfit. It was a good-natured way of showing off a bit, but perhaps more importantly, it showed that Billy *never forgot* his mates, and always remembered the friends who had helped to put him where he was in the present. There is no doubt that Aberdare certainly *were* a superior outfit, henceforth they – *and Billy* – undoubtedly expected to win.

HE WHO DARES

In the event, class *did* tell, as the semi-professionals were to prove too strong for the amateurs. On a wet and stormy afternoon in south Wales, Aberdare beat Arlington by four goals to nil. The pitch was slippery, but this appeared to have no real effect on Wedlock, who was reported to have played well. Hugh Williams scored twice in the first half for Aberdare, who led 2-0 at the break, then in the second half, Berryman and Osborne completed the scoring to wrap up an easy victory for the home team. At 4-0, Arlington got off lightly, for if it hadn't been for Clapp, the Rovers 'keeper, then Aberdare's margin of victory would have been much greater. The **South Wales Daily News** reported that "*the spectators were treated to several good bouts of passing, Shenton and Wedlock leading their forwards in fine style*". It is interesting to note that two of the beaten Arlington team, Marsh and Harding, were the same two players who (aside from Wedlock) had made a handful of appearances as trialists for Bristol City in the previous season.

As for Wedlock and his Aberdare men, the good times appeared to continue - early in March 1902, the team went to Blaina FC and thrashed them 6-1, in the semi-finals of the interestingly-named *Leominster 'Bright' Charity Cup*.

But there were still at least *three more* exhibition games to be played between now and the end of the season, and at least *two* of these matches, in their own different ways, would be of considerable importance...

If Wedlock had been looking forward with great excitement to the previously-reported Christmas match against Arlington, then he would surely have been positively licking his lips having checked the fixture diary for the next *'Friendly'*. On Monday March 17th, the next visitors to *Ynys Meadow* were a team called Bristol City. Although not many in the crowd might have been quite aware of how much this game will have meant to Billy Wedlock, it was still a fair-sized attendance of around 1,500 who went along to watch. In the event, despite a gallant effort by Aberdare, City triumphed by two goals to nil. Banks headed the opening goal for City in the 37th minute, though it was reported that straight from the re-start Wedlock was within centimetres of equalising but his powerful shot hit the post, the **Western Daily Press** explaining that *"...Wedlock once putting a nice attempt that nearly took the upright"*. City were still 1-0 up at the break, after which, Aberdare – or rather more, Wedlock *in particular*, was struck with a little bit of raw irony. City on this particular day had given a rare outing to *yet another* local amateur, this time in the shape of young Vickerstaffe, of Eastville Athletic. And of course, it would be *he*, Vickerstaffe, who finished off Aberdare in the second-half, netting City's second goal, the youngster also having had an effort disallowed in the first-half. The **Western Daily Press** perhaps seemed rather more amused at the hosts' line-up, it noting *"Aberdare...however, were perhaps more entitled to be termed a 'Bristol side' than the City, for no fewer than six men on the Welsh side were old Bristol players, these being Golding, Wedlock, Shenton, Smith, Osborne, and Woolacott"*.

It seemed that Aberdare simply could not get enough of playing Bristol-related teams, as next up on their 'Friendlies' list was a contest against a Select XI containing some of the best amateur players of the Bristol and District League, dubbed the '*Bristol*

HE WHO DARES

League XI' by the south Wales press. Included in the team were the two Arlington full-backs Smith and - *that man again* - Marsh. The match took place on Friday March 28th, at *Ynys Meadow*. After going a goal down early on, Aberdare led 2-1 at the break, with Wedlock then adding a third goal in the second half, thus helping his team to eventually run out deserved 3-2 winners. Once again, Billy Wedlock had shown a team of Bristol *non-professionals* that he had moved on...

After the League XI fixture, the second of the 'important' friendly matches occurred a few weeks later on Tuesday April 15th 1902, with Aberdare playing host to a touring Aston Villa side at *Ynys Meadow*. Although just an *'Exhibition'* match, this was probably the highest-profile contest yet experienced by Wedlock in his short career so far, and *certainly* his most glamorous opposition. With five English Football League Championships to their credit, as well as three FA Cups, not to mention an historic *'Double'* that had been won in 1897, Villa were probably the biggest and most famous football club in England at that time. For Aberdare, the opposition, quite simply, did not get any more *'glittering'* than *this*... The **South Wales Daily News** reported that a *'Record Crowd'* was there to see an enthralling game eventually won 5-2 by Aston Villa, with the local press yet again giving favourable reports as to the personal performance of Billy Wedlock, making various mentions of *"clever tackling"* and shots at goal that *"only missed by inches"*. But if *this* game had been classed as a *'Friendly'*, then the next one would end up being *anything but...* The match in question was a hotly-contested local derby between Aberaman and Aberdare, which took place on Monday April 21st

WEDLOCK – THE FIRST HERO OF BRISTOL CITY

1902, at the home at the former. Although Aberdare had led at the break, the game finished in a 1-1 draw. It then appeared that a number of the Aberaman fans had taken exception to the some of the tough-tackling by Aberdare's Sam Parker, believing that he had *'roughed-up'* two of the younger Aberaman players who had taken part as trialists that day. As the teams walked off the field at the final whistle, some of the aggrieved supporters ran on to confront a group of departing Aberdare players, Parker included. A full-scale fight was only *narrowly* averted, with Parker and Wedlock apparently needing an escort off the pitch for their own protection. A hot reception for the Aberdare team had *always* been on the cards, in the first league game between the two sides at *Ynys Meadow* on March 31st, the *Darians'* had walloped their neighbours by six goals to two, with Wedlock scoring twice, the first one coming after only three minutes. The match though, had been littered with a succession of crude fouls, Wedlock being on the receiving end of the worst of them, resulting in a sending-off for Aberaman's Hendy.

As the league season drew to its conclusion, Aberdare had an outside chance of winning the South Wales League title, but needed to win their final two games at home to leaders Barry *and* then against Porth, in order to overhaul both Barry and second-placed Rogerstone. Unfortunately, Aberdare failed at the first of these hurdles, only gaining a 0-0 draw against Barry at *Ynys Meadow* to effectively end their chances.

For Aberdare, the season's end had a slightly anti-climactic feel to it. In one way, the campaign *could* be seen to have progressed satisfactorily, especially given the problems which had marred the start, and taking their first-ever South Wales Cup, via the thrashing of Llandrindod by seven goals to one on April 5th, *did* go some way towards making up for the disappointment of not winning the League. For Wedlock *personally* though, it was a different matter. *He* had made tremendous progress, he had been a fixture in the team, and his influence over that team seemed to be *growing.* In the following season, it would grow even stronger...

It must have seemed an odd life for Rose Wedlock, Billy's wife, finding herself living in a strange place, in a strange *land*, and often alone with nothing much to do except house chores and looking after the baby. There was Billy's football at the weekends, *and* his regular training sessions – not to mention the fact that he also had rather tough old 'day job' - it was a wonder they could ever have found much time to spend together. Billy would have simply been *so* busy all of the time, and the couple quite often would have been like ships passing in the night. Many years later, the **Nottingham Journal** (November 3rd 1920) painted a rather amusing picture of the daily rush that a busy Wedlock must have experienced -

"A Lad's Enthusiasm -
Wedlock hails from the Bristol district, but was at that time engaged in the building trade at Aberdare, and was often to be seen dashing from work to the hotel in his corduroys to strip ready for the match on the adjoining field".

There wouldn't have been all that much for Rose to do in the town either, Aberdare as a place wasn't like Bedminster and it *certainly* wasn't like Bristol. When a person walked outside the border of the town, they were out into the open country, out into the wild – effectively *cut off...* In the winter, when a thick white blanket of snow covered the ground, that was it, you were practically disconnected from the rest of the world.

Aberdare nestled in the rolling hills and valleys of the Cynon Valley. It lay roughly half way between the cities of Cardiff and Swansea, also being four miles south-west of the town of Merthyr Tydfil, and just outside the southern border of the area which is today known as the *Brecon Beacons National Park.* The town sat at the confluence of the Rivers Dare and Cynon, the former of which was also responsible for Aberdare AFC's club nickname, '*The Darians'*. Its population in 1901 would have been maybe around 50,000, which seems a lot, but then Bristol's population at the same time was more than six times that figure, standing at around 330,000. And to Rose, most of these people spoke in a very strange native tongue, both in terms of *accent*, and occasionally in terms of *language.* It wasn't quite as difficult for Billy, who had five other Bristolian team-mates to keep him company. Such were the trials and tribulations of being the wife of a semi-professional footballer! This, it seemed, and the potential and prospect of regular upheaval, and of the moving from town to town, seemed to be the territory that came with being married to a young, up-and-coming soccer player of the early 20th century...

Wedlock's second season for Aberdare, 1902/03, began late, as usual, in October. On Saturday the 11th of that month, Billy was present as the team defeated Brecon by three goals to nil, at *Ynys Meadow.* The proper business however, started a week later on the 18th, when the team played its first League match of the season, at home to reigning champions Barry. The result, however, was another clear 3-0 win for Aberdare - which represented a very encouraging start indeed. The return fixture with Barry took place only a week after *this*, on the 25th, the match ending in a 0-0 draw. Unfortunately, *this* occasion marked what was to be surely the only time in his career that Wedlock would ever be sent from the field of play, albeit in completely bizarre circumstances that had little to do with foul play, and *everything* to do with *mistaken identity*. Aberdare's Sam Parker, the man whose tough tackling had caused a near-riot in the derby match at Aberaman the previous spring, had again been at it with the Barry left-winger Bevin, the referee eventually warning the pair that any more rough stuff, and they would *both* be 'Off'. It was simply a running feud between the two of them, with no-one else involved. It then occurred however, that Wedlock and his Barry opposite number Tattersall collided near the usual left-flank position of Bevin, the pair falling to the floor. Rushing up, the referee - immediately mistaking the pair for Parker and Bevin - sent the unfortunate duo *off,* with the **South Wales Daily News** reporting that *"...visiting spectators and players are certain it was a mistake by the referee"*. In between these two matches with Barry, Aberdare also played a home friendly with Doncaster Rovers FC on Monday 20th, winning 5–2 after the teams had been level at two goals apiece at the break.

By now, Wedlock's increasingly consistent performances at the back had earned him the captaincy of Aberdare, at the very least on an *occasional basis*, the match against Doncaster being the first example of this fact being recorded in the local newspapers. *Captain Wedlock* certainly led by example *that* day, scoring one of the five goals that saw Doncaster scurrying back to Yorkshire with their tails between their legs. The **South Wales Daily News** was positively purring, claiming *"For the homesters, the two Hughes' were the pick, but Parker, Wedlock and Ingham played a sterling game".* Interestingly, a strong Bristol City side was *also* playing a friendly that day, just up the road in Aberaman, suffering a surprise 3-2 defeat. Had the City sent one of their 'spies' over to *Ynys Meadow* to watch the Aberdare game instead, they may well have been interested in what they saw...And perhaps - *rhetorically speaking - if* that spy had subsequently watched carefully enough, he may have then found himself reporting back to City with some rather gloomy news and a dramatic statement to the effect of - *"We have made a grave error in letting young Wedlock go!"*

Aberdare's league campaign meanwhile, had got off to an absolutely flying start, it being reported in early December that they had remained unbeaten over the course of the first six matches, winning five of these, with the only small blip being the 0-0 draw with Barry. Added to this, they had also scored a whopping 22 goals and had conceded *none,* the highlights of this run being a 3-0 win over Caerphilly and an astonishing 10-0 mauling of Treharris (the previous week). However, at Nelson on December 8th, Wedlock's boys suffered a bout of complacency, and having finally conceded their first league goal – albeit via a penalty – they only got away with a draw with thanks to a late headed equaliser from Hughes, scored in the semi-darkness.

HE WHO DARES

The ***South Wales Daily News***, in its Boxing Day edition of 1902, then became one of the first British newspaper to refer to Wedlock by his most enduring and iconic nickname. Giving their official match report on the contest played between Aberdare and Ebbw Vale at *Ynys Meadow*, a meeting that Aberdare had won by a single goal to nil, a cheeky sports journalist had the sheer temerity to reel off the following immortal line – *"...for the homesters, Ingham, Jack Hughes (left-half) and FATTY Wedlock were the most conspicuous..."*

On the following day, Saturday 27th, Wedlock was again specified by the local media as being the *captain* of Aberdare, the papers reporting that *this* time, his team had beaten Newtown 1-0 in a friendly.

A few weeks later, on Saturday January 17th 1903, Aberdare went to Treharris in the League, with the latter of these teams seemingly determined to gain some revenge for the 10-0 humiliation which Aberdare had thrust upon them earlier in the season. In the end, despite some newspaper accounts claiming that Aberdare had ridden their luck at times, Wedlock's boys *did* come out on top, by two goals to one. One reporter though, *did* have to admit that *"Parker, Wedlock and Hughes worked together in beautiful unison, passing on several occasions between them, taking play from one end of the field to the other..."*

Yet over the long winter months, Aberdare appeared to suffer a slight dip in form which would later have a crucial bearing on their chances of winning the league title. To make matters worse, their bitter rivals Aberaman were on a roll, *they* being the very team who would leapfrog them into pole position in the League table.

WEDLOCK – THE FIRST HERO OF BRISTOL CITY

On Saturday January 24th 1903, the two teams met at *Ynys Meadow*, in a vital fixture that the Aberdarians really needed to win. Unfortunately it was not to be, the game finishing deadlocked in a 1-1 draw, with both goals coming in the second half. However, the Welsh sports journalist for the **Daily News**, writing under the pen-name '*Arthurian'*, made sure the south Wales public became aware that, once again, the Aberdare skipper had been one of the stars of the show:- *"...the home half-back line was a strong one, and the captain, though small in stature, proved a veritable host in himself. He kept at his work from start to finish, and was one of the best on the field."*

Aberdare still had a chance of wreaking revenge on their neighbours, as the two sides were due to meet in the South Wales Cup Final on March 28th. Bizarrely, Aberdare had got to the Final without having to play a *single match*, with two teams having 'mysteriously' pulled out upon hearing the news that they had drawn Aberdare in the 'next round'. But in the Final, at the Mountain Ash Recreation Ground, Aberaman defeated Aberdare by two goals to nil, the result confirming that a power shift was occurring in the Cynon Valley, and unfortunately it was draining away from the *Darians* in favour of their near–neighbours.

By this time, Aberaman were moving well ahead in the League table as well, and by early April, although Aberdare were still in second place, it was all over bar the shouting.

In mid-April, a late flurry saw Aberdare win 5-0 at home to Porth in the league, with Wedlock connecting with a corner to score the first goal. But it all came too late, and Aberaman finished the season as worthy champions, leaving Aberdare to lick their wounds in second place.

WEDLOCK

Surely one of the oldest photographs of Billy still in existence, maybe even the OLDEST. Published in Welsh newspaper the 'EVENING EXPRESS' on September 3rd 1904, it shows a young Wedlock, moustache and all, in his Aberdare kit

Wedlock though, as had been the case at the end of the *previous* season, had sufficient reason to feel a good deal of satisfaction. From his *personal* point of view, yet *more* significant progress had been made. He was an automatic member of the Aberdare side, and there was certainly no question of his ever being dropped. As the most consistent performer in the team, he was now being selected as the club captain on a regular basis. He

was the club captain on *merit*. People were beginning to talk of Wedlock as being the best centre-half-back in Welsh football. From the opposition's point of view, he was a marked man.
Yes, Wedlock was the man they feared, even from the so-called 'defensive position' of centre-half, Wedlock was the *Danger-man*. Everything seemed to be going Wedlock's way, he was a *success*. His 'weekend job' with Aberdare was going well. His 'day job' in the building trade was going well. He was successfully providing for his family, and *his* was now a family of *four*, as Billy and Rosina's second child – and *first son,* William James Wedlock - had been born at Aberdare on December 22nd 1902.
Billy Wedlock had *every reason* to feel a sense of satisfaction. It was as if the Bristol City *debacle* had now long since disappeared over the horizon. It was as if the Bristol City *phase* had been virtually flushed from his system.
It was almost as if he had *forgotten* about Bristol City. One *could* have said that in his mind, he had left Bristol City firmly behind him.
But *had he?*

5] Two sides of the Severn

As Billy Wedlock was walking out of Bristol City around the spring of 1901, a moustachioed, bowler-hatted administrator and local businessman named Francis Noot Bacon had nearly bumped into him coming the other way. They hadn't *quite* passed like ships in the night, because the suited and booted gentleman, more usually known as simply 'Mr Frank Bacon', had arrived to take his place in the City boardroom some time *earlier* during that season, which had kicked off in September 1900. In other words, he had *certainly* been present at the club during the time when young Billy and his Arlington team-mates had effectively formed the City 'reserve team'. Whether or not Director Bacon had been *in favour* of letting young Wedlock leave the club is unknown, but one thing is *certain* – if he *had* been in favour of it, then he would certainly change his mind on the matter later on.

WEDLOCK – THE FIRST HERO OF BRISTOL CITY

Bacon was an absolute *authority* on sport in the Bristol area, taking a particular interest in the matter of junior sports. From an early age, sport had been Bacon's great passion, football, rugby, athletics, or cricket, it didn't matter – in fact, it would be far easier to list the sports that he *didn't like*, rather than the ones he *did*. Of all his sporting passions, however, the activities of football and athletics were the ones closest to his heart. He liked to encourage all young people to keep fit, and to take part in healthy outdoor activity, and any youngster who was making his mark, excelling in his sport, moving up the ladder and making a name for himself – Bacon got to hear about it.

From the year 1905, until the time he eventually died, in 1918, Mr Bacon was to have a tremendous influence on Billy Wedlock, the two men striking up a close friendship that quite possibly, was to affect Billy for the rest of his life. Bacon was to become Wedlock's friend, mentor and confidant, his advice and encouragement was to shape Billy both as a footballer, and as a *human being*. It was also quite possibly *his* influence that eventually guided Wedlock through the end of his footballing career, and beyond, easing Billy's passage from the role of *'sporting idol'*, into *another* calling...

Mr Francis Noot Bacon, AKA, 'Frank Bacon', had been born in Bedminster, Bristol, on March 22nd 1862. The son of John and Mary, his passion for all things sporting has already been mentioned. But he, like Wedlock, worked his way up from very humble beginnings, and, from an early age, he never had things easy. The 1881 census tells us that the 19 year-old Bacon was working as a machinist in the boot trade. He later moved on from this and eventually made some money through entering the licensing trade, whilst also becoming the proverbial *'pillar-of-the-community'* in the process. He was landlord of the *'Queen's Head'* in New Queen Street for five years, between 1891 and 1896. Then he famously became licensee of the *'Masonic Arms'* in North Street, Bedminster, staying there in this capacity in fact, until the time of his death, nearly twenty-two years later. Rumour has it, he knew of young Wedlock practically since the time of Billy's birth, and although this story *may* have been exaggerated, it *is* likely that the pair had been acquainted, at least from the time that the Wedlocks' had moved into *Ashton Place*, North Street, around the year 1890, when Billy was ten, and Frank was 28.

Strangely enough, Frank took over as landlord of the *'Masonic Arms'* in February 1896, not all that long before Billy had first joined the nearby Arlington Rovers. He also arrived in the boardroom at Bristol City during the same season (1900/01) that Arlington's amateurs had been on trial at the club, with Wedlock & co leaving at the end of the term. Another rumour once did the rounds that Bacon had originally known of Wedlock's footballing prowess at Arlington *specifically* because *he* (ie, Bacon) had once played as a *goalkeeper* with the Rovers, again, this does seem a little *unlikely* and may well have been exaggerated. What *canno*t be said to be in doubt, however, was Frank's sheer *breadth* of knowledge concerning all matters relating to sport. Bacon's sporting expertise apparently knew no limits, he was by all accounts a great authority on just about *everything*. In sporting and recreational circles, *he* was the man who knew all the right people, *he* was the man who had all the good connections, *he* was the man with a finger in every sporting pie. He was a member or Chairman of just about every local sporting club, society or committee going, later becoming, in-effect, Head of Bristol Athletic Club, and eventually even becoming its Life President. In footballing terms, his early connections were with, if anyone, *Bedminster*, rather than Bristol City. In 1898/99, he was part of a nine-man Syndicate Committee, whose job it was to make all the preparation and arrangements necessary for the first-ever International football match to be held in Bristol, namely, England v Wales, on March 20th 1899, at the ground *later* to be known as Ashton Gate. The staging of this match was a massive coup at the time, Bedminster were still in the midst of their great rivalry with Bristol City, and followers of the latter had reacted with great jealousy, claiming in vain that St John's Lane would have made for a better venue. The Syndicate Committee of which Frank Bacon had been a part had a good deal of other responsibility, for it was *their* job to make sure that one-third of all home gate receipts were paid as rent to Bedminster's landlords. When the amalgamation between Bedminster and Bristol finally occurred in the spring of 1900, Bacon, in theory, was out of a job. He could have simply rolled back to his pub, the '*Masonic Arms*', and sulked. But he didn't. As previously mentioned, the amalgamation between the two clubs had resulted in an almost *total takeover* by Bristol City. City had kept their name, club colours, manager and chairman. They also took most of the better Bedminster players and got rid of their own. The only two areas where there was to be a 50/50 split was in the retaining of the two grounds, and in the Boardroom. Henceforth, Bristol City, in season 1900/01, needed more *Bedminster* men to fill up the allocated spaces on the Board. It seems, therefore, more than a mere coincidence that Bacon should arrive specifically in *that* season, just at the very point in time when City were doing away with their reserve team, and taking on board the Arlington Rovers boys, to be trained, developed and nurtured. (Frank Bacon – with *his* knowledge and experience...)

Whichever way one looks at it, it seems likely that Bacon had been invited onto the City Board for his sheer *sporting expertise*, rather than for his money. At which point, as we now find ourselves up-to-date with *Bacon's* story - for his tale *now*, is fully aligned with that of Wedlock's – we shall continue the main narrative, through jumping from *one* side of the River Severn, to the *other*...

WEDLOCK – THE FIRST HERO OF BRISTOL CITY

At the end of the 1902/03 season, Wedlock was disappointed to see a good friend and team-mate leave the club. John *'Jack'* Hughes had played alongside Billy in the half-back line for two years, for in 1901 the two had joined the club at roughly the same time. But Jack had been recommended to Liverpool FC, and had subsequently gone for a trial at Anfield – he must have been successful, because he ended up signing a contract. A full-time professional career had *always* been his ultimate goal, and happily, Liverpool had *always* been the club he wanted to play for. In May 1903, he departed for Anfield to play in the First Division, quite a big step-up, because Liverpool had become Champions of England for the first time only two years earlier, in 1901.

There is no doubt whatsoever that Billy would have wished his mate Jack all the luck in the world, because Jack had deserved it, he was a good footballer, a very fine player. But Wedlock - being *only* human - when wishing his pal *"All the best"*, must, it would be imagined, have done so with just a private tinge of envy. Yes, Hughes was a good player. Yes, Hughes was a fine footballer who had *deserved* his move to a top-class club. But Billy...Billy was a *better* player. Wedlock *must* have been thinking to himself - *"Will my turn come too?"*

Hughes had great respect for Wedlock, and *vice-versa,* and Hughes knew that Wedlock should be playing higher-grade football for *someone,* for he was better than the only level that Aberdare could offer and *5s* was not a great wage befitting of someone of *his* talent. Just before Hughes departed, Wedlock is alleged to have asked Hughes – *perhaps*, tongue-in-cheek, but

perhaps *not* - *"Any chance of finding ME a decent club?"*
And with that, Hughes went away to Anfield, but he never forgot Billy's question. He soon recommended Wedlock's name to the legendary Liverpool and ex-Sunderland manager Tom Watson, but it was nothing doing. Hughes also saw for himself that Liverpool's stock of centre-halves in the First Division was already very strong, Alex Raisbeck (the captain), Andy Raisbeck (his brother), Maurice Parry, George Fleming – there was no way in a million years that Wedlock was going to get a game ahead of any of *these guys*. It is not known whether there continued to be any kind of written correspondence between Wedlock and Hughes, but one thing *is* known – Hughes would *never* forget Wedlock's request. Jack though, had to look out for *himself* first, and soon got on with the job in hand, becoming a first-team regular at Anfield, and playing in 31 out of Liverpool's 34 league games that season. But he continued to make enquiries on Wedlock's behalf, and in time, sent a letter off to Blackburn Rovers FC, a club not a million miles away from Liverpool...
Meanwhile Wedlock, as usual, just carried on with things. Like he *always* did. And the 1903/04 Welsh season commenced, and it began to make progress...
The highlight this term would not be in the League, nor would it be against a flashy opponent in an exhibition game. It wouldn't be in the Leominster 'Bright' Charity Cup. It wouldn't be in the South Wales Cup. No. The high-spot of *this* season would be a great run in the Welsh Cup, the major knock-out competition in the *country*, and the Welsh equivalent of the English FA Cup. Aberdare couldn't stop *winning* in this competition, and after

having a *bye* for the First Round, they eventually beat Porth, Rogerstone, Chirk and Oswestry to reach the Final for the first time in the club's history. It was to be held at the Racecourse Ground, Wrexham, on April 4th 1904 – Easter Monday. Aberdare's opponents were to be Ruabon Druids, more commonly known as *'Druids'* for short. Unfortunately for the Aberdarians', everyone knew that the Druids were going to be an extremely difficult nut to crack. The team was vastly experienced, and had already won the Cup *seven times* previously since the competition's inception in 1878. They were a long-established club, and very old hands in the north Wales game. As they were based in the village of Ruabon near Wrexham, the Final was also going to be played on virtual home territory for the Druids. In short, any other result bar a Druids win was going to be a major surprise. Druids as a team were roughly of the same quality of Wrexham, and in the previous year's final, Aberaman, who had *then* proved themselves as being superior to Aberdare in the South Wales competitions, had been walloped 8-0 by Wrexham. This fact highlighted the sheer *scale* of the task facing Aberdare *this year*. Having said that, it had been noted that the Aberaman men had clearly been affected by the long train journey, endured on the morning of the match. There would be no such chances taken by Aberdare *this year*, Wedlock's boys travelling up on the Saturday instead, and having a full day's rest before the Final on Monday. But what Wedlock may or may not have known was *this* – Jack Hughes had still been persisting with his enquiries on Wedlock's behalf, he had contacted representatives from Blackburn Rovers FC, and as it happened, the referee for the

TWO SIDES OF THE SEVERN

Welsh Cup Final was going to be a Blackburn native, Mr John Lewis. Accompanied by a separate footballing representative of Blackburn Rovers, Jack Hughes made the 75-mile journey to the Racecourse for the Final - the duo would be discreetly hidden amongst the 6,500 crowd, an estimated 700 of whom had travelled from south Wales to support Aberdare.
But how would Wedlock, and Aberdare, perform on the day? In the end, although the game would prove to be a highly-entertaining one, and Aberdare would be able to hold their heads up high, the Druids won the day, running out as narrow 3-2 victors. Frustratingly, *twice* the Darians' had taken the lead, only to *twice* be pegged back again by Ruabon. It had been all-square, 1-1, at half-time, and then 2-2 in the second-half, before a third goal for Druids in the latter stages of the game had won it. By all accounts, Wedlock *"was a wonder that day"*, being *"here, there and everywhere"*. But it had not been *quite* enough. The Druids had won the trophy for the *eighth* time in their history. Almost as if the officials were fed up with having to hand over the Welsh Cup to the same old team again, no trophy presentation formally took place, with Druids being told to simply take the trophy away. Aberdare later cried foul, complaining that Druids had fielded an ineligible player, W Davies, who had not been listed on the pre-match team-sheet. But the Welsh FA disagreed, and the result was allowed to stand. In the ground, immediately after the game, Jack Hughes turned to the Blackburn Rovers representative and asked *"Well? What did you think of Wedlock?"* The reply was simple and blunt – *"He is far too small for first-class football"*. And that, unfortunately, was the end of *that*.

WEDLOCK – THE FIRST HERO OF BRISTOL CITY

Billy Wedlock would never end up playing for Blackburn, and neither would he end up playing for Liverpool. In fact, the following season, he would still be playing for Aberdare...

At the beginning of the next season, 1904/05 – Wedlock's *fourth* with Aberdare – there were changes afoot. In April 1904, the **Merthyr Express** had reported that a new 'Welsh Football League' would be formed *in addition to* the normal South Wales League which had been going since 1891. The reason for its creation was apparently due to claims that the South Wales League was being *'overly dominated by Cardiff clubs'*, a bit of a flimsy excuse, as in reality there weren't all that many.

The new set-up would comprise three levels, a Third Division, a Second Division – and a seven-team 'elite' First Division, including Wedlock's Aberdare, along with Barry, Cardiff Corinthians, Ebbw Vale, Llanbradach, Rogerstone and Treharris.

Another view of Ynys Meadow, home of Aberdare FC

TWO SIDES OF THE SEVERN

As far as the Glamorganshire men were concerned, a programme comprising of twelve fixtures for the new competition - also to be known as the *Rhymney Valley League Division One* - was to be tackled in addition to the regular South Wales League games. Aberdare's campaign in the new League kicked off with a convincing 5-1 victory at home to Cardiff Corinthians on November 12th 1904. It would eventually come to be that Aberdare would write their names into the history books of the Welsh Football League, by becoming the first-ever *champions* of that inaugural season, in 1904/05. They would end the campaign by winning not only *their* very first Welsh League title, but also therefore, *the* first Welsh League title, *period...*

In other competitions, Aberdare's reward for another lengthy Welsh Cup run would be a second successive place in the Final, again at the Racecourse Ground, Wrexham. This time, the opponents would be Wrexham *themselves*, meaning another tricky-looking match to negotiate...

And in their *domestic lives*, the Wedlock family's 'reward' would be the addition of a third child, as Billy and Rosina's second son, Thomas George Wedlock came into the world on September 11th 1904. The Wedlocks' would eventually produce seven children during their happy marriage, and of these, all but two of them would be Bristol-born. The two exceptions, sons William James and Thomas George, would be the two born under the *Baner Cymru* – in other words, under the Welsh flag, during Billy's spell at Aberdare.

 Back over the Severn in Bristol, Frank Bacon was getting anxious. He was getting twitchy. Bristol City were not moving on.

WEDLOCK – THE FIRST HERO OF BRISTOL CITY

Bristol City were staying still. Bristol City were stuck in a rut. The team had finished in sixth position in 1901/02, their debut season in Division Two of the English Football League, and also the first term under the *second* management spell of Sam Hollis. They had got 40 points from 34 matches. Everyone at the time had agreed that this had been highly satisfactory, for their *first* season, for their *first-ever* campaign in the Football League. Then in the following year, they had advanced two places in the table and had finished in fourth. With 42 points from 34 matches. *Progress.* Everyone agreed that *this* had represented *progess*. Then, in 1903/04, their third season, they had finished, once again, in fourth place. With 42 points, again, from 34 matches. Of course, the ultimate goal was a top-two finish, which would mean promotion to the First Division. Season 1904/05 saw City move operations *permanently* to Ashton Gate, the former home of Bedminster FC, and the ground they had used alternately (with St John's Lane) during the 1900/01 campaign. St John's Lane was now going to be consigned to the history books. Ashton Gate was clearly the *future*. But would it change City's luck? On the evidence of season 1904/05, it appeared *not*. For at the end of *this* campaign, City would finish in fourth position yet again, this being for the *third season* in a row. Their points total was 42, from 34 matches – *again*. It was as if Bristol City were standing still. It was as if they had reached their zenith, and would never be able to finish in a position any higher than *fourth*. It was as if the proverbial needle had got stuck in its groove, resulting in the record sounding as if it were playing the same burst of tune over and over again. It was as if the City were bereft of *one* vital instrument from their toolbag. It was as though they were missing a single piece of the jigsaw, which – if it were *found* - then the puzzle would henceforth become solved.

Bacon felt that he knew what – or rather, *who* – that missing piece was...

Wedlock.

The player that City had inextricably let slip from its grasp four years ago. And Frank Bacon had begun to realise that City had made a mistake. They should not have let him go after all. But then again, maybe it *hadn't* been a mistake. Because Wedlock had not been *ready* then. Not four years ago. But he certainly appeared to be ready *now*.

The Bristol City squad for the 1904/05 season, including Frank Bacon, seated on the middle row, facing the camera - far right

Because Bacon always made it his business to know when a young native of Bristol was performing outstanding feats in his field. Because *he* was Frank Bacon. He *always* got to know! And Wedlock *was* performing outstandingly well – for Aberdare. Bacon had heard all the gossip. He well knew what all the south Wales papers had been printing, week after week, month after month – that the boy Wedlock was a *genius*. Bacon knew all the scouts had been watching him, for ages. Scouts from Second Division clubs, from First Division clubs. He knew all the rumours about the Aberdare manager, Bob Jones, allegedly turning down *bribes*. Yes, clubs had actually been offering bribes to make sure that Wedlock was pushed in *their* team's direction. Bacon knew all this. But Bacon was still not deterred. He simply knew that City *had* to get their man. Wedlock *had* to be persuaded to come back to Bristol, the city of his birth, the city of the first twenty years of his life – in order to sign for Bristol City. Sam Hollis, the City manager for the *whole* duration of their Football League existence, had departed once more. He *knew* that City were going to miss out on promotion again, he probably knew they would finish in fourth place again as well. He had seen the writing on the wall, and, knowing that his contract was about to expire, had walked, with seven games still to play before the season's end. And so that was *that*. Hollis departed, on March 19th 1905, to concentrate on his business interests. He went off to manage the *Southville* pub just up the road. In the meantime, the club had advertised the post for the vacant manager's job, and an answer had speedily arrived – from within the City's own ranks. In fact, from within their own *playing* ranks...

...Harry Thickett, the sturdy Yorkshireman, that famous old Sheffield United and England right-back, who had joined City only a year ago. Who had made 14 appearances for the club that very season, but who was approaching the end of his playing career. Whose CV and application had so charmed the board of City directors...And Thickett had thus been appointed, in double-quick time, only eight days after Hollis had left the club in fact. The directors had decided that Thickett was their man at an evening board meeting on March 27th, with the Yorkshireman's name being released to the press the following day, on *his* (Thickett's) 32nd birthday. And so Harry would be the man charged with getting City through their '*stuck record*' phase, he would be the man trusted to end the stigma of '*fourth place again*'. But Bacon knew that Thickett would need to have *all* the tools at his disposal. Thickett could not be expected to complete the puzzle if he did not possess all of the pieces.

Frank Bacon   *Harry Thickett*

Bacon knew that he, *and City – had* to have Wedlock. Bacon's big idea was a trip, with Thickett, to see Aberdare in action, so that Thickett could see for *himself* just what a football genius Billy Wedlock actually was!

But – would Wedlock actually sign for the club? Could he be persuaded? The newspaper reports concerning Wedlock and his outstanding form were becoming more and more frequent. The gossip and whispers were getting louder and louder...

On Saturday April 8th 1905, Wedlock was present as usual as Aberdare squared up to Treharris in a 5pm kick-off at *Ynys Meadow* in the *Rhymney Valley* Welsh League. Treharris were simply swept aside, Roberts, Ingham, Grant and Shenton putting Aberdare 4-0 up at the break, with McKiernan adding a fifth in the second-half to make it 5-1 to Wedlock's boys. *"Archie Davies, Wedlock and 'Mac' were the pick of the home team."* boasted the **South Wales Daily News**. Two days later, on Monday the 10th, Aberdare squeezed past Ebbw Vale 3-2, with the papers, of course, confirming that *"Wedlock was the best of the home lot."* The games were really coming thick and fast now, and on Wednesday the 12th, Barry District drew 2-2 at home to the Aberdarians, the single point meaning that Wedlock's men had failed to conclusively wrap up Welsh League title on the night. But - *"Twice Sutton had to save a warm shot from Wedlock..."*

"...Wedlock, Yarr and Stillman were the best halves on the field..."

Back in Bristol, Frank Bacon was in a state of some considerable agitation, he was now well past being anxious...All these reports had come filtering back to him, '*Wedlock this, Wedlock that*'........he had heard them *all*. Newspaper reports, scouting missions, it didn't matter – they all said the same thing. He had also been to watch Wedlock, himself – *personally*. He *knew* how good Wedlock was. He knew what Wedlock could do for Bristol City. He could transform the team, and propel it into the First Division. He was the spearhead. The linchpin. Wedlock was an out-and-out *attacking* centre-half, the like of which no-one had ever quite seen before. He advanced well up the field and joined in with the attacks. He took long-range pot-shots at opposing 'keepers for fun, and just kept trying them until he scored. Bacon knew that in one season with Aberdare, Wedlock had scored *twenty goals* – all from the centre-half position! He seemed to the opposition to be some kind of human-dynamo, having this uncanny knack of simply popping up unexpectedly, all over the field. The opposing teams simply couldn't pin him down. It was one thing man-marking a 'danger man' when he stayed in *one* position, but how to do it when he drifted all over the pitch, and wouldn't stay still for a second? At Aberdare, he seemed to have almost a free-role, a 'license to *wander*' – and opposition teams simply couldn't handle it. Through this, Wedlock seemed to take all the free-kicks, the corners, the throw-ins, *everything*. The only thing he didn't seem to take was the penalties. Yet the whole team seemed to revolve around what *Wedlock* was doing. He could pass, he could shoot, he could dribble, he could tackle, he was good in the air, he scored, dead-balls, free-kicks, corners – there was simply *nothing* this man could not do. He also had a 'tank', he never stopped running, and had great stamina. He could play comfortably in practically any position on the field, bar goalkeeper.

These were the skills he could bring to Bristol City, he was surely capable of rejuvenating a club that had grown stagnant...

WEDLOCK – THE FIRST HERO OF BRISTOL CITY

But Bacon now also knew that City had to act – *fast*. There were rumours swirling around, rumours that Stoke City were preparing a bid for Wedlock, that Blackburn Rovers – of *all* teams – were also in the running. Both these teams had obvious advantages over Bristol City – they, unlike City, were already *in* the First Division. These were well-established clubs, big clubs. Clubs with a history, clubs who - especially in the case of Blackburn - had *won things*. But then City had one clear advantage over the northerners – namely, that Bristol was Wedlock's *home*.
Bacon got his diary out, and circled two dates, two *critical* dates – dates that *he* hoped, would hold the key to Wedlock's eventual signing for Bristol City. The two dates were April 25th, and April 27th, 1905...

On Saturday April 15th, a late, late equaliser by Billy Ingham gave Aberdare a 1-1 draw away at Treharris, on a day that a special train had to be laid on in order to carry the great number of travelling Aberdare supporters who wanted to see the game.
In its match report on the Monday, the **South Wales Daily News** once again referred to Billy by his nickname, *'Fatty Wedlock'*, and indicated that, in their opinion, he had for once been out-foxed by his centre-forward opponent, in this case, Treharris's former Aberdare player, Hughie Williams.
On Monday April 17th, it was Aberdare's turn to concede a late equaliser, doing so in the very last minute of the game, this giving Ebbw Vale a 1-1 home draw with Wedlock's boys in the Welsh League, Billy gaining no more than a passing mention in Tuesday's newspaper match report.
The countdown to the Welsh Cup Final was well and truly on, for

TWO SIDES OF THE SEVERN

Wedlock and his team-mates. There was now only one more league fixture for Aberdare to play before facing their illustrious opponents in the showpiece Final in north Wales. This was at home to Rogerstone in the Welsh League on Saturday April 22nd. – Easter Saturday. This particular game also signalled, however, the beginning of the final frenetic week of the season which would see Aberdare having to negotiate five gruelling games within the space of *eight days*. This arduous schedule would also include the nightmare prospect of playing three punishing matches inside *72 hours*. On the face of it, this already seemed bad enough, before you even considered the fact that the three games in question were a Cup Final, a virtual title-decider and a high-profile 'friendly'!

On the Easter Saturday before the Cup Final, an injury-hit Aberdare side beat Rogerstone in the Welsh League by five goals to two. As soon as the game finished, the Wrexham-bound Aberdare squad rushed off to the station to catch the train to north Wales, where they would prepare for the Final, which was to take place, once more, at the Racecourse Ground, Wrexham - on Easter Tuesday, April 25th 1905. Unfortunately, the opponents were this time going to be Wrexham *themselves*, who, as with the Druids in the previous year, were the old, established club, past masters at this competition. They had won it five times before, and would also be playing on their 'home' ground. Henceforth, it went without saying that Wrexham were seen as being hot favourites for the Cup. The Aberdare players spent Easter Sunday in the city of Chester, resting up on Monday before the big day finally arrived...

WEDLOCK – THE FIRST HERO OF BRISTOL CITY

Frank Bacon, meanwhile, had persuaded his new Bristol City manager, Harry Thickett, to accompany him to the Final, specifically of course, to check out Wedlock's performance. At long last, the time for talking was over – Thickett was actually going to *see* Wedlock with his own eyes, Thickett was going to find out if all of Bacon's stories had been accurate. A small band of 'secret *Bristolians*' thus mingled in the stands, in keen anticipation of what they were going to witness. The small group included Bacon, Thickett and Walter '*Cocky*' Bennett, a former Sheffield United and England right-winger whom Thickett had made his first Bristol City signing only twelve days earlier. Thickett and Bennett were long-standing mates, old Sheffield playing colleagues from Bramall Lane. Both men had been born and raised in the Doncaster area, they were nearly the same age. Bennett was also a very experienced footballer, being a former League Champion with Sheffield United and having played in multiple FA Cup Finals with them. Back in the day, he had also won two England caps. In short, Thickett undoubtedly valued his opinion. Unfortunately, in many ways Messrs Bacon, Thickett and Bennett could barely have picked a worse game in which to make a judgment on Wedlock. Wrexham overpowered their rivals from the start, eventually winning 3-0 in front of a crowd of more than 6,000. As far as Aberdare were concerned, the day had been a big anti-climax. For the second season running, they had finished as runners-up in the Welsh Cup Final. But Bacon, Thickett and Bennett had still seen enough to enable them to make a positive judgment on Aberdare's star man. They could still see that Wedlock was a class above his team-mates. After four years,

TWO SIDES OF THE SEVERN

Billy's talents had slowly outgrown those of *Arlington Rovers* – now, four years later, they had equally outgrown those of Aberdare. During the game, Walter *'Cocky'* Bennett had been asked for his opinion on Wedlock, and Bennett, watching Billy in action for the very first time, subsequently replied with his famous line, namely that City had found *"a second Johnny Holt!"*
This was of course, a reference to the pint-sized former Everton and England centre-half, who has been mentioned previously.
The **South Wales Daily News** indeed concurred, writing *"the Aberdare defenders played a fair game, while Wedlock was a tower of strength at centre-half"*.
And *that* did it, for Thickett and for Bacon.
Bacon now had just one more date left in his diary...one last, *crucial* date...
Aberdare meanwhile barely had time to catch the train back south, before having to play a vital away game the *next day* at Rogerstone in the penultimate Welsh League fixture. As long as Aberdare avoided defeat, then they would be as good as champions. Despite a late equaliser for Rogerstone, the match finished 1-1, just about guaranteeing Wedlock's boys' place as top dogs in the new *Rhymney Valley Division One* of the Welsh League. By all accounts, Billy had *yet another* great game, with the **South Wales Daily News** reporting that *"Wedlock was the chief factor in the visitors defence and continually cut up Rogerstone's efforts..."*
But as for Frank Bacon, and his one *last* remaining date...
It would be just two days after the Welsh Cup Final, on Thursday April 27th, 1905. For it was on this day that Bristol City *just*

happened to be coming to *Ynys Meadow* to play Aberdare in an end-of-season friendly match. This game had *always* been scheduled, and - *allegedly* - wasn't pencilled in at the last minute as part of a dastardly plan to nab Wedlock. It was simply the stroke of good fortune that Bacon had been hoping for. Because *now* the City directors finally had their chance - Thickett, Bacon and *all concerned* must have almost been waiting to intercept Wedlock in the players' tunnel after the game! Yet they needn't have bothered being in a sweat over whether or not Wedlock would agree to come to Ashton Gate. Deep down, Billy knew that City were *always* going to be the club for him. Secretly, there had *never been a doubt* that - if the opportunity had *ever* presented itself – he was going to come back...

The Bristol City friendly at *Ynys Meadow* would prove to be Wedlock's penultimate game for Aberdare. City won 1-0 with a first-half goal by inside-forward Albert Fisher.

Four days later, Billy Wedlock signed for Bristol City – on Monday May 1st 1905. Before he did so, he had one last remaining engagement to complete for Aberdare, on Saturday April 29th 1905. This was the last game of the season, finally completing an exhausting closing week of football for Billy and his Aberdare boys. After the home match against Barry at *Ynys Meadow*, the Welsh League Championship trophy, AKA the *Rhymney Valley Division One Cup*, was presented to Billy Wedlock, the proud captain of Aberdare, on the occasion of his farewell match...

And this must have gone at least some of the way towards making up for the disappointment of losing the Welsh Cup Final. Wedlock in his post-match comments was typically modest to the end, the **Evening Express** reporting that he had *"felt highly proud of the Cup, not so much for my own sake as for the sake of my fellow players, who have worked hard to win the trophy"*.

As for the game itself, after finding themselves 3-2 up at half-time, Aberdare went goal-crazy in the second period, running out astonishing 10-2 winners. Billy signed off with a couple of goals *himself*, taking his end-of-season tally up to a highly-impressive 17.

By this time of course, Wedlock must have known that he was playing his last-ever match for the Welshmen, that he was about to become a Bristol City player. And subsequently, two days later on the Monday, he signed for the Ashton Gate club.

The following day, May 2nd 1905, saw news of Wedlock's transfer appearing in all the papers, and not just *Bristol* papers, lots of papers – papers from all across the country. From the *Eastern Daily Press*, in Norfolk, to *the London Daily News*, from the *Birmingham Daily Gazette*, to the *Portsmouth Evening News*, and from the *Nottingham Evening Post*, to the *Bolton Evening News* – all these newspapers felt it justified and newsworthy to print the story that Wedlock was coming home to the city of his birth.

Billy had been hero-worshipped by the townsfolk of Aberdare, they were going to miss him, more than any words could say...

But Wedlock had bided his time, and Bristol City – mainly due to the sheer dogged persistence of Frank Bacon – had finally corrected their 'mistake'. Everyone was happy.

After four years in the wilderness, Billy Wedlock was coming back to Bristol City – this time, as a *full-time professional.*

And *this* time, it would be for *keeps...*

WEDLOCK – THE FIRST HERO OF BRISTOL CITY

"THEY USED TO CALL ME THE *INDIA-RUBBER MAN* – SEEMS I USED TO BOUNCE FROM ATTACK TO DEFENCE, AND FROM DEFENCE TO ATTACK…"

6] Up, up and away...

On their return to Bristol, the first thing the Wedlocks' needed to do was find somewhere to live, for theirs was now a growing family, Billy and Rose having left for south Wales with *one* child, but now coming home with *three*. For this reason, they couldn't very well move back in with Wedlock's parents at Ashton Place. Billy however, was now in a better financial position than the one he had been in upon leaving four years previously. As a newly signed-up *professional footballer*, he had, for the first time in his life, a bit of decent money in his pocket – he was now in a position where he was able to buy his *own* house. Henceforth, by the end of the year, the Wedlocks would be settling into this very house, on the slopes of lower Garnet Street, not too far from the Chessels, but heading down the hill towards Palmyra Road. The family were next door to *Potticary's Hardware shop*, which straddled the corner of West View Road, and this was the first house that Wedlock ever bought. It was fairly small, but respectable – just the thing for a growing young family, just the house for an up-and-coming professional footballer. It wouldn't be a permanent fix, but just right to tide the family over for the time being. Early the following year, Wedlock would move his family into No 70, South Street, virtually opposite the entrance to the school of the same name, though this too would not prove to be a *permanent* solution for the ever-growing family, the Wedlocks moving out again after a year or two...

WEDLOCK – THE FIRST HERO OF BRISTOL CITY

Meanwhile, Billy had his football to concentrate on, for there was a *big* season approaching. As far as Bristol City was concerned, there was to be no mucking about this time – Billy had been purchased to play in the first-team, right from the 'off'. The guidance of that team this time round of course, was to be placed in the hands of Thickett, that stocky 32 year-old Yorkshireman, a man who was to take his managerial duties very seriously, now appearing in his formal black suit and bowler hat to boot. A former Doncaster Rovers and Rotherham Town player, he had gone to Sheffield United in 1893, becoming their first-choice right-back for about ten seasons. At Bramall Lane, he would enjoy a great career, winning the First Division Championship title in 1898 and finishing as a runner-up on two other occasions, whilst he also gained two FA Cup winners medals in 1899 and 1902, with a runners-up medal sandwiched in between in 1901. Full of typical northern grit, he had been a hard worker and a fearsome tackler, qualities which had endeared him greatly to the United supporters. He was an interesting character in many ways, and there were a number of legendary stories concerning him that had been talked about for years, such as his allegedly playing in the 1899 FA Cup Final *"swathed in forty yards of bandages and fortified with copious amounts of whiskey"*. This story was almost certainly highly-exaggerated, but it did somehow reflect the kind of tough guy he was. Also a very conscientious man, he had offered to take a pay cut in 1895 because he believed he had missed too many first team games after contracting typhoid fever. With his career seemingly coming to an end, Thickett had eventually moved to Bristol City in May 1904, making his 14 appearances for the club the following season, after which, he had applied for – *and got* – the manager's job. Thickett's remit for the season ahead was simple – '*Promotion*'. This could only be gained through a place in the top two of the Second Division. If – not *when* – they achieved it, they would be playing in the First Division, the very top league in English professional football.

Following on from Walter '*Cocky*' Bennett and Wedlock, Thickett's main summer signings were four Scotsmen, Archie Annan, Andrew Burton, Billy Maxwell and Pat Hanlin – plus Yorkshireman Frank Hilton and Bristolian Joe Cottle.
Annan was a Scottish-born right-back, who, like Bennett, had effectively followed Thickett from Sheffield United. Ironically, Annan's initial emergence at Sheffield in the first place had threatened Thickett's own position in the team, leading to *his* (Thickett's) eventual departure as a player to City.
Signed from Motherwell, Andrew Burton was a left-sided inside forward who was a native of Lochgelly in Scotland, and he would go on to make the No 10 shirt his own. His transfer had come about because a contact of Thickett's – Peter Boyle, *yet another ex-Sheffield United full-back* – had agreed to do some scouting for his old friend in Scotland.
Goal-getter Billy Maxwell was a right-sided inside forward, yet another Scot, very experienced, who had joined City from Millwall at the age of 28.
Pat Hanlin, from West Calder was a former Scottish Junior international who had been signed as a left-half from

WEDLOCK – THE FIRST HERO OF BRISTOL CITY

Bristol City, season 1905/06

UP, UP AND AWAY...

Everton, despite never having made a league appearance for the Toffees. His job was to provide stiff competition for existing half-backs Billy Jones and Peter Chambers. Barnsley-born left-winger Frank Hilton had been signed by Thickett from amateur side Doncaster St John's.
The local lad was 19 year-old Joe Cottle, like Wedlock, a Bedminster boy who had risen up through the Bristol and District Leagues. About six years Wedlock's junior, he had been recruited from amateur club Dolphins, after having a trial and having played in two subsequent reserve games for City the previous season. He would replace City's regular left-back Bill Tuft six games into the season and from then on, would never look back, making that position his own for the next five and a half years.
The *existing* squad members, *retained* by Thickett for the upcoming season included Billy Jones, Sammy Gilligan, Arthur Spear, Harry Clay and Peter Chambers. Jones, who had been City's only footballer capped by England, would start the campaign in his normal right-half position, though his City career was coming towards its end, and he would eventually be replaced by local lad Arthur Spear in mid-season. Scottish centre-forward Sammy Gilligan, who was about to start his second term at Ashton Gate, was an ex-Dundee and Celtic man who had signed for City in the summer of 1904, and had then established himself with 15 league and Cup goals in his first season.
Arthur Spear, another Bristolian – *again, from Bedminster* - had been signed as a 21 year-old in the summer of 1904, making his debut in a 1–0 win at Glossop on December 27th.

WEDLOCK – THE FIRST HERO OF BRISTOL CITY

He had made twelve appearances at half back, deputising at times for Peter Chambers and Billy Jones. Along with new arrival Pat Hanlin, he was again expected to be pushing both Jones and Chambers for their place.

The established goalkeeper was Nottinghamshire-born Harry Clay, he had been a fixture of the team pretty much since signing for the previous manager, Sam Hollis, in November 1901.

Holding the team together was skipper and experienced ex-Bedminster stalwart Peter Chambers, a 27 year-old Cumbrian who, previous to his time in Bristol, had played First Division football at Blackburn Rovers.

Aberdare striker Billy Ingham, who had played alongside Wedlock in the Welsh League during the previous season, had been brought to Ashton Gate *with him* during the summer, though Ingham, unlike Wedlock, was not destined for City greatness, and he would play only a single league game for the club during the coming season.

Of Thickett's eight major signings, four would start the first match on September 2nd at Manchester United, who, like City, were one of the teams strongly fancied to be in the promotion mix come the end of the season. The debutants (not including Bennett, who technically, had played his first game the previous season) were Annan, Maxwell, Burton and Wedlock. But the matter of Wedlock's first-ever match as a professional footballer for Bristol City, and the occasion of his official bow in English League football, turned out to be an utter calamity. Most observers expected a close game and a fascinating contest – what they got was a *walkover*.

UP, UP AND AWAY...

City's problems at Bank Street began early in the match when skipper Chambers was felled and hurt his knee. This being the era of *'no-substitutes'* of course, meant that any potential of injured players during a game spelled terrific danger, with the possibility of playing a man short looming large...

Chambers limped on and did the best he could, but was a passenger for large parts of the first-half, when ironically, his team-mates were playing quite well. When United took the lead through their new striker Charlie Sagar, it was against the run of play, but in the confusion, he soon added a second goal with an unstoppable shot. When Chambers' knee gave way for a *second time*, just before the break, the alarm bells were ringing for City. The Manchester men couldn't believe their luck when they saw that Chambers hadn't reappeared *at all* for the second-half, it meant that City would have to play with ten men for the entire second period, and United could go for broke. Confusion reigned in the Bristol back-line as the game-plan went out of the window, Burton being tried at left-half, and then being moved back up front again. United piled forward and pressed the ten men into submission, scoring three more goals, including a hat-trick strike for Charlie Sagar. Maxwell scored a meaningless 'consolation' for City at the death, but the Ashton Gate men had been hammered 5-1. It had been a *disaster*. The curious thing was that City had probably been the better team up until the point of the first United goal. Chambers' injury would keep him sidelined for weeks, though ironically, a serious knee injury later on in the season for *Sagar* would prove to be *his* undoing, it eventually bringing about the end of his professional career at United. Wedlock's name barely got a mention in the Monday match reports, it was not exactly how he had been expecting his City debut to pan out, and he – like Thickett – would remember this grim day for a long, long time to come...

At a rain-soaked Ashton Gate the following Saturday, only 4,000 turned up for the first City home game of the campaign against Glossop. It would turn out to be City's lowest home gate *all season*. It was as almost as if an air of resignation had filled the place, the 'United debacle' having already cast a *"here we go again..."* spell of gloom amongst the supporters. Even as City stumbled to a 2-1 victory, with goals by Maxwell and Bennett either side of half-time, there was nothing in the performance to suggest that a record-equalling sequence of *14 successive wins* had just begun. *Nothing* to hint that a *24 match unbeaten run* had now commenced. Yet amazingly, this is *exactly* what happened. The incredible run of victories, which *equalled* a Football League record set previously by – of *all teams* – Manchester United – began on September 9th (with the victory over Glossop) and was completed on December 2nd with another Ashton Gate triumph over Burnley. The match they would have needed to win in order to *break* the all-time record took place the following week at Leeds City, on December 9th, but the game ended in a 1-1 draw, meaning that City and Manchester United would have to share their place in the record books. But a 24–match unbeaten run would still continue until *February...*

UP, UP AND AWAY...

After Glossop, City went to Stockport County and won 3-2. Next up, Bradford City in midweek were narrowly beaten 1-0 at Ashton Gate thanks to a goal by Gilligan. This result pushed City up to fourth place in the Second Division after four matches – Manchester United meanwhile had won four out of four and were top with maximum points.

City next laboured to a hard-fought 2-1 victory over Blackpool at home in a match where, as had been the case in Manchester, the Reds' were forced to play the second-half with only ten men due to injury. But City – *and Wedlock* – had clearly learned a lesson from their hiding at Manchester, and this time had a contingency plan in place, though it was a scheme, admittedly, which left Wedlock having to do most of the donkey work. As the **Western Daily Press** explained, *"Wedlock, who has been attracting considerable attention in the City games this season, eclipsed all his previous work. It was undoubtedly his day and when, through the injury to Tuft, the Reds might have become disorganised, he did the work of two men, and a break-up was avoided. He assisted both wings and the defence, whilst also skilfully reinforcing the attack from the centre - a combination which has made many great centre-halves. His success had the doubtful advantage of being popular – doubtful, because in such a case future defects may be eyed too kindly..."*

The win over Blackpool put City into up into second place... Wedlock's young Bristolian colleague Joe Cottle made his City league debut at Bradford City the following week, this match providing the platform for successive win *No 5 –*

WEDLOCK – THE FIRST HERO OF BRISTOL CITY

by a 2-1 score-line. The result kept City hard on the heels of their Manchester rivals after six games, United though, having now won *six out of six*.

The tide was turning, however. On the day that City beat West Bromwich Albion 1-0 at home (October 7th), United finally dropped their first point, with Charlie Roberts' boys only drawing 0-0 at home to Bradford. This meant that Wedlock's City, although still second, were now only one point behind the leaders. When a late winner by Walter Bennett secured another 2-1 win, this time away at Leicester Fosse on October 14th, news then came through that United had been beaten 1-0 at West Brom, a result which put Bristol City at the summit for the first time. *And they would stay there.* This occurred after City's eighth game – their seventh successive victory.

Peter Chambers, now recovered from his knee injury sustained in Manchester, returned to the side the following week, at home to Hull (October 21st) whilst Wedlock's old Aberdare colleague Ingham was selected up front for his only game of the season. The match resulted in yet another narrow 2-1 victory for the Bristol men, but *another* victory nonetheless, their eighth successive one in the 'record run'. Lincoln City were next swept aside on their own patch by a score of 3-0, then Chesterfield came to Ashton Gate and were promptly despatched by three to one. An away match at Burslem Port Vale saw the home side narrowly beaten 1-0, then Barnsley came to Ashton Gate and were soundly defeated by three goals to nil. Further City successes against Clapton Orient (away) and then Burnley at home –

UP, UP AND AWAY...

both by 2-0 score-lines – finally completed the golden 14 - match sequence of successive victories. Although the 1-1 draw at Leeds City brought an end to the incredible winning streak, City bounced straight back to winning ways the following week by trouncing Burton United 4-0 at home. Of the long, winning run, the personal highlight for Wedlock must surely have been the match at home to Barnsley on November 18th, a contest that signalled the occasion of his very first professional goal for Bristol City. The match finished up as a 3-0 win for the Reds', with Wedlock scoring City's opener early on, and the **Western Daily Press** described Billy's goal and performance accordingly -

"After ten minutes play some remarkably fine work by the City left and Wedlock gave the latter a chance of gaining further distinction. He received the ball a good way out, and dribbling beautifully, got into position, and completely beat Thorpe with a magnificent low shot. There was unbounded enthusiasm at this, his first goal of the season. He seemed to take the Colliers' defence off their guard, and it was an excellent stroke of business all round....

...the game was a trifle erratic all through. Wedlock distinguished himself early in the game by a fine individual effort, which ended in the scoring of his first goal for the season....

...Wedlock was taking his part in attack as well as defence, frequently shooting splendidly..."

The **London Daily News** added – *"Wedlock, the leaders' sprightly centre-half, shot unexpectedly and hard, Thorpe hardly seeing the ball before it was in the net..."*

The season meanwhile had already rattled on into December and although the City were doubtless employing the old adage of *'taking each game as it comes'*, secretly, all eyes were turning ominously towards the calendar that showed *who* they would be facing on December 30th, on the first Saturday after Christmas...

City faced a particularly arduous Christmas programme, consisting of three successive away games inside the space of just five days, a 3-1 Boxing Day win at Gainsborough Trinity being sandwiched in the middle of draws against Chelsea (0-0) and Grimsby Town (1-1) respectively.

But the top-of-the-table excitement had reached fever pitch by the time Manchester United arrived at Ashton Gate on December 30th 1905, for the long-awaited return meeting of the top two – the first clash between City and United since the former's 5-1 mauling on the opening day of the season. City though, had improved beyond all recognition since that grim September day. *Hadn't they?*

The Bristol public was eager to find out and a record League crowd of 19,000 packed Ashton Gate for the festive showdown, not quite beating the 19,371 who had come for the FA Cup tie at home to Preston the previous February. The City team though, was desperately tired, having played two strenuous away games in two days over the Christmas period. Goalkeeper Harry Clay was one casualty, having to be replaced in goal at the last minute by the reserve, Bristolian Bill Demmery. Spear and Burton had barely recovered from the rigours of the Grimsby game, but they would play nonetheless.

UP, UP AND AWAY...

United on the other hand, were as fresh as daisies, having come down to Bristol straight from their Christmas Day home fixture with Chelsea. They had spent the rest of the week quietly training on the Downs, knowing as they did so, that City were away and tiring themselves out in between various long journeys. When the game kicked-off, it was obvious who looked the most energetic team, United capitalising on City's heavy legs, ripping into the Reds' straight from the first whistle, and having a goal disallowed after only three minutes for a foul on the debut goalkeeper, Demmery.
City successfully weathered the storm though, and despite a frenetic opening 45 minutes, it was goal-less at half-time. Fifteen minutes into the second half however, the ground erupted in delight when, from a corner, Sammy Gilligan forced the ball home amidst an almighty scramble. United though, would not be denied, and Charlie Roberts fired an equaliser late on which ultimately meant the game finished *'honours even'*.
The result meant that City started the New Year still in pole position, and even a shock FA Cup exit at the hands of Brentford could not dampen the spirits as far as the League was concerned - the team simply *kept on winning*.
January's big highlight was the 7-0 slaughter of Stockport County at Ashton Gate, an astonishing game that saw Gilligan score *four*, and Maxwell *three*.
City's critical game of the season now looked like being the clash away at West Bromwich Albion on February 10th. City and Manchester United had *nearly* pulled clear of the

chasing pack, the pack in question mainly consisting of West Brom and Chelsea. But a City defeat at West Brom would potentially leave them (ie, *City*) firmly in the Midlanders' sights, whilst perhaps also letting in Manchester United to take over at the top. A City *win* however, would place clear daylight between them and West Brom, and Thickett's boys would be firmly in the driving seat for promotion. In the modern era, such a clash would doubtless be dubbed a '*six-pointer*', this however being the year 1906, meant that it was still very much a '*four-pointer*'. The importance of the match was not lost on the Bristol public, who responded in a *big way*. It would be the largest fan following that City had ever taken to a league match outside of Bristol, with the **Western Daily Press** proudly reporting after the game that *"no fewer than 3,000 Bristolians made the journey"*. Once the snow had been cleared from the pitch, City roared into all-out attack, Gilligan quickly putting them a goal up and Walter Bennett, playing a stormer on the right-wing, adding a second before the opening fifteen minutes had been played. It remained 2-0 to the West Countrymen at half-time, and although West Brom rallied strongly in the second half, it seemed as if their luck was out. Despite Pheasant reducing the deficit from the penalty spot, the Baggies then had two goals ruled out for offside, much to the anger of the home fans among the estimated 15,000 crowd. City, riding their luck, then raced away on the counter-attack, resulting in Billy Maxwell adding a third and *decisive* goal. City had *done it*, they won 3-1 and when the team's train pulled into Temple Meads that night an enormous crowd was waiting to greet

UP, UP AND AWAY...

the players, the **Western Daily Press** reporting that *"...the cheers were deafening as the train steamed in. The bridge inside the station was densely packed, and as the players passed along, each one was addressed by name and patted on the back by enthusiastic admirers".*

Over-elaborate celebrations from the fans however, were proved to be premature as, only *one week* later, on February 17th, Leicester Fosse caused an almighty shock by coming to Ashton Gate and winning 2-1. It would be City's *only* home defeat all season, and their first league reverse of any kind for nearly six months! Henceforth, it sent shock waves reverberating not only around Bristol, but throughout the Second Division as a whole. Luckily, City kept their heads and retained their balance. As February rolled into March, the leading teams of both Bristol and Manchester continued to pull away from the chasing pack - it was now a two-horse race and the one last thing that remained in doubt was *which* of the pair was going to end up as *Champions*.

But City still looked favourites...

The only point the team dropped during the whole of March was away at Barnsley, on the 24th of that month,
this game ending in a 'mere' 2-2 draw. Perhaps Wedlock was a little off-colour that day, perhaps Wedlock had other things on his mind...

Because back down in Bristol, on the same day that the City were scrapping for their vital point up in snowy south Yorkshire, Billy's wife Rosina was at home, in the Wedlocks' *new house* - 70 South Street, Bedminster - giving birth to the couple's fourth child. James Wedlock (later to be known as

WEDLOCK – THE FIRST HERO OF BRISTOL CITY

'*Jim*') was also the third boy of the family, with eldest child Rosina Ellen - now five and a half years old - being the only girl.

City's promotion campaign eventually all boiled down to the Easter weekend of 1906. After a 2-0 Good Friday win over Gainsborough Trinity at Ashton Gate, it then became clear that if Thickett's men could manage to beat Leeds City at home on the following day, Saturday April 14th – then promotion to the First Division would become *guaranteed*. And it would be supremely fitting that on this crucial occasion, two of the three *Bristol-born* members in the City team that day, Arthur Spear and Billy Wedlock, would score the goals that sent City hurtling into top-flight football for the first time in their history.

*Arthur Spear and Joe Cottle,
the two other local lads in the side*

UP, UP AND AWAY...

On the biggest day of the season, perhaps understandably, it took City a good while to get going. They laboured and toiled in the first period, but could not find the net and half-time brought a 0-0 score-line. Seven minutes into the second period though, City's nerves were settled when Spear fired the Reds in front with a long-range effort, after a Maxwell shot had cannoned off Leeds defender Murray. In the 72nd minute, City won a corner-kick, and Bennett, floating it over, found Wedlock at a very acute angle to goal, Wedlock though, scoring *"with a swift, low shot"*, when – according to **The Sportsman**, he "*had only the narrowest view of the goal*". It was still 2-0 to City at the end, and, when the final whistle blew, everyone knew that promotion had finally been accomplished, as a local brass band entered the field of play and gave a lively rendition of '*See, the Conquering hero comes*' in recognition of the great achievement. It completed a magnificent Easter weekend for Bristol City Football Club, and an equally *perfect* one for Wedlock. According to the newspapers, Billy had played a stormer against Gainsborough on the Friday ("*Wedlock played a marvellous game, and his display throughout can only be described as brilliant*") - he *scored* against Leeds on the Saturday, and he would score *again* against Bristol Rovers on the Monday...

On Easter Monday, the morning papers reported the fact that Spear, Hanlin, Cottle, Burton, Gilligan, Maxwell, Hilton and Wedlock had all been signed up for the *following* season, which was to be the *first* in Division One. City then celebrated by giving a Gloucestershire Cup walloping to

WEDLOCK – THE FIRST HERO OF BRISTOL CITY

Bristol Rovers at Ashton Gate in the afternoon. 8,000 fans turned up to see it, with Bennett (penalty), Burton, Gilligan and Wedlock scoring the goals in an easy 4-0 win. Afterwards, acting-captain Harry Clay picked up the trophy and was seen still waving it above his head as he disappeared down the tunnel with his happy team-mates. Such was the severity of the Holiday schedules in those days, that, incredibly, City had *yet another* Easter match the *next day*, on Tuesday April 17th. This time, Grimsby Town would be the visitors to Ashton Gate, and the Reds', although somewhat weary, still had enough in the tank to force home yet another 2-0 victory, Maxwell and Hilton on this occasion scoring the goals.

Although City now had only two league matches remaining, they also knew that a single point from these games would be enough to secure *first place*, and therefore the Championship Shield. In the penultimate game away at lowly Burton United, on April 21st, Thickett's men swiftly achieved their target by inevitably gaining *two points*, duly clinching the title in Staffordshire with a game to spare. It came down to left-winger Frank Hilton to score the only goal in a 1-0 win before just 5,000 spectators.

All that now remained was the big party at Ashton Gate on the following Saturday (April 28th) for the final match, at home to Chelsea, who would be experiencing their first-ever league visit to Bristol. But despite a 14,000 crowd generating a carnival-like atmosphere, City remained professional to the end, winning 2-1, as goals from Burton and Gilligan secured an astonishing 30th win from 38 matches.

UP, UP AND AWAY...

Only *now*, with the season finally at an end, could people begin to draw breath and really look back to dissect the things which had actually been accomplished over the nine months...

The list of achievements covering the entire season by this team was simply staggering. And even allowing for the very high standards they had set over the course of the year, their record over the 'run-in' *alone* was nothing short of phenomenal. In between the shock home defeat to Leicester Fosse on February 17th, and the end of the season, twelve matches had been played, these resulting in ten victories and two draws. The only team they failed to beat in the League was Manchester United. They suffered only two defeats *all season*, and one of those had been in the opening game. The astonishing statistic of 30 wins from 38 matches was a new record, as was the final points total of 66, the previous record having been set by Liverpool only the season before, though admittedly, this had been achieved in less games. There had also been the much-lauded sequence of 14 successive wins (*another record*), set between September and December, *and* their unbeaten run of 24, set between September and February. Statistically speaking, *this* Bristol City team set the standard for every Reds' team that came afterwards, yet well over a hundred years later, no Robins' side has ever replicated it, or even come close. As far as the players were concerned, Gilligan, Maxwell and Bennett had stolen most of the headlines, if only because of their *goals*. Of City's 83 in the league, an incredible 65 had come from the boot or head of the aforementioned trio, Maxwell leading the way with 25 (plus one in the FA Cup), with Gilligan and Bennett notching 40 between them. But *every* player had done his bit and much, much more. Even Joe Cottle, who had come into the team for the first time as a 19 year-old at the end of September, had slotted into the left-back position and played as if he had been there for a decade. And Wedlock *himself* had been an utter *revelation*, he had played in every single match, and had probably been the most consistent performer of the lot, Frank Bacon's faith in him having been handsomely rewarded. He also scored two goals in his first season - three, if you counted the one against Bristol Rovers in the Gloucestershire Cup.

The secret of the team's success?

According to the **Western Daily Press**, it was *"the perfect understanding (of each other) and earnest effort, combined with the requisite doggedness in front"*.

On Wednesday May 16th, the players were rewarded and their achievements commemorated by an official banquet at the Royal Hotel, College Green, where the Lord Mayor and of High Sheriff of Bristol were also present. There were various important speeches made, 21 in total, and the players and staff were treated to the piano playing of Percy Smith, whilst Mr J M Dingle sang the club's song '*Play up, play up Bristol City!*'

Having gained official permission from the FA, the directors presented all playing squad members with heavy gold medals, engraved accordingly, and bearing the Bristol Coat of Arms. But the manager, Harry Thickett, was not forgotten as he got one too, alongside a bonus cheque for £100, *also receiving*, amusingly, the gift of a snuff box as a present from the players. Thickett declared that of all the medals he had won in his career, *this one* – his *first* as a manager – would be treasured above all others. The Second Division Championship Shield and Gloucestershire Senior Cup were also on show for all to see, and the songs, piano-playing and general festivities went on until the early hours of the morning.

Bristol City, a night on the town, 1906.
Wedlock is in the centre of the front row

Guests included John McKenna, a leading official of Liverpool FC (newly-crowned Champions of England), a future chairman of that club and also a future President of the Football League. He said that he wished Bristol City the very best of luck in the First Division, and hoped that they

WEDLOCK – THE FIRST HERO OF BRISTOL CITY

could follow in the example of Liverpool FC (in becoming the First Division Champions, only twelve months after gaining promotion as *Second Division* Champions).

There must have been a fair few Thursday morning hangovers on May 17th, but the players were justified in letting their hair down for once, for they had more than earned the right to a decent night out. It had been a truly historic season, a campaign of supreme brilliance – the season perhaps, to end *all* seasons. But it also been a long, hard slog – and now, finally, it was time for a break.
And so, in the summer of 1906, Wedlock went off to rest, to recuperate – though typically of Billy, it was *not* to be in a *non-sporting way*. He and Fred Fenton went off to play cricket for Long Ashton...

> BRISTOL CITY – the pride of the West –
> Have climbed to the topmost bough.
> To keep this position they'll try their best,
> They cannot do more you must avow.
> They'll stick to the game, nor will they yield
> So cheer them well as they take the field

7] The rise of the 'Babes' – an unforgettable journey!

'Bristol City Football Club are building for the future...' is a phrase that many generations of supporters will have heard down the years, and in the summer of 1906, it was no different. The club were preparing for life in with the 'big boys' and Ashton Gate needed to be updated and extended accordingly. At the end of May, just as the promotion celebrations were finally beginning to die down, the club placed an advert in the local papers offering *"4d per Full Load of Suitable RUBBLE TIPPED on ASHTON GATE GROUND for Banking* (terracing) *Purposes – Apply Groundsman"*...

The stadium in 1906 was capable of holding perhaps 20,000 spectators, and the biggest crowd in the promotion season had been the 19,000 present at the game with Manchester United, the lowest being the 4,000 who turned out against Glossop.

The average gate for the season worked out at around the 9,500 mark. The City directors though, were naturally expecting to be dealing with much higher numbers in the First Division, and they had visions of a 30,000 capacity stadium, hosting regular crowds of 20,000 and more. The race therefore, was well and truly *on*, to get Ashton Gate fit and ready for the rigours of top-flight football. The end of the ground that would later famously become known as the '*East*' or '*Covered End*' was in those days known as the '*Country End*', and from photos of the ground taken in September 1906, it can indeed be seen that a small form of '*Covered End*' equivalent had already been put into place, this being a rather quaint slope of *'terracing'* positioned behind the goal, with a thin layer of corrugated iron for a roof (*'Country End cover'*). There were stands on both sides of the pitch, and open *'banking'* or *'terracing'* behind the (Ashton) Park end. The directors wouldn't get their 30,000 capacity stadium *at this stage*, the summer extension of Ashton Gate resulting in a crowd-limit that was perhaps nearer 25,000. The Club had put money aside for these ground improvements, their annual accounts having shown a rare end-of-season profit, of £425 19s. Total income had been £5,505, whilst wages had cost £2,935. The directors had also calculated that *"Five years' work of the club in the Second Division"* had resulted in *"a net profit of £669"*.

In August, players and staff were treated to their annual excursion – to Cheddar Gorge, where they visited Gough's Cave amongst other things.

Then it was on to the serious stuff. The City team needed strengthening of course, and the major signings were to be two south Yorkshiremen, Reuben Marr and Fred Staniforth, who had both happened to be playing for the same team, Mexborough Town, of Doncaster. Marr was a 22 year-old powerhouse of a right-half, Doncaster-born, he would be challenging Arthur Spear for his shirt in the new season, but was really more of a long-term replacement for the club's former talisman Billy Jones, who had departed for Spurs of the Southern League. Staniforth was a 21 year-old flying right-winger, from Kilnhurst in Yorkshire, meaning Walter Bennett would be the City man looking over his shoulder in *this* instance, though for now, at least at the *start* of the season, Bennett would still be in the team.

THE RISE OF THE 'BABES' – AN UNFORGETTABLE JOURNEY!

Bristol City team photo 1906/07 season, complete with the Second Division Championship Shield and the Gloucestershire Professional Cup. Wedlock is seated on the end of the second row from the front, right-hand side as we look

The first game of the campaign would be against, *that team again* – Manchester United, though this time it was to be at *home*, so Ashton Gate was to get an early test as regards to the worthiness of its extension in capacity. The match was played in sweltering late-summer heat, on September 1st 1906, and a massive 21,000 crowd turned up, another home record figure for Bristol City.
The two new signings did not feature against United, Thickett, perhaps symbolically for this *first game*, staying loyal to the XI who had gained promotion, though Reuben Marr would make his debut in the following game, two days later at Birmingham FC. Soon after the kick-off, and following a massive goalmouth scramble at the United end of the field, Bob Bonthron handled the ball and a penalty was dramatically awarded to City, which

WEDLOCK – THE FIRST HERO OF BRISTOL CITY

Bennett duly converted, putting the Reds of Bristol a goal up with only four minutes on the clock.

Bennett's early penalty gives City their first-ever goal in the top flight – Wedlock appears to be the dark-shirted figure on the extreme left

Within another eight minutes, however, Charlie Roberts had levelled after a corner-kick, this being the second time running that he had scored an important equaliser at Ashton Gate in a league match. After half an hour, United's Scottish striker Jack Picken fired the ball through Harry Clay's legs and into the net, meaning the Lancastrians had a 2-1 lead at half-time, and City, despite a lot of huff and puff in the second-half, could not change the score-line, it remaining 2-1 to United amidst the 100°F heat. But City gained their first-ever Division One point via a 2-2 draw at Birmingham two days later, in an evening game that saw big Reuben Marr make his City debut alongside Wedlock in the half-back line.

THE RISE OF THE 'BABES' – AN UNFORGETTABLE JOURNEY!

*Bristol City v Manchester United at Ashton Gate -
the first game of the season, September 1st 1906. Such was the severity
of the heat, Wedlock was reported to have been carried off with
exhaustion in the first-half, though he later returned*

Then they got their first win, a tremendous 3-0 success at struggling Stoke City on the following Saturday. When Blackburn Rovers were also soundly beaten by the same score-line (3-0) at Ashton Gate on September 15th, it seemed as though City had simply picked up from where they had left off in the previous season. Expectations were raised even further when an exciting 3-3 draw at Sunderland, one of the most famous teams in the land, put City into the top six. It *did* indeed appear, the United result apart, that City were still riding the crest of a *promotion* wave, the momentum remaining very much with them from the previous – *unstoppable* – campaign. A 0-0 draw at home to Birmingham in front of 17,000 on September 29th failed to dampen the spirits, despite the Reds' dropping to into seventh position.

WEDLOCK – THE FIRST HERO OF BRISTOL CITY

The players and staff of Bristol City who travelled to the league game at Stoke City on Saturday September 8th 1906. City won the match 3-0

THE RISE OF THE 'BABES' – AN UNFORGETTABLE JOURNEY!

City had been beaten only once in their opening six games, they had won twice and drawn three times. Another long unbeaten run seemed as though it could be on the cards. But the team was brought back down to earth with a bump after a 2-0 defeat against Everton at Goodison Park in early October – their first away defeat for *thirteen months* – with Staniforth's debut on the right-wing doing nothing to alter the result. Wedlock's first-ever goal in the top-flight followed a week later when the Ashton Gate ground broke its attendance record once more – but the City were beaten *again*, 3-1 by leaders Woolwich Arsenal, in front of 22,000, the biggest home crowd all season.

***City v Woolwich Arsenal – Wedlock appears to be watching
the play, on the extreme right of the picture***

Wedlock's goal was merely a consolation, for City were already 3-0 down with only six minutes to play when he scored it, the **London Evening News** reporting that *"Wedlock's lightning drive*

WEDLOCK – THE FIRST HERO OF BRISTOL CITY

struck the post and rebounded into the net off Ashcroft's (goalkeeper) back. The game had a dramatic finish, as, just on time, a penalty kick was given to Bristol for an alleged offence by Bigden, which the referee tried to explain to the Arsenal players for fully a minute. However, Bennett shot within Ashcroft's reach, and with the latter's save the game came to an end".

A slightly unlucky 3-0 defeat at Sheffield the following week, against The Wednesday, represented three defeats in a row and the definite low point of City's season, the team falling into the bottom half of the table for practically the only time, now sitting in a lowly 13th. But everything thereafter got better. Manager Harry Thickett reckoned the forward line simply needed tinkering with – the team was playing well and creating chances, but they simply weren't taking them. When Billy Maxwell was injured, the team struggled for goals. Accordingly, Thickett brought in versatile winger or inside forward George Smith, from Gainsborough Trinity, whilst Wedlock's old Aberdare team-mate Ingham, who had failed to establish himself at Ashton Gate, moved in the opposite direction. Bristolian Bill Demmery had already replaced Clay in goal at The Wednesday, and he would keep his place for the rest of the campaign. *'Cocky'* Bennett was axed after the Wednesday game and would never play for City again...

Things got neatly back on track with three successive wins, against Bury at home, Manchester City away, and Middlesbrough at Ashton Gate, a game which saw George Smith open his account for the club in a 3-0 win. Despite an away loss at Preston on November 17th, Wedlock was back on the score-sheet the following week as the Reds' defeated Newcastle United in a simply massive game at Ashton Gate. City went a goal down early on, but equalised after 25 minutes *"through a shot by Wedlock after a melee in the goal mouth"*. **The Sportsman** elaborated further – *"a long kick from a melee at the goalmouth sent the ball to Annan, and this player returned so promptly that Wedlock at once shot into the corner of the goal, and Bristol were on equal terms..."* It was 1-1 at half-time, but Andy Burton scored the winner in the 65th minute, thus securing a famous 2-1 win which sent City up into 8th. The 20,000 Ashton Gate crowd were ecstatic, and the **Western Daily Press** described the result as *"the greatest win in the history of Bristol City"*.

Despite slipping to a narrow 3-2 defeat at Aston Villa seven days later, City then enjoyed another famous Ashton Gate triumph, this time a 3-1 win over Liverpool in front of 18,000, all three goals coming in the second-half after the Liverpudlians had been a goal up at half-time. Burton was now in a rich vein of goal-scoring form, grabbing eight from six matches starting with the Newcastle game. And Staniforth was establishing himself on the right-wing, meaning that Bennett was struggling to get into the team, but somehow the XI felt settled again. The Liverpool result was special, it meant that City had defeated *both* the 1906 League Champions and the 1905 League Champions in successive home matches. More importantly though, it signalled the beginning of a tremendous long run of unbeaten games, *thirteen*, that would stretch all the way up to March 16th, belatedly thrusting City into the thick of the League Championship race...

The Reds' were no longer merely *holding their own* at the top level, they were daring to challenge the 'big guns', and threatening to upset the stability of the *established order*. The whole football world began to talk of the '*rise of the Bristol Babes*', and national newspapers spread the buzz on the new '*hope of the South*'. As one of its star players, Wedlock in particular began to become a source of much fascination for fans up and down the country, and they began to gossip over what they'd heard about the small, spring-heeled young centre-half who'd allegedly been running rings around experienced forwards up and down the country – *"Who is he?"* - *"You mean he's honestly THAT good?"* - *"Is he really as short as they say he is?"* At every Bristol City away game, curious home supporters flocked in their thousands to find out.

Yes, the rise of Bristol City, the '*Bristol Babes*', had been noticed. Their top stars were being watched, put under the microscope, and weighed up as potential *international* players...

...And chief among this group of footballers was, of course, Wedlock *himself.* Wedlock's name was being considered as a possible England player. He showed *potential*. He was put onto a list of '*Players to watch*'. Yet the story of how exactly Wedlock came to get his chance, the crazy tale of how, in a mad dash against the clock, he managed to make sure he *got* his opportunity, is a legend that has been passed into the annals of West Country folklore...

Trials for the England team were to take place at Owlerton, Sheffield, at the stadium which was later to become known as 'Hillsborough'. The trials would effectively serve as a match played between the '*Professionals*' and the '*Amateurs*', this taking place on Monday December 3rd 1906. The contest was to pit the

THE RISE OF THE 'BABES' – AN UNFORGETTABLE JOURNEY!

best of the up-and-coming young professionals, the potential *England-to-be's* - against their amateur counterparts. Wedlock's name was not on the list of trialists, but unbeknown to him, he *was* down as a *standby*. On the Saturday night before the game, it became apparent that Newcastle United centre-half Colin Veitch, who was due to captain the *'Professionals'* team, was injured, and therefore, not going to recover in time. An urgent message to that effect having been duly despatched to the FA on Sunday afternoon, it then became apparent that Wedlock, as reserve, was suddenly required as a replacement. The FA, having subsequently realised that no-one had a record of the Bristolian's home address then faced a predicament, there being no-one working in the office at Ashton Gate that day, which was a Sunday... Instead, an urgent telegram was hastily sent to City director Frank Bacon via the *'Bristol Times & Mirror'*, he not receiving the communication, however, until quite late in the day. Bacon, from his pub in North Street, subsequently shot across the Chessels and went knocking on Wedlock's front door...
"You're needed, for the England trials in Sheffield – pack a bag!" was the gist of Frank's excited ravings upon Billy answering the door – *"Who are you getting at?"* being the alleged words of Wedlock's bemused reply. Having convinced the young City centre-half that he was most definitely *not joking*, Bacon, determined that his young protégé should *not* miss his big chance, accompanied Wedlock to Temple Meads station early the next morning – having made the grim discovery however, that the normal 1am train from Bristol to Sheffield did not run on Monday mornings. The next available locomotive needed to be

WEDLOCK – THE FIRST HERO OF BRISTOL CITY

boarded if Wedlock was to stand *any chance* of getting to Owlerton on time. This was subsequently done, however, the train itself, a *Midland Express*, ironically turned up late, this not leaving Bristol until 9:45am. Scheduled arrival at Sheffield railway station was at 2:00pm, the match at Owlerton however, was due to kick-off only fifteen minutes after *this*, with the football ground being positioned approximately three miles from the station!
The preparation for one of the most important matches of his life was hardly ideal, but Wedlock, adaptable as ever, had a plan, an '*off-the-top-of-his-head*' scheme consisting of having to get changed in the railway compartment as it rattled along on the outskirts of south Yorkshire...
At Owlerton meanwhile, the two opposing teams had been lunching together before the game, it being suddenly noticed on entering the dressing rooms that Wedlock was not yet present. It was then stated that the Bristolian was due to arrive at the railway station no later than 2pm, however, no plan had been drawn up to combat the problem of how he was going to get from a railway platform to the football pitch in *less than fifteen minutes*. None of the other footballers *knew* Billy, or had seen him play. But in a stroke of luck for Wedlock, also present that day was J.A.H. Catton, one of the great sports journalists of the day, who usually wrote in the **Athletic News** under the pseudonym '*Tityrus*'.
Catton was subsequently asked "*Had he seen Wedlock play? Would he be able to physically recognise him? And if so, could he meet him direct at the railway station, and bring him to the stadium, in double-quick time?*" Catton, replying in the *Positive*, confirmed "*Yes*" - he *had* seen him play, and therefore, *should*,

THE RISE OF THE 'BABES' – AN UNFORGETTABLE JOURNEY!

recognise him. Catton was then despatched in a car being driven by Sheffield United full-back Fred Milnes, another player who had been placed 'on standby' for the *'Amateur'* side... Meanwhile at Sheffield's railway station, leaping hurriedly out of the *Midland Express* and onto the platform came Frank Bacon and a fully-kitted out Billy Wedlock, studded-boots and all - it didn't take much 'recognising' for a waiting Catton to know that *here* was his man! As Catton, or *'Tityrus'* later recalled, *"When the train drew up, out stepped a sturdy little fellow fully dressed in football clothes and wearing his studded boots. He had evidently realised the position and turned the railway carriage into a dressing room....I went up to him and said* 'Wedlock?' 'Yes, zur!' *was the answer – the Western dialect was most convincing –* 'Then come with me - quick!'" Incredibly, there was still a crazy three-mile car journey through the streets of Sheffield ahead of them before Billy would be able to reach his destination. Wedlock and Bacon were promptly bundled into Fred Milnes' car, the vehicle apparently breaking the city's official speed-limit several times during a manic, *"tortuous"* journey that *Tityrus* never, ever forgot; *"As we literally flew along the thoroughfares of the city of Sheffield, I mildly intimated that the speed was rather high for crowded streets. The reply of Mr Milnes was that the police knew him, and that he had some influence with the Watch Committee if any trouble arose. The town was soon left behind..."* Despite this highly-dramatic motor car dash through the streets of Sheffield, it was *still* not enough to get Wedlock into the dressing room in time to meet his team-mates, though he *did* make it onto the pitch – *just* – as the teams were having their pre-match photos.

WEDLOCK – THE FIRST HERO OF BRISTOL CITY

By all accounts, Wedlock went sprinting onto the field straight from Milnes' car, and Billy, perhaps understandably displaying a rare moment of nervous over-excitement, promptly went sliding into a clumsy challenge on his future England team-mate Vivian Woodward, completely up-ending the unfortunate Spurs striker.

Thankfully, it resulted in nothing more than a free-kick for the *Amateurs*, though free-kicks, it has to be said, being very rarely given away by Wedlock. After that, Billy settled down and forgot his nerves, turning in a fine display and creating exactly the right impression for the watching England selectors. In the words of *Tityrus*, *"after that unfortunate first step, Wedlock played like a man"*. The *Professionals* were understandably the stronger side, eventually winning the game by a 4-2 score-line. Even imagining a scenario where Wedlock *had not* impressed the England selection committee, then it may have been a small consolation had he known that he *did* at least take the eye of the **Yorkshire Post (and Leeds Intelligencer)**, that newspaper reporting that *"there were several bursts by the Amateurs....but the active*

THE RISE OF THE 'BABES' – AN UNFORGETTABLE JOURNEY!

spoiling efforts of Wedlock, and the fine defence of Stokes and Layton, preventing any of the attacks reaching close quarters...". It later added *"Wedlock delighted the crowd with his versatility. He hung onto Woodward persistently, and succeeded in beating the Tottenham international on many occasions, while he was exceedingly smart and cool in giving his own forwards possession. The Bristol centre-half came into the Professionals' team as a substitute, but he was one of the most conspicuously successful players on the side".*

So despite the most incredible shenanigans that had taken place before the game, Wedlock had *done it*. His trial had been a complete success, and he appeared to be on the verge of playing for the England team. There was one further trial match to be played in January, at Stamford Bridge, Chelsea, namely, *The North v The South*. Wedlock, as a Bristolian, was naturally picked for the Southern team, who were subsequently outclassed on this particular occasion, losing by a score of 4-1. Wedlock though, once again excelled, appearing on the day to be a class above many of his team-mates. And so it came to be that on Monday January 28th 1907, pretty much as soon as the *North v South* game had ended, the FA Committee selected its next England team which was due to face Ireland in the *'Home International'* match at Goodison Park, Everton FC, on Saturday February 16th. The friends and colleagues of young Billy, no doubt including Frank Bacon, held their collective breath... Henceforth, the committee's *'number five'*, and therefore, its *centre-half*, was soon revealed as being – *'W. Wedlock' (Bristol City)*. Interestingly, Colin Veitch, the Newcastle centre-half whose

WEDLOCK – THE FIRST HERO OF BRISTOL CITY

unfortunate injury had presented Billy with his big chance in the first place, was *also* selected – as one of two *reserves*.

The team was released to the newspapers in time for publication on Friday February 1st. The **Kentish Independent** had distinctly *mixed* feelings about Billy Wedlock - however, it should be made clear that *this* was a *Woolwich Arsenal-supporting paper, and their team was due to face Bristol City in the Second Round of the FA Cup on the following day (City would lose, 2-1). But as far as the England team was concerned, the paper looked forward to his international involvement, saying, *"A man in the South side on Monday who seems likely to cause us* some anxiety is Wedlock, the Bristol City centre half, who showed himself a master hand and was chosen to operate also against the Irishmen at Everton on February 16th. The words of one critic are* **"There is no doubt about the qualities of this man"**. *Even a past master like Colin Veitch was completely eclipsed by the strength and subtlety of this new star of the West. He has all Needham's ubiquity, and he has also not a little of Needham's reserve power. When one thought he must be beat, he would trump his opponent's ace with an unexpected and brilliant manoeuvre. In tackling he was great, man or ball – sometimes BOTH – he was sure to stop. And when he got the ball, he knew what to do with it. Gone in a flash to wing or centre, he seemed to know instinctively where the unmarked man was waiting. Nor was he afraid to risk his legs. He performed the 'splits' in a manner that made me shudder, and yet, when I came to think of it, he is not a likely man to get hurt. After seeing Wedlock, I can understand much of Bristol City's success this season. The tip for tomorrow (for Woolwich Arsenal*

THE RISE OF THE 'BABES' – AN UNFORGETTABLE JOURNEY!

v Bristol City) *is* – *"WARE WEDLOCK"*...
However, there often being two sides to the story meant of course, there was a flip-side to the England centre-half debate... For there is no doubt whatsoever that from a *national* point of view, Wedlock was not everyone's cup of tea, and his selection would ruffle more than a few feathers. In the doubters' defence, he was *not*, in any way, shape or form, a 'classic' centre-half. They perceived him as being the wrong size and the wrong shape. He was not six feet two and *not*, therefore, a Colin Veitch or a Charlie Roberts. He did not stand in his central defensive position and simply win the ball in the air, pass to a forward, and then take a breather. He covered acres of ground, and simply ran all over the field, assisting his forwards in *every attack*.
He worked like a trojan and his stamina was limitless.
He possessed deft footwork, and on the ground, knew every trick in the book. The skills he brought to the centre-half role were totally unique, Wedlock firmly stamping his own interpretation of what a centre-half *could be* if he didn't have height, hence the inability of *some* journalists to get their heads around, and simply, *accept,* his selection. With the possible exception of Everton's Johnny Holt, there had never been one like Wedlock *before*, and there has certainly never been one like him *since*. Many journalists constantly referred to his *'jack-in-the-box'* style, and this was intended as being both complimentary *and* insulting, depending on who was saying it at the time...
But any critics of Wedlock's England selection were going to have to lump it, for as it turned out, Billy was going to be in it for the *long term*. Not only did Wedlock play against Ireland at Goodison

WEDLOCK – THE FIRST HERO OF BRISTOL CITY

Park on February 16th, he would also be selected for the other two 'Home internationals' that season, against Wales and Scotland, on March 18th and April 6th respectively. These in fact, would actually represent the first three of 25 *consecutive* international appearances, Wedlock eventually receiving 26 caps in total across his professional career – earned between 1907 and 1914.

This however, is neither the time nor place to enter into great detail on the *international* aspects of Billy Wedlock's career – a special section on that subject being placed *elsewhere* in this narrative...

Wedlock in his England strip – and with his first (1907) international cap

What *is* worth saying, however, is that it would become clear in the future that Bristol City were going to be significantly affected

THE RISE OF THE 'BABES' – AN UNFORGETTABLE JOURNEY!

by the popularity of Wedlock with the England selectors.
The problem for City would all be about learning to cope without him for two or three matches a season. That didn't matter quite so much as long as City were languishing in mid-table obscurity. This however, would not *always* prove to be the case, and the future possibility of Wedlock missing crucial Bristol matches at the 'business end' of the season, in March and April, spelt danger as far as manager Harry Thickett was concerned.
And at the tail-end of the 1906/07 season, there were vital games *indeed* still to come...

A thirteen match unbeaten run, as has been previously mentioned, had elevated Bristol City up the league table and within striking distance of the leading teams. The excellent run of results had started with the 3-1 defeat of Liverpool at Ashton Gate, it also included a very creditable goalless draw away at Manchester United on December 29th, this going *some* way towards making up for the 5-1 tanking that City had suffered at Bank Street in the opening game of the previous season. January and February of 1907 had seen City *creeping* up the table almost un-noticed, they got into the top six, then the top five, and then, the top four...
The early-season leaders Woolwich Arsenal had fallen away somewhat, but of the other autumn pace-setters, Everton and Aston Villa were still there or thereabouts. Newcastle United though, were now at the top of the pile, and threatening to pull away from the chasing pack as the season headed towards the all-important Easter weekend. City were now inside the top four and, on current form, looking like a good bet for runners-up

– *at least*. Bristol's whole season now looked like hanging on two critical games to be played over the holiday period. These tough-looking matches though, were not only *both* away from home – they were *also* scheduled to take place only 24 hours apart...
City faced a long journey to Bolton Wanderers on Easter Friday, and then had to make up a lot of extra miles overnight by visiting leaders Newcastle on the following day, Saturday the 30th of March. Even with a fully-fit team, this would have seemed an ominous prospect for the Reds'. The Geordies had proved to be utterly *invincible* at home all season, winning 16 out of 16, including a ruthless 5-0 drubbing of Manchester United.
In the event, City went to Bolton on the Friday and won – *narrowly* – by two goals to one. But the biggest test of all was *still to come*....
On Friday night, City travelled to Tyneside knowing they were now *third* in the table, though level with second-placed Everton on both points *and* games played. They were still six points behind Newcastle, but had *two games* in hand. It was a very tough ask, but a win at St James' Park followed by two victories in the matches they had spare, would potentially put City level on points with Newcastle, with only four games left to play.
In the end though, City might well have not bothered working out all the various scenarios, for the long journey was to end in vain. The gruelling schedule that had demanded the playing of two games in two days would ultimately prove to be fundamentally too much for Harry Thickett's travel-weary troops. When the City party finally arrived at St James' Park, it was clear for all to see that the team was badly fatigued, and in no real condition to face

THE RISE OF THE 'BABES' – AN UNFORGETTABLE JOURNEY!

the onslaught that Newcastle were inevitably going to release. They were simply *physically incapable* of being up and ready for the fight. When it came, the Newcastle bombardment was just as fierce as City had feared in their wildest nightmares...
The Geordies tore into them right from the start, going a goal up after only five minutes. City tried to steady the ship and made occasional journeys towards the United penalty-area, but these became increasingly rare. The Reds' held the score-line to 0-1 at half-time, but their energy levels were beginning to flag – it was simply a case of *hanging on* and trying to keep the score down. Newcastle though, were even *more* rampant in the second-half than they had been in the first, and City could barely get out of their own penalty-area. The Geordies accordingly turned the screw, and in time scored twice more, the game finishing 3-0 to Newcastle. But for the gallant efforts of Wedlock & co at the back, it could have been a lot worse. Even the City *supporters* had a hard time that day, any noise made by the 350 *'excursionists'* from the West Country being drowned out by 40,000 screaming Geordies. Yet despite the men from Tyneside going eight points clear, it wasn't *quite* the end of the Championship race. City still had their two games in hand and simply had to try and *win them* - and hope that Newcastle somehow blew up. And *that* – <u>at least from the Newcastle end of the 'bargain'</u> – is pretty much what happened. As the Geordies stumbled and stuttered towards the finishing line, City faced two critical home games, against Bolton on Easter Tuesday (April 2nd), and then Aston Villa on the Saturday (April 6th). Unfortunately, Wedlock would be absent on England duty for *both* of these matches, and agonisingly, City

ended up getting beaten – *twice*. Ironically, on April 6th, Billy was back at St James' Park, Newcastle, to play for England against Scotland – this being on the day that City lost the second game of the two, against Villa. It was very telling that when Wedlock returned, City immediately kicked back into life, winning their last four games in a row, including a fine 4-2 victory over Liverpool at Anfield on April 13th. But by then, it was *too late*, and Newcastle claimed the league title by three clear points, with City finishing in second. City would later regretfully look back on that fateful Easter weekend as the being the two days when the league title slipped away. That regret would also extend to the two vital home matches which had immediately followed. The season inevitably ended on a disappointing note, and there would be a lot of 'ifs', 'buts' and 'maybes'. Yet the fact remained that if a *fully-fit* City had only been given the chance to take on Newcastle on Easter Saturday, with the benefit of fresh legs and ample preparation, then the result *might* have been different. Alternatively, if Wedlock had been allowed to play in the two home games that followed it, and Thickett's men had *won* them – then City *would* have clinched the title. Alas, it was simply not to be. The players, of course, were beside themselves with disappointment, but in the pit of their stomachs, they knew they had simply been *not quite* good enough. And deep down, they also knew that it had *still* been a tremendous season, for if anything, Bristol City had *over-achieved*, gaining second place in their first-ever campaign in the top flight.

What *no-one knew,* however, was that *this* was going to be as good as it got. 1907 would ultimately prove to be the *closest* that

THE RISE OF THE 'BABES' – AN UNFORGETTABLE JOURNEY!

City would ever get to winning the English League title...
As it was, Billy Wedlock would have to move on from this disappointment, because for Billy, time never stood still, he *always* moved on. There would already be other things to look forward to – the *following* season, the possibility of additional England appearances, the chance of more success with Bristol City. The cricket season was *also* now upon him, and Wedlock had a new team to play for - Bedminster. There was also a new house on the horizon, in Chessel Street. And more importantly, Wedlock was to become a father for the fifth time, as his wife, Rosina, was pregnant once again...

WEDLOCK – THE FIRST HERO OF BRISTOL CITY

"WE LIVE TO FIGHT AGAIN, AND IN THE REPLAY WE SHALL PLAY BETTER — YOU CAN TAKE THAT FROM *ME*...
...FOR THE *TIME*, WE ARE HAPPY"

8] On his way to the Palace

The work to extend the capacity of Ashton Gate during the previous close-season had certainly been worth it, because as the City directors had correctly predicted, average gates had risen significantly across the 1906/07 season – from 9,500 in the previous year to over 16,000 in *this*. The biggest crowd had been the 22,000 who came flooding in to watch the Woolwich Arsenal game on October 13th, and it was *this* figure which now held the official attendance record at Ashton Gate. But gates of 20,000 or more had also been attracted by the visits of Manchester United, Newcastle and Everton. And as the players were once again rewarded through the presentation of medals – though this season, of the *runners-up* sort, rather than the *Championship* kind – the board of directors began to count their profits and assess their various stats and figures. Needless to say, the figures looked *good*, and the directors perhaps dared to dream that next the team might be able to go one better in the following season, and actually *win* the League Championship.

But any such aspirations were actually to prove very premature – in reality, such dreams were the stuff of fantasy, rather than of genuine ambition. Unbeknown to virtually everyone, the club had *already* reached its zenith... Indeed, if the previous two campaigns were to be regarded as having been the *'champagne'* seasons, then there can be little doubt that 1907/08 was to prove very much the *'hangover'*, as City would find it very, very difficult to replicate the success they had achieved in 1907.

The bubble, it seemed, had burst...

WEDLOCK – THE FIRST HERO OF BRISTOL CITY

Bristol City FC, season 1907/08

Bristol City, 1907-08. Back row (left to right): Batten (trainer), Gale, Rippon, Young, Demmery, Spear, Mr Bacon (director), Harry Thickett (manager). Seated: Marr, Staniforth, Maxwell, Gilligan, Connolly, Hanlin, Cottle, Mr Deveridge (director). On ground: Wedlock, Hilton.

A brief flick through the history books shows us that City would finish their Division One campaign in tenth place that season, suggesting a distinctly average year and mid-table mediocrity.

ON HIS WAY TO *THE PALACE*

But the final table paints a very false picture and doesn't even tell half the story...

After two games, having beaten Everton 3-2 at Ashton Gate in front of 14,000, and then walloped Woolwich Arsenal 4-0 in London, City were fourth in the table and it looked as though they were simply going to carry on as before. Although they faded as the season went on, they remained in the top half of the table practically all the way up until New Year, in fact they had barely dropped out of the top eight by the time the Christmas period arrived. But a dire run of form in the second half of the season, which came to a head when Wedlock, once again, was absent on England duty, soon plunged City towards the foot of the table. During this miserable sequence, the Reds' would only gain *one* win in all league fixtures between Christmas Day and Easter Saturday (April 18th). In the week leading up to Easter *itself* it was looking like the game was up, and City seemed doomed to relegation. But Wedlock's timely return, once again, sparked a four-match winning upsurge in the home straight, they managed to win three times out of these final four fixtures, with the other match being drawn, and because of this, City were able to save themselves at the death...

Some minor changes to the playing staff had been made from the previous season. Scottish junior international defender Bob Young had arrived from Dundee Violet in May 1907, and he would go on to share the right-back duties with Archie Annan. Also arriving in May 1907 was Kilnhurst Town striker Willis Rippon, a south Yorkshireman, and a former team-mate of City's current outside-right Fred Staniforth. Rippon was seen as being very much 'one for the future', and for now, he would have to bide his time...

Inside-left Fred Connelly, a forward from London, had actually been signed in 1906, but he had only made his first-team debut at the tail-end of 1906/07, when City's final four games had been won during that last, vain effort to win the League title. Having not played a competitive match since October 1906, Walter '*Cocky*' Bennett had been released, and he then elected to drop out of professional football altogether. Apparently now disillusioned with the game, he returned to his south Yorkshire roots and became a coal miner in the village of Denaby Main, whilst also turning out as an amateur footballer for the local side, Denaby United. His place on the right-wing had been taken by, first George Smith, and then, on a more long-term basis, by Fred Staniforth. Also released was ex-skipper Peter Chambers, whose long spell in Bristol had dated all the way back to the late 1890's, when he had first played with Bedminster. But Chambers had not played a first-team game for 14 long months – going back to the 1905/06 promotion run-in – and was simply no longer a part of Harry Thickett's plans, eventually ending up at Swindon Town of the Southern League. Goalkeeper Harry Clay had been the captain for much of the calendar year of 1906, but having been dropped for the game at Sheffield versus The Wednesday on October 20th, that honour was duly passed on to the vastly-experienced striker Billy Maxwell.

It had been around this time, between the conclusion of the '*runners-up*' season and the beginning of the *next* campaign, that the Wedlocks' had been on the move again, swapping one part of *the Chessels* for another. 70 South Street was accordingly sold, and Billy and his young family next arrived in Chessel Street *itself*, moving into No 64. It was while they were settling into this new home that Rosina gave birth to the couple's fifth child, daughter Lilly Wedlock, on Monday October 21st 1907.

Billy and Rosina had now been married for over seven years, he was nearly 27 and she was 25. By this time, they also had a fairly sizeable family, of five children, three boys and two girls... Wedlock would celebrate the birth of his baby daughter by scoring his first goal of the season in the very next match, on Saturday October 26th 1907, away at Aston Villa. It had been 3-1 to Villa at the break, and then 4-1 to the home side in the 53rd minute, but Wedlock's goal *"from a long shot"* in the 55th sparked a dramatic comeback for the visitors, the game eventually finishing in a sensational 4-4 draw. The **Western Daily Press** additionally described Wedlock's strike as being *"a grand surprise shot"*. The goal also came two days before the event of his 27th birthday, but Billy was in no mood to stop celebrating just yet, and on the following Saturday (November 2nd), Wedlock scored his second goal in successive matches by grabbing the first in a 2-0 victory over Liverpool at Ashton Gate. City scored a goal in each half, and Billy caught the Liverpudlians napping at a very early stage of the game. From a corner, *"Wedlock scored in ten minutes, the ball going through a crowd of players and being diverted into the net by West. Another shot by Wedlock was caught by Hardy, and Burton shot at the scoring side of either post, but in each case the custodian cleared... a second goal for the City was scored in the concluding half by Hilton....*

WEDLOCK – THE FIRST HERO OF BRISTOL CITY

Wedlock, although sometimes defeated when trying tactics that might have been of advantage to his side, was again in splendid form.... Cottle and Wedlock are both likely candidates for International honours this season".

City's new striker Willis Rippon meanwhile, had made his City debut some weeks earlier, on October 5th against Manchester City at Ashton Gate. But this game hadn't been merely a career milestone for *Rippon* – it had been one for *Wedlock too*. Rippon was playing in the first place only because of injury to Billy Maxwell – the *club captain*. Maxwell's absence therefore meant that City's *acting*, or vice-captain had to be called upon. The selected vice-captain for *this season*, but as yet, not used, was one – *Billy Wedlock*. This meant that the Manchester City game at the beginning of October 1907 became something of a pointer to the future, a *history-maker*, it becoming the first-ever occasion that Wedlock would proudly captain *his* Bristol City team...

Rippon was later to become City's star striker, but he didn't score that day, though City won the match 2-1 in front of 15,000 fans. Wedlock's duties as skipper were also a complete success, as he even won his first-ever 'toss of the coin'!

Billy was stand-in captain again the following week away at Preston, though City on this occasion were beaten 3-0.

The veteran Maxwell soon returned and normal service was henceforth resumed, though when his next absence occurred in March 1908, Billy was once more called upon to provide stand-in duties, against Aston Villa at home, on Tuesday 11th, and then again on the following Saturday, away at Sheffield United.

Billy reached another City landmark on March 21st, the 0-0 draw

ON HIS WAY TO *THE PALACE*

at home to Chelsea signalling the occasion of his 100th league match for the club. Wedlock's subsequent call-up to the England team however, whilst clearly a positive thing for *Billy*, was becoming a massive headache for Bristol City, who simply couldn't seem to cope whenever he was absent from the team. The annual international trial match *this year* had been held at Hyde Road, the home of Manchester City FC, on Monday January 27th 1908. This time around, thank goodness for Wedlock, there was to be no mad dash for Temple Meads, no changing into his kit on the train, and no wild car chases through town to get to the stadium on time. Everyone knew in advance that Wedlock was picked for the trial match, with the likelihood being, he would *also* be selected for the *team*. The trial game once again was contested under the banner of '*The North v The South*', with Billy playing for '*The South*', and the match ended in a highly-exciting 4-4 draw, watched by 10,000 spectators.

As a result, Wedlock was indeed re-selected for his country. This news pleased some of the journalists no end, and the February 1st edition of the **Cricket and Football Field** was full of praise for the City man, as it concluded its exclusive rundown on some of their 'favourite' England stars - *"The insatiable Wedlock dominated the proceedings for quite half the battle at Hyde Road on Monday, for the little Bristol man was forever obtruding himself to despoil the enemy and then to ply his forwards. 'Wedlock the wonderful' is one of those remarkable bundles of activity who is a full-back, all three halves, and a forward rolled into one. One moment you see him hugging the touchline to stop a dangerous run by the opposing wing man with a tap into touch, and as likely* *as not, he secures from his opponents' throw-in to set his own aggressive machinery going. Then as an attendant upon opposing inside forwards he is 'par excellence', despoiling them so persistently that it seems to take a man all his time to avoid either losing his temper or giving up in despair. In brief, Wedlock is a second John Holt, without the latter's tendency towards 'tricky', hoodwinking tactics".* In a separate section containing its match report, the same paper added – *"...somehow I think it would be an injustice to pass over the game little Wedlock. He's a regular box of tricks, and very few can teach him anything. He certainly shadowed Brown from Sheffield in a way that seriously hindered his usefulness, whilst he was a trier to the very last..."* Once again then, Billy was called up for all three *Home International* matches, against Ireland, Wales and Scotland – all to be played away from home. For the Wales game, Wedlock was strangely allowed to play for City - as captain - in their 2-0 defeat away at Sheffield United on Saturday March 14th, despite only getting 48 hours 'recovery time' before starring for England at Wrexham on the Monday. It didn't seem to do Billy much harm however, he scored his first international goal as the highly-unfortunate Welshmen were trounced by seven goals to one at the Racecourse Ground. The first game against Ireland in Belfast, on February 15th however, had been a different matter...

Because of the various preliminaries, training, trial match and selection process, Wedlock was forced to miss three City matches in a row. As a consequence, the Reds' lost two games by 3-1 score-lines – at home to Preston and away at Liverpool – and drew the other match away at Bury.

ON HIS WAY TO *THE PALACE*

Then on April 4th, whilst Wedlock was starring for England against Scotland at Hampden Park, in front of a new world-record crowd of 121,452, City were scrapping for their First Division lives against old rivals and Champions-elect Manchester United at Ashton Gate. In front of a 15,000 crowd, Maxwell levelled for Bristol in the second-half enabling the Reds' to gain a crucial point, this game, like the England match in Glasgow, resulting in a 1-1 draw. In any other circumstances, this would have been regarded as a satisfactory result, but what City desperately needed now, more than anything, was *wins*...

When Wedlock hurriedly returned from international duty, the team had high hopes of gaining a win, a draw – at least, *something* - from their fifth-from-final match away at Blackburn Rovers the following weekend. Yet City were thrashed 4-1 to leave them staring down the barrel at likely relegation after just two years in the top-flight. Three or four days before the game, though, the club had received the devastating news from Yorkshire that on April 6th, their former star winger, Walter '*Cocky*' Bennett, had been killed in a mining accident at Denaby.

City, of course, had let Bennett go at the end of the previous season, and '*Cocky*', who upon seeing Wedlock play for the first time three years previously had memorably uttered the line *"A second Johnny Holt!"* – was tragically no more. It appeared that as Bennett had been ascending to the surface at the end of his shift, the roof of the mineshaft had caved in, killing the ex-England international instantly. Bennett left a widow and four children. The news caused great sadness across the city of Bristol, but nowhere was the loss more deeply felt than amongst the players, staff and supporters of Bristol City FC. Without trying to make excuses for the 4-1 defeat which subsequently occurred at Blackburn on April 11th, many of the players must surely have been playing with heavy hearts indeed...

This result however, appeared to leave City with a mountain to climb as regards to their precarious position in the Division One table. Yet incredibly, with just four games now remaining, the Reds' managed to save themselves, winning three times and drawing once, scoring nine goals in the process, and conceding *none*. Crucially, *this season* City were scheduled to play *both* their Easter games at Ashton Gate, and both Bolton and Sunderland were soundly beaten in those two critical matches inside three days. Another vital point was picked up in a goalless draw at Manchester City, and then Birmingham were thrashed 4-0 at Ashton Gate in the final game of the season, to ensure City's survival. Although they finished in the rather *false* position of tenth, half-way up the table, and despite avoiding the relegation trapdoor by nine places, City still ended up only three points above the drop-zone, the Reds' leading a pack of *six clubs* who all finished on 36 points. The final burst of good form in the last four games, which, the previous season, had not been enough to steal the League title, had thankfully, *this season*, been *just enough* to save their First Division skins. Despite the expectations at the start of the season, the feeling amongst all at the club *now* must have been one of sheer *relief*. No doubt, *next* season, the board of directors wanted improvement, and *expected* it as well. But before Wedlock even had a chance to think about that, he was off on his travels with the England team again. The FA had arranged a four-match Whitsun tour of the Austria-Hungarian Empire, which offered Billy an excellent chance to add to his record of six international appearances. The fortnight's tour was accordingly undertaken between June 3rd and June 16th, and Wedlock indeed played in every game, taking his tally up to ten.

After returning and spending the rest of the sporting summer on the cricket field for Bedminster, the new season soon crept up... Whatever the City directors' expectations for the 1908/09 campaign were, they almost certainly didn't get what they thought. Yes, league form would be *improved*, though only slightly – City would finish the season in *eighth* place. But this year was really to become all about the Cup...

In the meantime, as has been mentioned earlier, Wedlock in the previous season had been 'stand-in' for the position of Billy Maxwell's captaincy, but *this* term Maxwell's first-team appearances would become less and less frequent, due to the emergence of Willis Rippon, City's latest star striker. As a result, Wedlock would be the captain in 1908/09 almost from the word *'Go'*. By the end of the season, as Bristol City closed in on an FA Cup Final appearance, it somehow seemed as if Billy had been leading his team for *years*, he being the most natural and obvious candidate for the Reds' skipper that there had ever been, and probably, ever *would be*. Indeed, Wedlock would remain as the official club captain from this point onwards, until pretty much the end of his playing career... Maxwell meanwhile *did* figure in the opening game of the season away at Blackburn on September 1st, in fact he scored City's equaliser in a 1-1 draw. But after

WEDLOCK – THE FIRST HERO OF BRISTOL CITY

Everton won at Ashton Gate in the next game on the following Saturday, the veteran striker was forced to give up his No 8 shirt first to Rippon, and then to Bob Hardy, an England amateur international and the new signing from South Bank. But longer term, it was *Rippon* who was going to be the big star... Harry Clay, who had lost his place in goal for much of the 1906/07 season, and a good portion of the following term, was now back as the No 1 'keeper. Centre-forward Sammy Gilligan, as ever, was still banging in the goals, though with slightly less frequency than had been the case before. Wedlock's Bristolian colleague Joe Cottle was still ever-dependable in the left-back position, and he was starting to gain the interest of the England selectors. Cottle would be picked for his one and only England match - *alongside Wedlock* - against Ireland at Bradford on February 13th 1909. Despite a 4-0 win, he was never selected again. At City, Cottle would be an ever-present *all bar* the two February games that coincided with the England / Ireland match. Scotsman Andy Burton, at inside-left would remain as reliable as ever, indeed, Wedlock apart, he was probably the most consistent performer in the City team. Archie Annan and Bob Young, meanwhile, would fight over the right-back berth.
City's half-back line was a reasonably settled one, playing alongside Wedlock at right-half was Reuben Marr, with either Bristolian Arthur Spear, or Scotsman Pat Hanlin operating on the left. In general though, City's league form was annoyingly inconsistent. If ever two matches were to sum up their season as a whole, it would surely be the visits to the two Manchester clubs.

ON HIS WAY TO *THE PALACE*

[ALL RIGHTS RESERVED.]

The Tricks of a Light-Weight Half-Back

BY

W. WEDLOCK
(Bristol City and England).

Ever since football has been regarded as the winter pastime of Great Britain and Ireland, there have been men included in sides of national repute who have been what is known in sporting parlance as "on the light side." Therefore it seems almost fitting that in that line, the middle of the side, where offence, strategy, and defence should all be prominent factors in a man's work, tricky little players should have predominated. In the history of half-back play some of the most conspicuous men who have appeared in first-class football have occupied, for years, the full eye of the spectatorate of the country. Where was there ever a more popular little half-back than John Holt, of Everton, a name which is still spoken in a whisper in Liverpool? Holt helped to build up the Everton team to the perfection it attained.

THE "NIPPY" MAN.

Then at a later decade came Ernest Needham, of Sheffield United, one of England's most brilliant and consistent half-backs. It is the boast of his team that it could at one time have formed an International side for England; indeed, at one period, it was almost comprised of men who had figured in the white jersey of their country. Miniature models of muscular mankind—to drop into alliteration—have always been prominent in half-back play, and I will tell you why. The little nippy man, whose tactics are always changing as the moods of a game alternate, seems better able to get about in a fast game than does a big man. Let me do justice, however, by agreeing that some big men have been brilliant half-backs, and have made history in International football. I refer especially to 'Varsity men—; they breed them big and they play them big.

THE "HALF" AND HOW TO MAKE HIM.

There is no getting away from the fact that the half-backs are the most important trio

As well as an outstanding footballer, Wedlock was also an articulate writer on the game. Here's a little snippet from a column he wrote for the 'St Andrews Citizen' (Fife, Scotland) - edition dated December 12th 1908

WEDLOCK – THE FIRST HERO OF BRISTOL CITY

Bristol were hammered 5-1 by Manchester City at Hyde Road, the Lancashire men being a team who were doomed to relegation at the end of the season. Yet Thickett's men also went to Manchester United, League Champions of the previous season, and secured a 1-0 victory – their first win over United for more than six years! In similar fashion, City again did the league 'double' over Liverpool, and forced a fine 3-3 draw at home to Champions-elect Newcastle United – and yet they failed in two attempts to beat a Leicester Fosse side who were easily relegated at the end of the season. City though, retained a top-half position throughout most of the campaign, and despite occasionally having cause to look over their shoulder, they were never really sucked into a repeat of the previous season's relegation scrap.

Wedlock in each of his first three seasons at the club had contributed two goals per term, but that little run was broken in 1908/09, when he only managed *one*. It came in the aforementioned 5-1 loss at Manchester City on October 31st, when Billy scored in the last five minutes for the Reds', who, having completely collapsed in the second-half, were already 5-0 down at this point! This result, no doubt, brought back painful memories of the identical score-line in the opening day defeat at Manchester *United* three years earlier, when City had again scored a consolation goal in the last few minutes, having already found themselves 5-0 down prior to it being registered.

After the Manchester City debacle, City went on a lengthy

ON HIS WAY TO *THE PALACE*

Bristol City FC 1908/09 Cup Squad

unbeaten run that took them into the top five by Christmas, but this came to an end with a 1-0 home defeat against Bradford on Boxing Day, a game that saw a new record crowd of 23,000 come flocking into Ashton Gate. Yet nobody could have guessed that by the end of the season, this latest attendance record would be smashed again – *twice over*...

In the meantime, City's league form dipped somewhat after the Bradford defeat, and they soon settled back down into mid-table obscurity. But *again*, as has been mentioned – *this* campaign was *never* going to be remembered as a vintage one in terms of the *league* – it was all going to be about the Cup. And a good run in the English FA Cup had certainly been well *overdue*. City's record thus far had been pretty bleak. Up until this point, the team had never made it past the second round 'Proper', not even during their most-recent seven campaigns in which they had operated as a professional outfit within the Football League structure. In fact, they had been eliminated in the first round twice during the previous three seasons. Nevertheless, the great run began with a first round 1-1 draw against old Southern League rivals Southampton at Ashton Gate on January 16th 1909, watched by a crowd of 18,531. Four days later, City went to The Dell and won the replay 2-0 to secure their passage into the last 32. When Bury came to Ashton Gate in the next round on February 6th, a new record crowd of 23,528 turned out to see it. Despite City taking a 2-0 half-time lead through goals by Burton and Gilligan, the Reds' conspired to throw it all away, and the game ended in a 2-2 draw. This meant that once again City would have to do things the hard way, but in the midweek replay at Gigg Lane, Gilligan notched the

only goal and Bristol squeezed home to enter the third round for the first time in their history. The momentum and excitement was now building tremendously, and City once again landed a home draw, this time against Norwich City on February 20th. The Reds' saw no reason for replays on *this occasion*, and goals either side of the break from Andy Burton and Willis Rippon secured victory at the first time of asking, the Ashton Gate attendance record being shattered *yet again,* with 24,009 squeezing into the ground. Wedlock and Cottle had rushed back from international duty in order to play in this crucial contest, the duo having both been involved for England in the previously-mentioned Ireland match at Bradford. But City were now in the *last eight* of the Cup, and the people of Bristol had barely known greater excitement. Expectations were lifted even higher when the draw pitted the Reds' against Second Division Glossop, perhaps the weakest team left in the competition. Although they were away from home, City were still expected to *win*. But as Thickett's men were preparing for their crucial quarter-final in Derbyshire, news arrived on March 3rd that poor Billy must have been dreading - his father, Thomas James Wedlock, had died at the age of 70 years.
City's great Cup run suddenly paled into total insignificance. Billy's mother later wrote of her husband *"Ever remembered by his loving wife and children. A light is from our household gone, a voice we loved is stilled; a place is vacant in our home which never can be filled"*. Three days later at Glossop, Wedlock must barely have felt like playing *at all*, yet Billy, professional as ever, plodded on bravely... Because *participate*, he most certainly *did*, though perhaps in the end, everyone might not have bothered

starting, as a blizzard-hit North Road ground meant the pitch was practically unplayable. The game henceforth was almost farcical as a spectacle, it being no surprise at all that it ended goalless. The replay took place four days later on the early-evening of March 10th, and in front of 15,932, a record attendance for a midweek game in Bristol, Sammy Gilligan dramatically slipped the ball past Glossop 'keeper Joe Butler for the only goal, just five minutes before the end. It was a highly-charged moment that sent the City hordes into ecstasy – and Wedlock & co were now into the *last four*. It all meant that either Manchester United, Newcastle, or *preferably* Derby County would have to be negotiated in the semis, but in the end, City got exactly the tie they would have wanted – Second Division Derby at Stamford Bridge, London, the home of Chelsea FC – on March 27th.

In the first-half, although the Reds' did most of the attacking they failed to take their chances, and Derby, on the break, always looked dangerous. The **Western Daily Press** dramatically reported that *"the idols of the teams, Wedlock and Bentley, were at last brought into desperate conflict..."* The latter of these, Derby centre-forward Alf Bentley, then struck a shot that City 'keeper Harry Clay touched onto the post, this being the only outstanding moment worthy of conversation of half-time.

Ten minutes into the second-half though, a scramble in the City penalty area led to Ted Garry firing Derby into a surprise lead, for the Bristol men had mostly been on top until this point. Content with their efforts, Derby then *shut-up shop,* pulled men back and decided to concentrate solely on *defending* their advantage. It so *nearly* worked, because for the next 35 minutes

ON HIS WAY TO *THE PALACE*

1909 FA Cup semi-final action from Stamford Bridge. Clay safely gathers the ball for City as Wedlock (right of picture) looks on

City desperately bombarded the County penalty area without being able to score. It just seemed as though Bristol's Cup luck was finally going to run out, and as the game ran into its closing minutes, some fans started heading for the exits, including one or two journalists who had actually travelled with the City team on the way to the match! However, with less than *five seconds* left on the clock, a Staniforth cross led to sheer panic in the Derby penalty-area, and with the 'keeper Harry Maskrey already well-beaten, Bob Hardy's goal-wards shot was desperately fisted away by Derby defender Jack Nicholas, when the ball *appeared* to be heading into the far corner of the net. It was a clear and deliberate infringement, and left the referee, H S Bamlett of Gateshead, with no choice other than to award City a last-gasp spot-kick. As he did so, he made clear to the players that, whether scored or missed, the penalty would be the very last kick of the afternoon, as time had already fully elapsed. For City then, it all came down to a nerve-shredding, *'one-kick shoot-out'* – it was effectively score, or *bust...*

This then set the scene for arguably the most dramatic and exciting penalty-kick the FA Cup had seen in its history, thus far...but the big dilemma for the City team was – *who* was going to take it? Despite the fact that Willis Rippon had been the penalty-taker that season, nerves got a hold of him, and because of the crucial nature of *this* one, he did *not* fancy taking it. Wedlock looked hopefully around the rest of his team for potential volunteers, but – nothing doing...

Some years later, Rippon recalled the incident when in conversation with a journalist – *"When the referee pointed to the penalty spot"*, he said, *"Billy Wedlock was the only one of us whose knees were not shaking visibly. He took me on one side, and it made me feel good to look at his happy face. 'Take it Willis', he said, 'and kick hard. Never mind direction.' Afterwards I realised what sound advice that was. Had I gone at that ball in half-hearted fashion anything might have happened. Billy saw the state of nerves I was in, and knew a good lusty kick stood the best scoring chance. I believe I closed my eyes when I kicked..."*

Wedlock's own version of the story differed, though only slightly. *"I knew it was no good ME having a shot at it, so I told Willis he would have to have a go."* 'What shall I do, Billy?' *he asked. He looked very shaky about the knees, and it was then I had an inspiration. I knew it was no good telling him to take careful aim, or anything of that sort, so I just said* 'Just close your eyes and kick it like blazes'. *That may sound like stupid advice, but I knew my man. He took a long run, hit the ball as hard as he knew how, and well – that's how we reached the Final".*

It didn't *quite* get them into the Final – *yet* – but it certainly saved City's skins, and they lived to fight another day. Legend has it that Bamlett, the referee, later sent the match ball to Rippon as a token of his coolness and bravery! Derby skipper Charlie Morris believed that Bristol had been slightly fortunate to get away with the draw, Wedlock however, was not in agreement, and he remained bullish on City's chances in the replay. The **Sheffield Evening Telegraph** recorded his comments accordingly:-

"We ought to have been a goal up in the first-half, but the forwards did not play up to their form. And the ground, which was slippery on top, put us off our game more than you might think, until we got used to it. Well, we live to fight again, and in the replay we shall play better – you can take that from ME. Derby are a better side than I thought, and their defence is great. When I think of it, I don't wonder we didn't get more than the penalty goal. This was, of course, rightly awarded, but what a terror Rippon is, to be strong when so much depended on him. We were unlucky with many shots, but here we are, going to meet again. We all had a good game, and for the time we are happy".

The semi-final, then, required a replay, and this took place on the following Wednesday afternoon, March 31st, at St Andrews, Birmingham. In preparation, the City squad hid themselves away for a few days of special training at Portishead, and as they did so, no doubt there were a few jokes doing the rounds concerning

WEDLOCK – THE FIRST HERO OF BRISTOL CITY

the '*bravery*' of Willis Rippon and the last-gasp drama which had occurred at Stamford Bridge. Little did they realise, however, that it was going to happen all over again in the replay – though *not* at the end of the game. At St Andrews, the game kicked-off with the same two line-ups and referee who had started the first match. And incredibly, a few minutes before half-time, there was *indeed* to be a near-exact replication of the penalty incident that had so marked the climax to the first game, *again* due to a Derby County handling offence in the penalty area, and *again,* down to the same player, Jack Nicholas, though on *this* occasion, the handball was said to have been more *accidental* in nature. Once more however, Willis Rippon stepped up to take the spot-kick, presumably in a somewhat cooler manner than had been the case with regards to the previous game on Saturday. At any rate, Rippon again made no mistake, and City walked in at half-time a goal to the good. Derby though, quickly equalised in the second-half thanks to a goal by winger John Davis in the 48th minute, though it was the Reds' who continued to do all the pressing. It was no real surprise therefore, when Bob Hardy slammed the ball home for a deserved 53rd minute winner. City had made it through to the Final at the Crystal Palace, and there was no doubt whatsoever that the Bristolians had been the better side over the two matches.

City had learned after the *first* clash with Derby, that in the other semi-final, Manchester had triumphed over Newcastle in the '*battle of the Uniteds*'. It meant that Charlie Roberts & co would be lying in wait for Wedlock's boys in London, on April 24th.

So when City went to Manchester United in a League game on

April 9th, it was already known to the spectators that they were witnessing the Cup Finalists *to-be*.

Man United 0 Bristol City 1, in a league match played at Bank Street, Clayton, Manchester – on Good Friday, 1909

Andy Burton scored the only goal, and City won 1-0. The omens then, appeared *favourable*. Three days later, an enormous crowd of 20,000 turned up to see the return fixture at Ashton Gate, but the game ended in a disappointing 0-0 draw. Experts then, were none the wiser as to which of the two teams would end triumphant on the big day in London, twelve days later.
Amidst all the excitement and *hubbub* of the Final, it was barely noticed that against Sunderland in the league at Ashton Gate, Wedlock was clocking-up his 150th league and cup appearance for the Reds' – meaning the United game in London the following week would be his 151st. It appeared though, as if the City team was *also* struggling to keep their minds *off* the Cup Final – for

despite early goals from Gilligan and Hilton, Bristol threw away a 2-0 half-time lead to inexplicably lose 4-2! Cup fever also appeared to be reflected in the attendance on this occasion, with only 7,000 turning out for a *league game*, on a day when the only thing people seemed to be talking about was the Final against United at the Palace.

In the end though, it was all destined to finish in tears. Willis Rippon suffered cartilage damage in the league game with Blackburn on April 13th, another embarrassing home loss (4-1) which had immediately preceded the Sunderland debacle. Despite a race against the clock, Rippon wouldn't make the Final. Similarly, Reuben Marr had injured an ankle at home to the Villa on April 3rd. He too faced a futile battle that was to end in great disappointment. It was originally thought that Marr might recover in time, but he broke down in training at the eleventh hour...

Marr (left), and Rippon – City's injured pair on Cup Final day

ON HIS WAY TO *THE PALACE*

The City were two quality players shy of being a potential Cup-winning side. When it came to the big day in London, the Reds' came up short, losing 1-0 to United in a Cup Final that was to prove a big let-down. Marr and Rippon, and the latter *in particular*, had been sorely missed. City had no cutting-edge up front, and had Rippon been able to play, then the result *might* have been different...

To rub salt into City's wounds, the deflated team had to hang around in London for another 48 hours in order to face Chelsea at Stamford Bridge in what was for Wedlock's team, effectively a meaningless league match. This wasn't the case for Chelsea however, who needed the two points to guarantee their First Division survival. They promptly *got* them, unsurprisingly defeating an emotionally—battered City side by three goals to one. The Reds' season then ended on a very anti-climactic note, beating an already-relegated Manchester City team by a goal to nil, in front of a desperately small crowd of only 5,000 fans at Ashton Gate. Even the solitary City strike was a trifle underwhelming that day – it was an own-goal by the unfortunate men from Lancashire...

Action from the 1909 Cup Final

ON HIS WAY TO *THE PALACE*

The Manchester United players await the presentation of the FA Cup

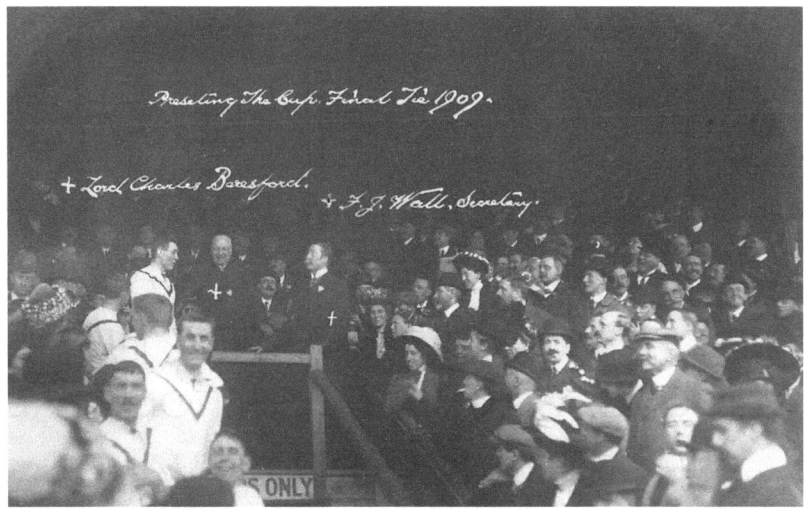

"WE CANNOT SEEM TO STRIKE A WINNING VEIN, AND CANNOT GET A BIT OF LUCK, WHICH GOES A *LONG WAY* IN FOOTBALL. I HOPE THINGS WILL CHANGE…"

9] Against the tide and on the slide

The Cup Final defeat would have been another massive disappointment for Wedlock and his boys, first they had been runners-up in the league, and now *this*, second place in the Cup. But Billy would move on from this failure in the only way he knew how, by remaining positive, keeping in good cheer, and looking *ahead*, in contemplation of the *next* group of matches...
And the next set of games were indeed already right on top of him. On May 26th 1909, Wedlock was off abroad with the England team again, for the FA had arranged a second mini-tour of the Austria-Hungarian Empire, and Billy's presence, once more, was to be required in *all* the matches the trip could provide. This time, it meant just the three games, but Wedlock was now becoming something of an experienced England performer, he now being the proud possessor of 16 internationals caps.
When he returned to Britain, his thoughts began to turn towards the following domestic season, and having provided another summer of excellent service to Bedminster on the cricket field, Wedlock soon found himself back for pre-season training at Ashton Gate. A number of small changes to the squad had taken place since the end of the previous season. The veteran striker Billy Maxwell had finally retired from playing, and he had taken himself off to Belgium in order to forge a career in coaching and management. Although he still remained with the club, there were continuing signs that Gilligan's goals were beginning to dry up somewhat, whilst Willis Rippon, although potentially *brilliant* on his day, was injury-prone and inconsistent. In order to beef up his attack therefore, Thickett had brought in striker Jack Cowell from

WEDLOCK – THE FIRST HERO OF BRISTOL CITY

Rotherham Town at the very end of the previous season, and he had made his debut in the closing game when Manchester City had been beaten 1-0 at Ashton Gate. Also coming in from Rotherham was Cowell's club-mate Ben Shearman, a speedy left-winger who was essentially recruited to replace Frank Hilton, the latter of whom was starting to be seen as being past his best. The ultimate results of these changes were to become clear as the season unfolded. Rippon and Hilton were to end up playing only a handful of games between them, whilst Shearman on the left flank was to become the new regular, and would generally be deemed to have been a success.

Gilligan, for the greater part of the campaign generally *kept* his place, although his goals tally was to drop off *even further*.

City's line-up in season 1909/10

This meant that a great deal of the goal-scoring responsibilities would fall onto the shoulders of the newcomer Jack Cowell, who was pretty much '*in*' from the start – and he did not let the club down, scoring 20 goals in his only complete season with Bristol City. In fact, without Cowell's goals, the club would surely have been relegated, and it was no coincidence that within six and a half months of his eventual departure in the autumn of 1910, the Club *would be* demoted at the end of the campaign.

Season 1909/10 though, is where City's slide really began, although some would argue that it had all started in the Cup Final against United at the Palace. Either way, the alarm bells *should* have been ringing after a number of embarrassing home defeats that had taken place towards the end of the previous season, but these losses had been camouflaged, or else simply hidden away and ignored, because they had generally occurred in the midst of all the Cup Final excitement. As it turned out, the whole season was to prove an almighty struggle, from start to finish. Privately, it must have been a campaign of utter frustration for Billy Wedlock, who was in the prime of his life, at the peak of his powers. But he was simply playing in a *struggling team.* City's problems were *not* at the back, because defensively, they were as strong as any side in the country. The troubles were all further up the field, most notably in attack. Apart from Cowell and his 20 successful strikes, regular goal-scorers from elsewhere were few and far between, and the spread of goals and 'shots on-target', from across the rest of the team, was very thin on the ground. Rippon started up front for the first game of the season, away at Bradford City, and despite scoring Bristol's goal in a 3-1 defeat, he was immediately ousted by Cowell, who promptly scored in the next game, a 1-1 draw with Bury at Ashton Gate.

A typical example of City's difficulties though, would be

highlighted in the goalless stalemate at home to newly-promoted Spurs' on October 2nd. The Reds', capably marshalled by Wedlock, remained safe and tight at the back, yet laboured and toiled up front without being able to convert any clear chances into goals. But as far as the history books were concerned, this otherwise forgettable match was to go down in the annals as an afternoon of shame with specific regards to the story of race-relations within the game of football. And for the venue of Ashton Gate, and in particular, because of the actions of its native *Bristol City supporters*, the occasion of *this game* is today looked back upon as being a day of pure *infamy*. The Spurs' had a relatively new player starting at right inside-forward that day, and his name was Walter Tull, a young man of dual-heritage, meaning, candidly, that he was dark-skinned. Tull was only the second-ever black professional player to have starred in the English football league, this being an era when the sight of a black man in British *society* was still relatively uncommon. Unfortunately, Tull's eager, all-action performance that day was wrongly interpreted by some of the Ashton Gate faithful as being over-the-top and aggressive. The home fans laboured under the delusion that Walter Tull was a wild-man and a cheat. As a result, every touch of the ball from Tull, for the rest of the game, was accompanied by a cowardly chorus of whistles, boos and cat-calls. But regrettably, it was to get *even worse* than this – personal insults, cruel taunts on his appearance, the colour of the skin, and, in short - a sheer *torrent* of racial abuse, that didn't let up for the rest of the game. The trigger for the obscenities appeared to be an innocuous incident in the first-half, namely, Tull's challenge on City full-back Archie Annan, a firm shoulder-charge, that, despite leaving Annan sprawled flat on the deck, had most sensible onlookers that day judging to be perfectly fair. **The Sportsman** reported that "*Tull and Annan got at loggerheads, and for a time scrambling tactics were introduced, the referee frequently stopping the game for illegal acts*". But the **London Daily News** was particularly damning in its criticism of the Bristol City crowd, observing – "*His* (Tull's) *tactics were absolutely beyond reproach, but he became the butt of the ignorant partisan...*

...a section of the spectators made a cowardly attack upon him, in language lower than Billingsgate. Let me tell these Bristol hooligans (there were but a few of them in a crowd of nearly twenty thousand) that Tull is so clean in mind and method as to be a model for all white men who play football, whether they be amateur or professional. In point of ability, if not in actual achievement, Tull was the best forward on the field...

...Cottle (Bristol City) *has acquired the temper of a spoilt child. A bad foul of his upon Curtis – the second offence – at once brought him applause from the hooligans above referred to and a caution from the referee. Cottle must get into a better frame of mind if he desires a second international cap...*"

For Walter Tull, the story is a sad one. Not long after the disgraceful scenes at Ashton Gate, Tull found himself dropped from the Spurs' first-team, and his career eventually waned. It is *believed* (although never been *proved*) that the powers-that-be at White Hart Lane were worried by the attention that Tull was attracting, and henceforth perceived that a repeat of the scenes at Ashton Gate would make Walter a liability to the team's chances of future success. Although over the next two years he was to play another handful of games for the Spurs' first-team, this period was spent almost exclusively in their reserves.

Walter Tull

In 1911, he departed White Hart Lane and joined Southern League Northampton Town, where he was a *success*, playing 111 first-team games. In December 1914, he signed up with the British Army and joined the First World War effort in France, fighting at the *Battle of the Somme* in 1916. Walter Tull was a courageous and heroic soldier, eventually climbing the ranks to become the first-ever black combat officer in the British Army. He was bravely killed in France, at the age of 29, on March 25th 1918. Today, there is talk of his lasting recognition with a posthumous awarding of the *military cross*, and a statue, outside the stadium of Tottenham Hotspur FC. But as of yet, nothing has materialised...

AGAINST THE TIDE AND ON THE SLIDE

For Bristol City though, it was going to be a long, hard winter, as, Cowell apart, their goal-scoring problems continued. After the infamous Spurs' game at Ashton Gate, City never reached any higher than 11th position in the league table, indeed, they spent virtually the rest of the campaign hovering dangerously around the bottom six or seven.

City would find no solace in other competitions, for there was to be no repeat of the FA Cup run that had been achieved so wonderfully the year before. In the first round, City safely despatched Liverpool 2-0 at Ashton Gate, but then West Brom defeated the Reds' by 4-2 after a replay, ensuring a second round exit for Wedlock's lads.

Meanwhile, the league match immediately following the Spurs' encounter at Ashton Gate saw City crushed 3-0 at Preston North End, mainly because Wedlock was away representing an English Football League XI against its Irish equivalent at Boundary Park, Oldham. Wedlock had a great game that day, and the English were triumphant by the tune of *eight goals to one*. But Thickett's City men seemed unable to learn old lessons about how to cope when Billy could not be in the team, and so yet *again*, at Preston, the Reds' appeared hopelessly outclassed in his absence.

Because of his England duties in the *Home International Championships,* City would have to endure two *additional* games without Wedlock during the course of the season, and both of these matches, away at Spurs', and then at home to Woolwich Arsenal, resulted in further damaging defeats...

There is little doubt that Billy's happy home and family life proved to be an excellent route of escape from the, at times, unhappy pressures and struggles of top-flight football. And, back at

WEDLOCK – THE FIRST HERO OF BRISTOL CITY

Chessel Street, the Wedlocks' were still a growing family *indeed*. Between the boys and the girls, an unofficial little 'competition' had been developing. Little James Wedlock had sent the boys storming into a 3-1 lead back in the spring of 1906, but Lilly had reduced the deficit for the girls a little over 18 months later... Now, Ivy Wedlock, born at Chessel Street on January 5th 1910, became the saviour for the 'fairer sex'. She was christened down the hill at St Aldhelm's on January 26th, and the Wedlocks' were now a family of *eight*. They were certainly outgrowing the dwelling of 64 Chessel Street, and before long, would need to be on the move again...

Unfortunately for Billy however, it didn't seem to matter what delights awaited him at home, as in the end he always had to return to the fray with his struggling Bristol City team, and, perhaps with a lesser degree of apprehension, with *England*... Billy was to miss City's return match with Spurs' at White Hart Lane on February 12th, because he was starring in the England v Ireland *Home International* match in Belfast, played on the same day. The England game ended in a 1-1 draw, but unsurprisingly, City lost *their* match 3-2 at White Hart Lane, though in reality, the team had been generally losing *anyway*, *with or without* the services of Wedlock.

The Spurs' defeat left City fifth from bottom of the table, but Wedlock's return then coincided with a mini-revival that saw successive wins recorded against Preston (home), and then Notts County and Liverpool (both away). A valuable 0-0 draw was also secured at home to Aston Villa, a game that doubled-up as a benefit match for popular striker Sammy Gilligan, and it drew a healthy 16,000 crowd. Fittingly, it was a rare Gilligan goal which had secured the 1-0 win at Liverpool the week *previous*. But the run-in was going to get *even tougher* now...

Wedlock again only scored one goal all season, but it was a *crucial* one, proving to be the winner in a 2-1 victory over old rivals Manchester United at Ashton Gate. It happened on Easter Monday, March 28th 1910, and City had badly needed the win for they were now in desperate trouble near the foot of the table.

A 4-0 loss at Sheffield United 48 hours earlier had left the Reds' sixth from the bottom, and sinking fast. And City's start against United, in front of 18,000 at Ashton Gate, was not the best either. Welsh legend Billy Meredith had given the Lancastrians the lead after 25 minutes play, but from Wedlock's pass Jack Cowell quickly equalised for Thickett's men and it was 1-1 at the break. The **Dundee Courier** then reported that, mid-way through the second-half, *"from a beautiful movement by Staniforth and Gilligan, Wedlock scored a beauty, and was loudly cheered. Manchester tried hard to equalise, but always failed in shooting..."*

Interestingly, the first league game between the two sides had taken place only three days earlier, when an enormous Good Friday crowd of 50,000 had flocked to Old Trafford, the new ground to which the northerners had moved, a little over a month earlier. *This* occasion then, marked the first time that the Reds of Bristol would perform at a venue that was later become world-famous. But it wasn't a good day for Bristol City, Fred Staniforth's late goal proving *'too little too late'*, and United won 2-1.

A 1-0 home defeat against Woolwich Arsenal (when Wedlock was away in Glasgow, playing for England against Scotland), followed by a 4-2 loss at Bolton plunged City *even deeper* into the mire – they were now *third from bottom*, with the relegation places consisting of the *bottom two*. A narrow 1-0 victory over Chelsea at Ashton Gate was to prove only a *temporary* fix, for a disastrous 3-0 home loss to a severely-weakened Newcastle team in the penultimate game appeared to leave City dangling over the precipice...

It was Bristol's worst performance of the season, and the team was now only two positions and *one point* above the drop zone with one match remaining...

It all now came down to the last game of the season, at home to Nottingham Forest, at Ashton Gate, on April 30th 1910. It was actually strikingly *simple*, for City *had* to win, to guarantee their safety. Two points would be enough, but anything less, and the Reds' would be left relying on other results, and praying that the complicated mathematics of 'goal average' might come to their aid. But in the end, the mathematicians might not have bothered - for incredibly, the City were to save their best performance of the season, for the *final game*. On an enthralling afternoon, Forest were simply *blown away*, their defence being pierced four times to no reply, with Jack Cowell scoring *all four goals* in sensational style. After being set up by Fred Staniforth, Cowell steadied City's nerves by scoring first in the 19th minute, but there then followed an agonising 51 minute spell, split either side of half-time, when the match remained in the balance. Wedlock and his fellow backs, Annan, Cottle, Young and Hanlin worked like trojans to keep Forest out and, for once, City always looked dangerous up front. Jack Cowell settled it with the crucial second goal after 70 minutes, and shortly after that Bob Hardy was fouled in the box, so Jack Cowell took the penalty to complete his hat-trick. In the last five minutes, Cowell struck his fourth to compound Forest's misery. The transformation across the two performances against Newcastle and Nottingham had been utterly astonishing. The ***Athletic News*** reported that *"Wedlock never gave (Enoch) West much latitude, so certain was his tackling. He was here, there, and everywhere, and constantly made splendid use of the ball when he had robbed an opponent."*

It was just a pity that only 11,000 fans turned out to see it. City finished the season in *sixteenth position* – in other words, fifth from the bottom. As other results had panned out, a point would have been enough anyway, and City survived relegation by three places and two points.

Wedlock *himself* had so often been the saviour for City in the past, but on *this* occasion, he had good reason to thank Jack Cowell for single-handedly saving City's place in the First Division, not only because of his 20 goals, but more directly as a result of his *four golden strikes* in the final game. Incredibly, these were also to be Cowell's final goals for the club. Although he was to start five matches at the beginning of the following season, he was unable to score, and was soon sold to Sunderland – a move that was to cost City dear. Interestingly, his final game would be at Ashton Gate on October 8th 1910, a league contest with Manchester United that would double-up as Wedlock's benefit match...

On May 20th 1910, Billy and Rosina Wedlock celebrated their tenth wedding anniversary, though this may have been done *separately,* for on that day the former was at sea, on board the vessel *Kinfauns Castle,* bound for South Africa with a touring FA party. To explain fully, Billy was off on his summer travels again, a lengthy close-season tour of *"the Colonies"* (comprising of 23 engagements) having been arranged by the Football Association. The tour lasted for the best part of two months, and Wedlock's 'big' three games were played in the 'high-profile' Test fixtures against the nation of South Africa. Billy earned no official 'caps' for his trouble, for this was a *Football League* Representational trip, rather than an *'England international'* one. The finer details of the tour are to be found in another place of this publication, but for now it simply remains to be said that Wedlock was to find himself a very popular man on the trip, both with his team-mates, and indeed, with the natives of South Africa...

When he returned to Britain for the new domestic season, Billy knew that he was about to embark upon – what would today be called - his *'testimonial season'.* Bristol City had thus arranged that the home league game with Manchester United on October 8th would double-up as Wedlock's benefit match. This was not an uncommon practice for the era, because on occasions when a player was deemed deserving of such a *'benefit season'*, 'one-off' end-of-term matches were not specially-arranged for the purpose. Instead, a specific home game was selected from the busy league programme, and all the gate receipts would then be put aside for the player in question. There can be little doubt that Wedlock, in this context, was a highly-deserving figure for such a reward. He was now closing in on 200 League and Cup appearances for the club, and had done so much to establish Bristol City amongst the elite during his five years thus far. In short he had done immeasurable amounts to put the club on the map...

In the meantime, City's fifth season in the First Division got off to a surprisingly good start when the mighty Newcastle were beaten 1-0 in front of 26,000 at St James' Park. Hardy scored the only goal, and it seemed there might be reasons for *optimism* in the campaign ahead. Unfortunately, it was to prove a *false dawn*, and City soon slipped back into their bad old ways...

The Reds' were promptly beaten 2-0 at home to Spurs', and then 3-0 away at Middlesbrough, results which started to put pressure on the manager Harry Thickett. Despite gaining a goalless draw at home to Preston on September 24th, another 2-0 defeat away at Notts County the following week plunged City towards the foot of the table, and Thickett's fate was finally sealed. His unfortunate dismissal, after five and a half years in charge, was decided at a special meeting of the directors on the evening of Wednesday October 5th 1910, and he was informed of the decision on the following day. It was a sad end to Thickett's managerial career, for he had done a tremendous amount of work to put City into Division One in the first place, but times had now moved on and he was no longer wanted. Still only 37, Thickett would subsequently drop out of football altogether, retiring from professional sport and becoming a licensee in Trowbridge, Wiltshire, remaining in this position until the time of his death at the age of 47, in 1920.

Meanwhile, as City continued their search for a new manager, the directors were placed in short-term charge of general team affairs, with tactics and team selections being ultimately made by Wedlock's friend Frank Bacon, who was now at the peak of his powers behind the scenes – as vice-Chairman.

Under these curious circumstances, Wedlock's benefit match, at home to Manchester United in the aforementioned league game, was played on Saturday October 8th. The **Western Daily Press** gave coverage to the event in the build-up by announcing that *"Each purchaser of a programme at the match will have a presentation autograph portrait of the International, which has been provided and splendidly produced by the Exchange Printing Company, 22 Clare Street, Bristol. It is a good photograph of Wedlock, who is attired in his international dress, and is printed on fine art paper. The picture should form an interesting souvenir of the event".* On the day of the game, a very healthy 20,000 crowd turned out at Ashton Gate to witness the grand occasion, but United – including Wedlock's rival Charlie Roberts - were clearly the better side and deserved to win 1-0, as they had done in the Cup Final. Harold Halse scored the game's only goal early in the first-half, the result leaving City third from bottom in the league table, with only *one goal* scored in six games; *that* having been netted in the opening game of the season.

The financial consolation for Wedlock though, was *considerable*, with the **Western Daily Press** reporting that he *"was guaranteed £200, in addition to the large number of subscriptions and a South African testimonial, and as he has played all his best club football with Bristol City, there was a complete unanimity of effort on his behalf".* According to the newspaper, the "minimum guarantee" of £200 constituted *"half the gross gate of the United game".* Gate receipts were £462.16s.10d.

Straight after Wedlock's benefit match came a smoking concert, held in his honour at Whatley Hall, Clifton, and Billy took this opportunity to make a speech addressing City's poor start to the season, whilst expressing his desire for a speedy improvement. The evening was a complete success, and the **Aberdeen**

AGAINST THE TIDE AND ON THE SLIDE

Evening Express reported that *"Mr Tayler, who presided, handed to Wedlock, amidst much laughter, a large rag doll, on the understanding that he did not undress it until he got home. Then he would find something worth having - the gift of an anonymous donor. The silver cup hidden in the interior of the doll presented to Wedlock was an exceedingly fine massive specimen of the 'celebrated two-handled Irish cup'. It was mounted upon a Chippendale mahogany plinth, and bore the Bristol arms and a suitable inscription. The weight of the cup was over 38 ounces. The doll was dressed in the Bristol City colours.*
W. Wedlock, who was received with great applause, musical honours, and cries of 'Good old Fatty', *in replying, did not attempt any high flights into the realm of oratory, but contented himself with a few simple sentences of thanks, which reminded one of his play, in that they were sincere. He thanked the donor of the lovely present that had been made to him, also Mr Phillips and the committee who had arranged the concert for his benefit, as well as those who contributed to the programme. In fact, he was grateful to everybody who had in any way assisted in his benefit match and concert. Concluding, Wedlock briefly referred to the present position of Bristol* (City), *and said he was sorry the team was not doing better.* 'We cannot seem to strike a winning vein' *he said,* 'and cannot get a bit of luck, which goes a long way in football. I hope things will change, or it will be a bad job for you, and me, and... (added Wedlock, amidst laughter)...the baby' *(pointing to the doll). The gate money at Wedlock's benefit was £460, and £10 had been collected for the popular centre-half by the band".*

For Billy however, it was just a terrible shame that his benefit season had happened to coincide with quite the worst league campaign that anyone at the club could ever remember. The main problem, as ever, was *scoring goals*. The Ashton Gate faithful had vented their anger when their idol, Sammy Gilligan, who had given six years loyal service, was transferred to Liverpool. But Willis Rippon had *also* departed in the close-season, leaving for Woolwich Arsenal. Then, in the wake of Thickett's departure, almost the first decision that the board of directors made was to sell Jack Cowell *as well*, to Sunderland! The team's difficulties escalated when it became increasingly clear that most of the replacements were not up to scratch, and City's goal-scoring drought became an even more prominent feature than it had been in the season before. Thickett's main summer signing Ebenezer *'Ginger'* Owers, a centre-forward from Chesterfield, had scored 52 goals for that team in the Midland League the season before, but for City, he had yet to really get going...

The home game with Manchester United accordingly became Jack Cowell's last-ever appearance for the club, as he was dropped for the next match away at Liverpool, and City, after a number of comical errors at the back that had the Scouse natives rolling around in stitches, were promptly crushed 4-0 at Anfield. But on October 29th 1910, the day after his 30th birthday, Wedlock reached another personal milestone by making his 200th league and cup appearance for Bristol City, away at Sheffield United. The team celebrated in fine style, gaining a relatively rare victory, and not simply 'winning', but utterly *trouncing* their rivals by the tune of four goals to nil. The downside for Wedlock was that he received a nasty knock to the head, leading to the game being stopped whilst City's skipper was allowed to recover from a bout of concussion. It was enough to keep him out the team for the Aston Villa home clash the following week, *and* the Sunderland match *the week after that*, making these the first-ever occasions – *thus far* – that he would miss Bristol City first-team matches through injury. And although City's 4-0 win at Sheffield was indeed a memorable one – it was to be a very rare high-point during a season of utter misery.

The only light at the end of a very long tunnel turned out to be the goals of new striker *'Ginger'* Owers, for he had starting scoring with some regularity at last. His highlight would be a hat-trick in the 3-2 win over Middlesbrough on January 21st 1911 - but come the end of the season, it looked like even Owers' 16 goals in 31 games would not be enough to save the Reds'...

In *this* campaign of *all campaigns*, Wedlock would manage three goals from the centre-back position, his best seasonal return so far, and the joint-highest of his entire professional career. The trio of goals all came inside a ten-day period in December 1910, in a little run that was spread over four matches. He netted a vital 51st minute winner in the 2-1 bottom-of-the-table clash with Manchester City at a rain-washed Ashton Gate on December 17th, and then scored again a week later at Goodison Park, Everton, on Christmas Eve, when City lost 4-3. After drawing a blank in the 2-2 draw at home to The Wednesday on Boxing Day, Wedlock then scored his third goal in four matches by notching a late, late winner in a crucial 3-2 win over Oldham Athletic on *the very next day*, December 27th. All three of these games were relatively exciting contests in their own right. For Billy's first goal, at home to Manchester City, the **Athletic News** described his strike in the following style; *"only six minutes of the second-half had gone when Wedlock restored the lead to the home men, shooting through near the post in a fierce melee after Smith had saved a grand shot from Marr"*.

Away at Everton, Wedlock was to score the Reds' third and final goal in a narrow 4-3 defeat, when City had attempted a late fight-back from 4-1 down, though this was partly helped by the dismissal of Everton striker Jimmy Gourlay fifteen minutes from the end. The Oldham match at Ashton Gate was held only 24 hours after City's previous Christmas holiday fixture (at home to The Wednesday), and it drew a pretty good crowd of 16,500. In a topsy-turvy game which had been deadlocked at 2-2 going into the 90th minute, Wedlock then struck a highly-dramatic winner to nick the two points for the Reds', described by the **Nottingham Journal** in the following words - *"The Oldham defence however, held out in resolute style, and it was not until the stroke of time that Wedlock scored the winning goal, this dramatic work gaining for him a remarkable ovation from the holiday crowd"*.

Frank Bacon's leadership had provided a degree of stability, but the problems were still prevalent, and he kept hold of the reins until a shock exit in the first round of the FA Cup on January 14th, when Crewe Alexandra beat City by three goals to nil.

Yet for a group of directors who had spent three months searching for a new manager, their choice, although an *understandable* one, did not show much imagination...

On Friday January 20th, national newspapers reported that, once again, Sam Hollis had been called back in order to save the day, his return to the club as manager meaning that he was now starting his *third spell* in that role. In one sense, he had never really left the club, because, despite running his pub, he had always maintained a keen interest in City's affairs, retaining his membership, and speaking at all the important meetings. Hollis was appointed until the end of the season - *for now* - but not even *he* was going to be able to provide a miracle cure for *this team*. The results were bad, but the *luck* was absolutely *atrocious* – virtually *everything* was going wrong for this team. Bristolian Joe Cottle, one of City's genuine 'Mr Reliables', had been an ever-present all season, but on January 28th at Preston North End, the week after Owers' hat-trick against Middlesbrough, he sustained a broken leg during City's disastrous 4-0 defeat in Lancashire. Cottle would be out for the rest of the season, but tragically for him, it ultimately meant that he ended up never playing for the club again. He was released by Bristol City – at the tender age of 24 - in the summer of 1911, later signing a short-term contract with Bristol Rovers of the Southern League. He ended up with Mid Rhondda in South Wales, and later became a publican in Bristol, most notably as the licensee of the *Leicester House*, in Mill Lane, Bedminster.

Once again, Wedlock was to miss four vital Bristol City games that season, this time for a combination of reasons – either injury, or because of his continued involvement in England international matches. Subsequently, yet again, the Reds' did not perform well in his absence. Because of the previously-mentioned head injury, he missed the Aston Villa home match (which doubled-up as Andy Burton's benefit game), on November 5th, and also the contest away at Sunderland the following week, when Jack Cowell netted for the Wearsiders. Both of these matches were *lost,* as was the clash away at *Champions-to-be* Manchester

United on February 11th (1-3), *and* the game at home to Bradford City on April Fools' Day (0-2). The latter two matches took place when Billy was starring for England - against Ireland at the Baseball Ground, Derby, and against Scotland at Goodison Park, Everton, respectively.

The trial game for the England team this year had taken place at White Hart Lane, Tottenham, on Monday January 23rd, this consisting of a match played between *'The Whites'* and *'The Stripes'*. Wedlock played (successfully) for *'The Whites'* and was subsequently selected for the English team as normal. England eventually ended the *Home International* campaign 'Top of the group', meaning that Billy was a British Champion for the second time, but for Wedlock, it was going to count for little if Bristol City ended the season going down the plughole...

Away at Aston Villa on March 11th 1911, Wedlock clocked up his 200th league game for the club, but there was to be no celebration on *this* occasion, the match being yet another one that ended in defeat, this time by a score of 2-0.

City's eventual fate essentially boiled down to the final three games, but as they prepared for the first of these, at home to Nottingham Forest, to most observers, the Reds' already looked practically dead and buried. Inexplicably though, the team suddenly kicked into life, and unexpectedly thrashing Forest by five goals to one, they next travelled to Manchester City praying for *another* miracle... Having gone behind at Hyde Road after 35 minutes, two penalty-kicks either side of half-time (scored by Logan and then Marr) subsequently gave City a narrow 2-1 victory, and in his sheer *desperation* to keep City up, this game may just represent the *only time* in his career that Billy Wedlock ever lost his temper on the field of play. It happened in the immediate build-up to City's second penalty, twenty minutes from the end, when a goalward shot struck by Wedlock clipped the corner of the post and crossbar, the ball then appearing to be fisted away by Manchester defender Tommy Kelso. The **Western Daily Press** explained that *"Kelso, it seemed, stopped a certain goal with his hand, and this produced appeals for a penalty, and led to the greatest excitement, in which Wedlock got at loggerheads with a Manchester player. The referee consulted BOTH linesmen, and finally awarded a penalty – Marr scoring with a fast drive..."* The Manchester City fans did not agree with *any* of the penalty awards, least of all the *second* one, and some spectators invaded the field, to make clear their feelings to the referee. But both penalties – and both *goals*, for that matter, *stood* – and City clung on for a critical 2-1 victory.

Incredibly, this result left Bristol with still *half a chance* of survival – with only *one game* remaining. But they simply *had* to beat Everton - no *'ifs'* or *'buts'* on that one - and *even then*, City were still relying on other results...

Yet when it came to the crunch, Wedlock's men weren't *quite* up to the task, and there were to be no *'last-day'* miracles this time – because on April 29th, in front of 10,000 hopeful fans at Ashton Gate, Everton won 1-0. The Reds' finished second from bottom of the First Division, two *agonising* points short of next-placed Bury, who escaped the drop. Had the City *won*, they would have *survived* on goal average.

But after five wonderful campaigns in the top-flight, the *'glory years'* were now officially at an end, and Bristol City – *Billy Wedlock and all'* – were on their way down...

WEDLOCK – THE FIRST HERO OF BRISTOL CITY

DIVISION ONE - FINAL TABLE

	P	W	D	L	F	A	PNTS
1. MAN UNITED	38	22	8	8	72	40	52
2. ASTON VILLA	38	22	7	9	69	41	51
3. SUNDERLAND	38	15	15	8	67	48	45
4. EVERTON	38	19	7	12	50	36	45
5. BRADFORD C.	38	20	5	13	51	42	45
6. THE WEDNESDAY	38	17	8	13	47	48	42
7. OLDHAM	38	16	9	13	44	41	41
8. NEWCASTLE U.	38	15	10	13	61	43	40
9. SHEFFIELD U.	38	15	8	15	49	43	38
10. WOOL. ARSENAL	38	13	12	13	41	49	38
11. NOTTS C.	38	14	10	14	37	45	38
12. BLACKBURN	38	13	11	14	62	54	37
13. LIVERPOOL	38	15	7	16	53	53	37
14. PRESTON N E	38	12	11	15	40	49	35
15. TOTTENHAM	38	13	6	19	52	63	32
16. MIDDLESBROUGH	38	11	10	17	49	63	32
17. MAN. CITY	38	9	13	16	43	58	31
18. BURY	38	9	11	18	43	71	29
19. BRISTOL CITY	38	11	5	22	43	66	27 (R)
20. NOTTM. FOREST	38	9	7	22	55	75	25 (R)

10] The Darkest Hour

Some time before the end of that fateful relegation season, the Wedlocks' had moved home again, leaving their house at *The Chessels* after more than three years, and crossing the main thoroughfare that is North Street, into No 44, Exeter Road, Ashton Gate, a smart little dwelling that possessed what the family desperately needed – an extra bedroom...

Because on June 28th 1911, Billy and Rosina's final child was born, Frederick George Wedlock, meaning theirs was now a family of *nine*, the seven children consisting of four boys and three girls. In order, there was now Rosina Ellen, who was ten, William James (aged eight), Thomas George (six), James (five), Lilly (three), Ivy (eighteen months), and little Fred - the latest, and *final*, addition.

In the wake of Bristol City's relegation, a number of First Division clubs were immediately alerted as to the possibility of Wedlock becoming available to play for *their* team. It would not be inaccurate to suggest that the vultures were circling...

They anticipated that Wedlock, being an established international player, would naturally want to continue in this vein, and they calculated that the possibility of it actually *happening* would be fairly doubtful, if he were to remain playing his club football with Bristol City - a relegated team - in Division Two. Additionally, even the sizeable group of cynics (journalists) and critics across the country, who had been desperately unhappy at Billy's continued selection for the England team, felt the prospect of Wedlock plying his trade in the Second Division was a simply *ludicrous* one, because *everyone* knew – friend or foe – that he was better than *that!* But then again, his England critics may well have been popping the champagne corks on hearing the news of City's relegation, because it meant in the unlikely event that Wedlock *did* elect to stay with the Reds' into the Second Division era, it therefore stood to reason that his England career would finally be *over. Didn't it?*

Meanwhile, Everton and Blackburn Rovers were said to be two of the leading clubs who were jostling for Billy's signature. Wedlock, after all, was still only 30, and appeared to have plenty of First Division life in him *yet.* At *that* level of football, he probably had two or three years still in him, maybe more.

But the *one* club, and as far as can be told, the *only* club, who were to submit a *genuine*, cast-iron overture to the Bristol City directors, was Chelsea, in May 1911. The west London establishment would allegedly offer Bristol City the princely sum of £1500, and it was a mouth-watering bid that was to severely tempt the directors of the Ashton Gate outfit, whose cash-flow was going to be hit significantly in the wake of relegation.

In some ways, it would have been a strange move. Chelsea at this point were not even in the First Division *themselves*, for they had been relegated to Division Two the year before City, and had yet to bounce back. Season 1911/12 though, as it turned out, was to be their second and final campaign at that level, for they would gain promotion at the end of the season.

Wedlock was certainly *prepared* to *go* to the Stamford Bridge outfit, but only on the understanding that it was going to save his beloved City from financial meltdown – *a factor which cannot be stressed enough*. That City *were* indeed financially embarrassed,

THE DARKEST HOUR

is a fact that cannot be disputed, for they seemed to be undergoing some difficulties in raising money for summer wages and other immediate costs. Wedlock though, whilst allegedly being *okay* with playing for Chelsea, was *not keen* on living in London, where house prices were not cheap, and Billy – candidly – feared that financial circumstances for his wife and large family would be hit significantly. Knowing of his apparent keenness to remain living in the Bristol area, Chelsea were even allegedly prepared to offer Wedlock a deal that would have accommodated this desire, in other words, they would presumably have allowed him to commute to and from Bristol, whilst offering him digs in London for *if* and *when* he needed to be *there*. Chelsea, it seemed, really *did* want Wedlock!

It then came to be, however, that Bristol City, after a meticulous round of budgeting, managed to straighten out their financial arrangements, and it became deemed no longer a necessity that Wedlock's transfer be sanctioned in order to balance the books. Wedlock *himself*, always consulting with the club, then approached the directors looking for a firm assurance that it was indeed no longer the case that City needed to sell him in order to get by. In other words, was it true that the club would *not* be on the verge of financial ruin if he did not leave for Stamford Bridge? The directors, having replied exactly in *confirming* words to that effect, then essentially made up Billy's mind for him - and Wedlock, probably with a good deal of relief, then elected to stay with Bristol City, *whatever* Division they happened to be playing in. *Football-wise*, it seemed that it was simply Billy's *destiny*, never to leave the Ashton Gate club.

Nevertheless, whilst Wedlock might have been staying, amongst his club-mates there was a mass exodus taking place, as the team of City's 1906 – 1911 glory years slowly began to break apart. Sam Gilligan had left the previous year, and now Staniforth, Burton, Annan, Hanlin and Spear were on their way to pastures new. Cottle, of course, had been released by the club in the aftermath of his broken leg, whilst the days of Harry Clay in goal were also coming to an end, though he would remain with the Ashton Gate outfit for another year or so. It truly was the end of a golden era, and City's Second Division teams of 1911 – 1915 would end up looking a lot different to their recent *First* Division ones...

After the birth of his son Frederick, Wedlock could finally relax a bit more and as usual for the close-season, went off to play cricket. But for *who* would he be playing this summer?
For it wasn't just in the game of *football* that Wedlock's team loyalties had been much-speculated upon. In fact, the first clue had been given away that Billy appeared be remaining with Bristol City, when newspaper reports suddenly revealed on May 11th that Wedlock had signed up to play for – *and coach* - *J S Fry & Son* Cricket Club, a post for which he was to be paid for his troubles. This move effectively brought down the curtain on Billy's four years' service to the equivalent establishment at Bedminster.
The summer code had always very much been Wedlock's No 2 sporting activity, he took the game very seriously and was in fact, not surprisingly, something of a supreme all-rounder. It would actually be an injustice to recount the complete sporting story of Billy Wedlock without giving at least a passing mention to his

prominent and lengthy cricket career.

By all accounts, Wedlock was an absolute *master* of the game, he being an outstanding batsman, a more-than-useful bowler – and a pretty decent fielder.

Wedlock in his cricket whites...

WEDLOCK – THE FIRST HERO OF BRISTOL CITY

His adult cricketing activities appear to have started at Long Ashton as far back as the summer of 1900, an era of course, which actually pre-dated his footballing days at Aberdare, and which *even* came before his *original* spell as a young player at Bristol City. There was no English cricket for Wedlock during his four-year footballing exile in South Wales – for he was busy playing the '*summer code*' for Aberdare (and later, Aberaman) *instead!* - but when he came back as a professional with City, he was straight off to the Long Ashton cricket field with the then-Bristol winger Freddie Fenton, in the summer of 1906.

From the summer of 1907, through to the end of the equivalent season in 1910, Wedlock spent four seasons dedicating his cricket services to the Bedminster club – though the latter of these campaigns would have been heavily interrupted because of Billy's lengthy English FA tour of South Africa, which had also taken place that year. One of Wedlock's regular team-mates in the Bedminster line-up for a number of those four seasons was his Bristol City footballing colleague Billy Maxwell, which is perhaps surprising because Maxwell of course was a *Scot*.

But interestingly, Maxwell *himself* had at one time made a single appearance for the county of Staffordshire, in a 1904 Minor Counties Championship match against Dorset, and was even named opening batsman in their second innings. In Wedlock's early Bedminster days, his friend Archie Annan – *another* Scots-born Bristol City team-mate – often had a go with the cricket bat as well...

The **Western Daily Press** covered a fascinating match in August 1909, played out between Wedlock's Bedminster side, and St George, reporting that; *"It was a curious Bedminster team that*

THE DARKEST HOUR

took the field against St George at Ashton Gate, the absentees being the brothers North, Dr Cook, W. Maxwell and E.H. Murdoch, but notwithstanding, Bedminster had no difficulty in winning. Clay (* Harry) came into the side, and as he took five wickets for 20 runs, his presence compensated for the absence of the Norths'. Another Bristol City player, J. Cottle, was in the team, but, for the second time, did not bat. Wedlock made 29, and in that score hit 4 sixes and a four – an innings which needs no words to describe its character. Wedlock also did some good bowling, so that the Bristol City element was strong. The first wicket partnership between W. Cox and E.R. Mellier settled the game in favour of Bedminster, who eventually won by two wickets, and 36 runs to spare."

Wedlock, by all accounts, was certainly good enough to have turned professional, and over the years a number of attempts were made to persuade him that he really could – and indeed *should* - be playing for the county of Gloucestershire. One such cheerleader for Wedlock in this respect was apparently none other than Gilbert (G L) Jessop, the long-time Gloucestershire skipper and England international batting supremo. According to many in the know at the time, the prospect of a Jessop / Wedlock partnership at Gloucestershire C.C. would have been a fearsome one indeed... On June 1st 1908, Wedlock accordingly took part in a trial match for that very county, a contest played between a selected *Bristol & District XI* and a strong XI representative of *Gloucestershire C.C.* Joining Wedlock on the Bristol team that day was City club-mate and goalkeeper * Harry Clay, yet another useful cricketer from within the Ashton Gate ranks. But Billy enjoyed a 'mixed' time of it on this occasion, as local papers

would explain. On the one hand, he had the temerity to see G L Jessop, the aforementioned international, caught *'out'* by Silverthorne for only 11 – after Wedlock had bowled a *corker*. Yet as a batsman, Billy's luck was *not* as good – he being *'stumped'*, and therefore – *'out!'* for only two runs. And as the **Globe** later wrote in 1920, when perhaps referring to *another* unsuccessful county trial:- *"G.L.J. (Jessop) was once very keen on making Wedlock into a county cricketer. He played him in a trial match, and Wedlock, though a frequent centurion for his club, chose the occasion to make 'a pair' and drop three sitters at cover-point!"* However in June 1911, as Wedlock and his *Fry's* batting partner W E Meyer produced near-on 200 runs between them in a match against Stapleton, the **Western Daily Press**, reporting on the contest, confirmed Billy's county credentials by claiming -
"If Wedlock could get and keep a place in the Gloucestershire team, everybody would be delighted."
Before his move to *Fry's*, another regular feature of Wedlock's sporting summer was the annual friendly match, contested every August, between Bedminster C.C., and the football players of Bristol City FC, who usually played under the banner of '*Mr H. Thickett's XI'*. But Wedlock's services *here,* if only for the day of this one-off contest, were always given over to the *footballers*. On these occasions, the soccer players were more often than not triumphant over the cricketers, and as the **Western Daily Press** reported on Monday August 16th 1909, *"Saturday was no exception, Mr Thickett's XI winning by 93 runs, after declaring with only six wickets down. Wedlock and Clay, both very fair cricketers, put up a capital partnership for the first wicket, which was only disturbed by the latter having to leave the ground*

THE DARKEST HOUR

through playing a ball from Macklin into his face. The footballers excelled, as one might expect, at short run-getting, but when Bedminster attempted to emulate these tactics they found the fielding too smart for them. Clegg, Staniforth, and Wedlock took the Bedminster wickets between them, whilst the popular half-back (Wedlock) *pleased the large crowd with two very smart catches."*

Yet the footballers didn't *always* have it all their own way. In the 1907 contest, played on Monday August 5th, it was the *Bedminster cricketers* who had been triumphant, seeing off Wedlock's boys who were all out for 127. Billy himself was bowled for 19, whilst Sam Gilligan was out for a *duck!*

The story of Wedlock's 'summer career' also leads to an odd little curiosity, for it meant that between 1907 and 1910, he was spending twelve whole months of the year playing on the turf at Ashton Gate – eight months for football, and four for cricket. That's because from the early 1900's onwards, *Bedminster C.C.* were actually sharing that sacred soil with Bristol City FC! It was only in 1912, by which time Wedlock had moved on, that Bedminster moved out to the ground they still possess today, over the road at *'The Clanage'*.

After transferring his allegiance to *J S Fry's,* who were based at Ashley Down (Gloucester Road), Wedlock soon got back into some fine batting form. In a match between *Fry's* and the *United Press*, played at the County Ground, Gloucester Road in August 1911, the **Western Daily Press** reported that *"the United Press also had plenty of leather chasing...W. Bennett and W. Wedlock got going, and the ball was hit to all parts of the ground, and even into the refreshment room, smashing, after passing through the* *open window, a bottle of whisky and a bottle of port. Wedlock survived a leg before appeal, which many thought should have sent him back, before he had scored, but afterwards he used the long handle to such good purpose that he scored 70..."*

Another good example of Wedlock's cricketing prowess for *Fry's* came a year later, in July 1912, when Billy took part in a match that might well have been dubbed the '*Chocolate Derby*'. Describing the event, the **Clifton Society** reported that; *"The annual game between J S Fry and Sons and Cadbury teams, played on the ground of the Knowle club, produced some high scoring, the home firm making 267 for five wickets, and the visitors 148 for one. Rain then put an end to the game. A great stand by H. Miller and W. Wedlock was the outstanding feature of Fry's innings, the latter getting 106, whilst the former failed by four runs to reach the century. Wedlock hit a six and 12 fours, and Miller 12 fours. By scoring 148 for one Cadbury's did well. The teams and friends were entertained during the day."*

Wedlock played for *Fry's,* it appears, for at least six years, from 1911 until the summer of 1917, and after that, he eventually returned to his old stomping ground, playing with Long Ashton. Billy was still turning out in cricket matches well after his retirement from football, and never lost his love for the game, never *quite* though, making it into the 'big team', by starring for the county of Gloucestershire. It just seemed as if it was simply never meant to be...

Yet Wedlock's services, it seemed - *as ever* - were in great demand. His sporting calendar, twelve months of the year, must have been totally *full-up*. In the summer, he was needed on the cricket field, first by Bedminster, and then by *Fry's*. That's when

THE DARKEST HOUR

he *wasn't* required by the Football Association on the occasion of a close-season foreign tour, either in the name of *England*, or under the banner of the *English FA*. From September through to the end of April, he was needed by *Bristol City.* But there was no guarantee, of course, that he was able to play in all the matches, as *here*, he was often wanted by the England team as part of their annual battle to win the *Home International* championships, or was required to play in the occasional Football League Representative match.
And the doom-mongers who predicted that Wedlock's England career would be over, in the wake of his decision to remain with Bristol City into their Second Division era, were once again to be proved *wrong*. To the chagrin and dismay of that small group of journalists and observers, who mainly hid themselves away in the London and Greater Manchester areas, Wedlock was subsequently picked *again*, for all three matches of the *Home Internationals'*, against Ireland, Wales and Scotland. England ended up *sharing* the trophy with Scotland, despite possessing a superior goal-difference.
But it was in the *following* season, 1912/13, when Billy's international career finally ran into trouble. Wedlock picked up a serious injury to his right ankle whilst playing for Bristol City against Fulham on the rainy Christmas Day of 1912 - it was enough to keep him out of all league action for *three months*, also meaning, therefore, that he had to miss the annual England trial match in January 1913. This was to prove *not only* the *worst*, but also the most *costly* injury of Billy's entire career. Never before and never again would he be forced to miss such a great portion of the football season through either ill-health, or injury. His non-

participation in the January 20th trial match for England (at Hyde Road, Manchester) meant that his taking part in the trilogy of *Home international* matches was now practically impossible, even if he *had* recovered in time...

Missing the Belfast clash with Ireland at Windsor Park on February 15th would have been *bad enough*, missing the match with Scotland at Stamford Bridge on April 5th would have been *even worse*. But for Wedlock, the biggest blow of all would concern the *middle fixture*, at home to Wales on Monday March 17th 1913. Irony was to play a cruel trick on Billy here, for *this year* it happened to be that *'Ashton Gate, Bristol'* was the designated venue for the match, and Billy must surely have had one eye on the calendar *all season*, in eager expectation of *playing*. Although Wedlock was closing in on full-fitness, and had already been out for more than *two and a half months* by the time the match was played, he *didn't quite* make it. Some newspaper reports had implied that Wedlock was to make his league return in City's home match with Lincoln on March 8th – nine days before the Wales international match – but the story turned out to be *false*, and Wedlock *didn't* play. A rumour then did the rounds that Billy's apparent 'transfer' to Tottenham Hotspur was *imminent*, a story which was hotly denied by City, and as it turned out, was something again that 'strangely' never materialised. His comeback match for Bristol City finally took place at Ashton Gate on March 29th, *twelve* agonising days after the Wales international game. Billy had badly wanted the chance to play for his country, *in Bristol*, before his *'home crowd'* - at Ashton Gate, for the only time in his career. But it was not meant to be – and Wedlock came to regard this upset as having been the biggest

THE DARKEST HOUR

disappointment of his footballing life...

Taking Billy's place for the Ireland match in February had been Burnley defender Tommy Boyle, earning the *only* international cap of his career. When Bristol City had hosted Burnley in a league fixture played at Ashton Gate one week *before* the Ireland game, a watching Wedlock had reportedly sought Boyle after the 3-3 draw to wish him all the luck in the world, though the **Burnley News** had clearly taken more of a 'tribal' approach in its take on the situation, when commenting - *"Boyle's selection for the International match has gone down very badly with the Bristol people, and their papers are full of excuses for Wedlock's non-selection..."* (**Note** – Billy had a long-term injury!)

"...Wedlock himself is showing a much better sporting spirit, for as soon as he met Boyle on Saturday last, he congratulated him upon his selection..."

 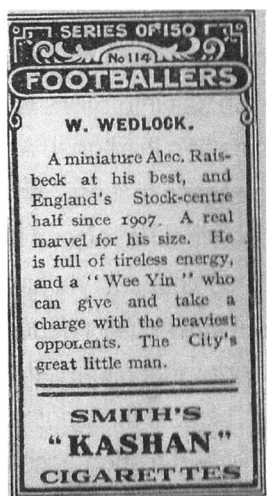

Wedlock perhaps caught in a rarely-seen negative frame of mind for this 1912 cigarette card image. But he had fair reason for bad moods in 1912/13 – injuries

But when it came to the day of the game, the Irish subsequently caused an upset by winning, 2-1. Interestingly, Boyle was only 5 feet 7 and-a-half inches tall. For the Wales and Scotland games, Wedlock's position was taken by *not* by Tommy Boyle, but by the Preston defender Joe McCall. *He*, like both Wedlock *and* Boyle, was a centre-half of, shall we say – '*less-than-average height*'. *He* stood 5 feet 8 and-a-half inches tall. It was almost as if the England selectors were trying to make a point to their critics. It was as if they were effectively saying *"It doesn't matter WHAT you say. If we WANT to pick Wedlock, we SHALL pick Wedlock. And if we CAN'T pick Wedlock, then we'll pick a 'Wedlock-alike' instead"*. Sure enough, McCall's selection, amongst the 'usual suspects', was *severely criticised*...

The reason? That McCall was *"too similar to Wedlock"*...

In the second international game, at Ashton Gate, England had just about enough in their locker to defeat the Welsh 4-3, in a highly-entertaining contest that was watched by 8,000 fans. Just to rub salt into Billy's wounds, his replacement Joe McCall scored England's third goal. And Billy *watched it all unfold*, for he was in the stands that day, an interested, but also, no doubt, a *frustrated* spectator. The size of the crowd though, was a big disappointment, yet had Wedlock been *playing*, then it surely would have been *doubled*. Billy confirmed to a Derbyshire sports reporter that his absence from this particular match was indeed the *"biggest disappointment of his life"*. The **Derby Courier** published a short account of the conversation in its paper the following week, and it reported that Wedlock had *additionally* claimed *"...he would willingly have given a year of his life to be able to have played for England before his own particular* *spectators..."* The paper then continued with a big compliment for Billy, by saying *"We* (England) *have not found Wedlock's successor yet - so far as ability is concerned, for despite anything that football critics may say to the contrary, he has undoubtedly been the most powerful centre half-back of modern times. I hope to see him back in his old position".*

But Wedlock's absence for all three *Home international* matches in 1912/13 meant that the flow and momentum of his England career had been interrupted in an almost *terminal* manner. It certainly meant that he would no longer be an automatic choice when it came to the *following* season. Subsequently, he was *not* picked for the first game with Ireland in February 1914. The centre-half berth *that* day was taken instead by a player who was later to become known as one of the most famous managers in English football history – Major Frank Buckley. But this was to be Buckley's *only* international appearance, because Joe McCall was now generally rated as the *number one* choice of the selectors. It wasn't *quite* all over for Wedlock however, as the aforementioned McCall was now *himself* injured. Billy was henceforth allowed to come back into the England team as a *'stand-in'* when they took on Wales in Cardiff for the second game of the tournament. This turned out to be Wedlock's *final* game in an England shirt, and he bowed out in style, scoring a fine goal as the team triumphed by two goals to nil. It was Wedlock's second goal in 26 international appearances – but he was dropped for the Scotland game, and he never played for his country again. *Internationally*-speaking, Billy's career had finally run its course. The coming of the First World War killed off any last chance that Billy *might* have had of *adding* to his collection of

England caps. But in reality, Wedlock could have no real cause for complaint – he had given his absolute *all* for the England cause, and in turn, the selectors had remained loyal to, and had been good to *Billy*. Wedlock had been given a good, long, extended run in the team, and the FA selectors – despite spells of stinging criticism from *some* of the newspapers - had always stuck *firmly* by their man.

Wedlock then, had *had* his day...

In previous years, a main plank of Wedlock's defence against his *newspaper critics* had been that he was a top-quality First Division player, who was playing high-level football *every week* for an established Division One club. That he was competing with the top players in the land, and mixing it with the cream of the crop. Unfortunately, Wedlock couldn't say this any longer. Back then, Bristol City had been a leading power in the land. They had been right 'up there', competing with the Newcastles, the Evertons, the Liverpools, the Manchester Uniteds and the Villas of this world. But they certainly weren't doing that *anymore*. Wedlock was playing for a *run-of-the-mill*, distinctly *average* Second Division side, who in the immediate years following their relegation in 1911, hadn't remotely looked like they were going to come back again. In the four seasons that covered the era set in between City's *demotion* and the suspension of professional football because of the *Great War* (1915), the team had finished in 13th, 16th, 8th and 13th positions respectively. *This* form was hardly setting the world alight – it was in fact, distinctly *underwhelming*.

In 1911/12 – *City's first campaign in Division Two since relegation* - Wedlock again scored three times, just as he had done during

THE DARKEST HOUR

the previous campaign in Division One. He struck first on November 4th at Stamford Bridge against Chelsea – the team who had tried so hard to secure his transfer the previous May. Wedlock's 61st minute goal was City's second and the *equalising* goal in a 2-2 draw, played in front of a 25,000 crowd.
The sports-writer '*D.D'*, of the **London Daily News,** who was never much of a Wedlock fan, and had even previously referred to him as being a '*midget'*, was *this time* forced to admit that Billy's strike had indeed been a good one, it consisting of *"a sharp, short shot just under bar, from* (Levi) *Copestake's centre"*. Interestingly, **The Sportsman** was a little kinder *still, this* paper noting that *"Copestake middled the ball neatly, and when it dropped, Wedlock shot first time to equalise brilliantly!"* The goal was a valuable one for City, for it finally delivered their first away point of the season, and this too against a Chelsea side who would be *promoted* at the end of the campaign. The following week, in the home clash with Clapton Orient at Ashton Gate, Billy struck *again* – this time it was the only goal of the game and it arrived in the 17th minute. The **Athletic News** reported that Clapton's *"overthrow was brought about by a clever goal scored by WEDLOCK...he had made a capital opening for Gould, and when that player centred, he met the ball and beat Bower with a fine shot..."*
Furthermore, *"...Wedlock has been the mainstay of the side all season, but it is doubtful if he has ever done quite so well as upon THIS occasion. He overshadowed Bevan, and still had time to pay some attention to Dalrymple and McFadden. When he got the ball, he parted with it in the most skilful style..."*
Billy's third and final goal that season came on Saturday January

27th 1912, at home to Leeds City - a game that saw City rush into a three goal lead after only twenty minutes play. Wedlock's was the first of the three, and City ended the afternoon as handsome 4-1 winners.

1912/13 was the wretched season in which Wedlock's Christmas Day injury sustained against Fulham would write off more than three months of his campaign. He actually played in City's first 18 matches of the season, from September 4th through until December 25th 1912, before his ankle gave way. After his recovery, he then participated in five of the final six matches, from March 29th until April 26th 1913. Wedlock's continued absence led to the team's dramatic slide down the table, and City finished the campaign in 16th position – *fifth from the bottom.* This was the club's worst Divisional finish since entering the English Football League twelve years earlier. There were subsequently *more* rumours to the effect that Wedlock's departure from Ashton Gate was *imminent,* these whispers coming hard on the heels of the previous story, a few weeks earlier, which had suggested that Billy was going to Spurs'. Come the end of the season, however, and Wedlock would be signed up once again. Billy's only goal of the season, which was scored *prior* to his injury problems, came at Glossop on October 19th, when the team had suffered a disappointing 3-1 defeat. It was ironic that Wedlock should choose *this* occasion however, for his only successful strike of the season – because it came on the day of his 250th league appearance for the club.

Manager Sam Hollis had announced his intention to stand down at the end of the season, and henceforth, on April 23rd 1913, 36 year-old former Sheffield United, Southampton, and Wolves centre-forward George Hedley was revealed as the new man in charge for the following campaign. Hedley was not only a 'single-cap' former England striker, he had *also* been a Sheffield United team-mate of Harry Thickett and Walter *'Cocky'* Bennett. When Hedley's name was announced, City still had a single league match to complete, and he was immediately to see for himself the difficult task that lay ahead, for in that final game, the Reds' were inexplicably thrashed 5-1 at home to Bury.

The back of another cigarette card featuring brief information on Wedlock, dating from the 1913/14 season

It seemed that Bristol City were attempting to resurrect old methods of appointing ex-Sheffield United Cup winners as their manager, *à la* Thickett. Hedley though, would not do particularly better than his predecessor, although he *did* steer his team into eighth position in his first season (1913/14). Wedlock once again netted a single *club* goal that term, and it came only twelve days after the occasion of his final game – and *goal* – for England. The City goal arrived on March 28th 1914, a second-half strike that sealed a 1-0 victory at home to Nottingham Forest in the league. Events abroad meanwhile, meant that dark clouds were gathering over Europe, and August 1914 was to bring the beginning of the First World War, yet for *now* at least, English domestic football continued in full flow... This gave Wedlock the chance to play his 300th league match for City, at home to Leicester Fosse in Division Two, on September 26th 1914. Thankfully, City won the game 1-0.

Although no one was to know it at the time – least of all Wedlock *himself* – his equalising strike in the 2-2 draw away at Wolverhampton Wanderers on October 17th 1914 turned out to be his final goal in first-class *peace-time* matches for Bristol City, that is to say, his last-ever strike in any league or cup game, either side of the First World War. *Likewise*, Wedlock's goal against Forest in the previous season would prove to be his final of its equivalent kind *at Ashton Gate*.

The conclusion of the 1914/15 season was to effectively signal the *end* of organised *League football* in Britain, for events abroad were spiralling out of control, meaning that a *different* kind of campaign was now taking place in northern France and other places...

It was certainly not a good time to be a professional footballer, for a whole *variety* of reasons. Wedlock did not take up arms in the *Great War*, for at 34 he was no spring chicken at this stage, and besides, he still had important roles to be performing at home in Bristol. Henceforth, it cannot be said that the War took Billy's best footballing years *from him*, for he was now at the 'veteran' stage

THE DARKEST HOUR

in his career, but it did in all likelihood rob him of another one hundred–*plus* league appearances for Bristol City, and *who knows* – maybe a few more England caps. Though he was to remain on City's books as a *professional,* the domestic football world was now a volatile and unpredictable environment - and the one thing it *wasn't,* was *profitable.*

From September 1915, for the next four years, Bristol City's annual fixture list was to consist of, in-effect, friendlies, fundraisers and exhibition matches. Not to mention a whole stack of 'derby games' against Bristol Rovers, because crowds in general were sparse, and local derbies were the only contests that generated *any kind of revenue.* Despite *'professionalism',* Wedlock still needed a *second income,* a fact which also highlighted his need to remain *ahead of the game* with regards to what he was going to do when his sporting career actually *finished.* This is exactly where the influence of his friend, Bristol City Chairman Frank Bacon, *appeared* to come in. Bacon, of course – who had been elected as the Chairman of Bristol City in July 1912 - had *also* been in the licensing trade for a good portion of his life, and he had famously been the landlord of the *Masonic Arms* for more years than anyone could care to recall. City's previous manager, Sam Hollis, it will be remembered, was also well-known outside football as a pub licensee. Countless ex-players and managers from within the world of football – meaning Bristol City, and *beyond* – had also gone into the pub trade at the conclusion of their sporting careers. Can it merely be *coincidental* then, that under the influence of Hollis, and – *in particular* – Billy's old mentor, Frank Bacon...*three* of Bristol City's defensive line from the 1905/06 promotion-winning team, and *specifically* –

the three *Bristolians* – Spear, Cottle and Wedlock – all went into the licensing trade at the conclusion of their careers?
Suffice to say, that by the end of November 1915, Wedlock had decided to move his family out of Exeter Road, thus ending a spell of five years or so of living at that address.
The family's next destination accordingly became the *'Star Inn'*, the public house and hostelry that stood at one end of Bower Ashton Terrace, right opposite the main entrance to the football ground that was known as *Ashton Gate*...
And so it was *now*, at the end of 1915, when he was *still* a professional footballer, and *not – as has often popularly been reported* – 1921, when he had retired from the game, that Billy Wedlock first began his carry out his duties as a pub licensee.
But just as the family were in the very business of moving their things – and they must *literally* have been almost *packing their suitcases* - tragedy struck, and on November 29th 1915, Rosina Wedlock suddenly died of pneumonia at the tender age of 33.
It was a devastation that will naturally have rocked the family to its very foundations, bringing to an end fifteen and a half years of happy marriage – and leaving Billy a distraught widower. In her final desperate hours, Rose had displayed the symptoms of syncope, which probably confirms that she suffered from low blood pressure, and henceforth from a lack of blood-flow reaching the brain. Her condition worsened, and it was the pneumonia at the very end that killed her.
Rose Wedlock had been the loyal, patient and loving wife who had been prepared to follow her young husband around the country during the era of Billy's long, hard efforts to forge a career in professional football. She had known him from the time that he

THE DARKEST HOUR

was an eager, wide-eyed inexperienced teenager, right through to where he was *now* – one of the leading footballing superstars in the land. Billy's first thoughts, of course, were with his remaining family, for he now had seven shell-shocked children who were grieving for their lost mother. Of his dear Rosina, Wedlock later wrote; *"I often sit and think of you when I am all alone...O, for a shake of her hand, or a word from the voice that is still..."*

In an almost unimaginable double-blow for Wedlock, just 17 days later, back at *Ashton Place*, North Street, his mother Sarah *also died* at the age of 74 – on December 16th 1915. It was naturally a period of great mourning, and a devastating way for the family to begin their new era at the *Star Inn*.

For the Wedlocks', the *darkest hour* had indeed arrived...

The Star Inn awaits...

WEDLOCK – THE FIRST HERO OF BRISTOL CITY

"I GOT 18 OF *'EM* IN SUCCESSION... - NOT BAD, EH?"

11] England Expects…

As previously mentioned, Billy Wedlock's first-ever match for England had been a *Home International* clash with Ireland at Goodison Park, Liverpool on Saturday February 16th 1907. Back in those days there were no such things as 'international breaks', League football continued, irrespective of whether certain players had been called up to play for their country – and every club *had* to continue their League programme using whichever players they had available. Accordingly, as Wedlock was making his England bow in the north-west, his City team was in London playing Woolwich Arsenal in the First Division.

This became the first match, League or Cup, in which Wedlock had been absent since signing for City 21 months previously. Strangely enough, City went to Woolwich Arsenal and beat them 2-1 that day, so Wedlock would have been greatly pleased when he heard the news. But it gets *even more strange* when you realise that City had *lost on the very same venue* only *two weeks earlier*, in an FA Cup match – when Wedlock had been *playing!*

Billy's priority on *this* occasion however, was purely about representing his country, and of attempting to establish a full-blown international career. The full England team at Goodison Park that day, including the club side of each player, was as follows:- **GOALKEEPER** – Sam Hardy (Liverpool), **BACKS** – Bob Crompton (Blackburn Rovers) (Capt.), John Carr (Newcastle Utd), **HALF-BACKS** – Ben Warren (Derby County), Billy Wedlock (Bristol City), Bob Hawkes (Luton Town), **FORWARDS** – John Rutherford (Newcastle Utd), John Coleman (Woolwich Arsenal), George Hilsdon (Chelsea), Joe Bache (Aston Villa), and Harold

Hardman (Everton). The two reserves were utility man Colin Veitch, a regular skipper of Newcastle Utd - *and the man whose place Wedlock had previously taken at the famous trial match in Sheffield* - and centre-forward Irvine Thornley of Manchester City. The attendance for the game was 22,235. Curiously, Ireland played in royal blue shirts that day, with shamrock crests. Perhaps the change of colours was made in order to flatter their hosts, Everton FC, but it didn't do them any good, as England won 1-0 with a 53rd minute goal from Harold Hardman - *"a long, splendid shot, high up in the corner of the goal"*.
Of the match, the **Nottingham Evening Post** reported that *"Wedlock was cheered for some fine tackling and accurate placing"*, whilst **The Sportsman** said *"We liked Wedlock immensely. He may not yet have attained the 'class' that marked the easier methods of Warren – who was very, very good – but the work he can accomplish is tremendous. On Saturday he gave the Irish forwards no quarter, and was a constant source of worry. He was equally good in defence and attack, always on the spot when wanted, and altogether a big success. What Wedlock requires is just a little 'rounding off', and that should quickly come in first-class company. Then, perhaps, he will achieve the dignity of being termed a 'great' half-back, in the sense that the word 'great' is applied to Crompton as a full-back. Sometimes, however, Wedlock's pace and energy impress one as too terrific to last. Let us hope that he is not a seven-day wonder..."*
There are a number of very interesting stories concerning three or four of Billy's team-mates that day. Hardman, who scored the goal, was of Everton at the time and the England match was therefore being played on his 'home turf'. But his later clubs

ENGLAND EXPECTS...

included Manchester United, and much later on, after becoming a well-known administrator, he was to return to the Old Trafford club as a director, later *still*, in 1951, becoming *Chairman*. He would be still running the club in fact, at the time of the Munich air disaster in 1958.

Chelsea and West Ham centre-forward George Hilsdon was nicknamed the '*Gatling Gun*' because his shots *"were simply unstoppable and which travel like shots from a gun."* However, during the period of the Great War, Hilsdon tried to avoid active service and was promptly caught by police hiding in a chicken run – he was later punished and sent to the frontline *anyway.*

When he got to France, he fought on the Western Front where he suffered a gas attack, which would affect him greatly, and in the words of his son, he *"copped the mustard gas at Arras."* It eventually also ended his football career.

Ben Warren, who played directly alongside Wedlock many times in the England half-back line, up until the year 1911, was a vastly experienced player who racked up more than 240 league appearances for Derby County. He later transferred to Chelsea, in 1908, making another 92 appearances at Stamford Bridge. He won 22 England caps between 1906 and 1911. However, his playing career was to end prematurely and tragically. Warren suffered a knee injury whilst playing for Chelsea in a 4–1 win over Clapton Orient, precipitating a dramatic decline in his mental health. Faced with a long lay-off on the sidelines, and with a young family to support in an era well before footballers were paid great fortunes, Warren suffered a mental breakdown and began to be plagued by hallucinations and delusions that he was being poisoned. By 1912, things would get so bad that he was admitted into a Derbyshire lunatic asylum. His condition deteriorated to such an extent that he was then placed on suicide watch. He died of tubercolosis whilst still an inmate of the asylum in January 1917, leaving a widow and four children. Tragically, he was just 37. Wedlock though, would never forget his ex-international colleague, writing, seven years after Warren's death, *"Of course, there are super-plodders, and they occasionally get international caps. But this type is extremely rare. Ben Warren, for instance, was one of the super-plodding type, and his value was fully recognised. You couldn't play alongside Ben without catching something of his enthusiasm for his job, and his willingness to 'pull out' to the uppermost..."*

Finally, John *'Jock'* Rutherford was a star at Newcastle, also later playing for top clubs such as Stoke City and Arsenal. Interestingly though, he was also the great-grandfather of the 2012 Olympic long-jump champion Greg Rutherford.

After his good performance at Goodison Park, Wedlock was again selected for the next game, the second match of England's *Home International* campaign, at home to Wales, at Craven Cottage, Fulham, on Monday March 18th. This contest gave Billy his first chance to play alongside the great Steve Bloomer, Middlesbrough's ex-Derby County striker, and a true goal-scoring legend of the game. In international terms, Bloomer's career was gradually heading towards its conclusion, but when it *did* finally end, he would gain the proud statistic of having scored 28 goals in only 23 matches for his country. But the real star that day was probably Welsh wing wizard Billy Meredith, who at times tormented the English defenders with his speed and dribbling on the right flank. Watched by 22,000, the match eventually finished

ENGLAND EXPECTS...

in a 1-1 draw. Meredith did most of his damage in the first-half (even though England won the toss and had played with the wind at their backs), so it was no surprise when Lot Jones gave Wales the lead in the 25th minute. Yet England, clamping down on Meredith, improved in the second-half and Jimmy Stewart grabbed a 62nd minute equaliser.

England completed their domestic programme with another 1-1 draw, this time at home to Scotland, at St James' Park, Newcastle, on Saturday April 6th. Strangely for Wedlock, this meant a swift return to the ground on which he had played only *one week* earlier, when Bristol City had lost 3-0 to Newcastle in what many people had dubbed the 'deciding match' in the First Division championship race. It must have seemed to Billy as if history was going to repeat itself, because in *this* instance, the English got off to a disastrous start when Crompton, the skipper, put through his own goal after only four minutes.

But Steve Bloomer, with one of his famous, rasping, 25-yard *'daisy-cutters'*, equalised just before half-time to save the day. By all accounts though, the Scots were unlucky not to win, and according to one of the leading newspapers north of the border *"...the English defence was sorely tried – Crompton and Wedlock were prominent in stemming the onrush..."*

The attendance was a good one, just short of 36,000. But the Welsh ended up becoming 'Champions of Britain', finishing top of the group (of four) after three matches. Wales had won two and drawn one, whilst England finished second having won one, and drawn two. Because of his further England commitments against Wales and Scotland, Wedlock ended up missing an additional three Bristol City games in the spring of 1907. By virtue of the

WEDLOCK – THE FIRST HERO OF BRISTOL CITY

Wales game on March 18th, he was not allowed to play in City's 1-0 defeat at Middlesbrough which had taken place two days earlier, on Saturday the 16th. Then because of the Scotland game on April 6th, he missed City's potentially *critical* home matches with Bolton and Aston Villa on April 2nd and April 6th respectively. Had City *won* these matches, they would have won the League Championship instead of Newcastle. Alas, in Wedlock's absence, they were *both lost*, and upon Billy's return, although City came storming back to win their last four matches in style - including a win at Anfield against Liverpool - it was too late, and Newcastle won the League title.

But as far as Wedlock's England career was concerned, he was now most certainly, firmly *in* with the '*in-crowd*' – he kept getting picked, probably to the great disappointment of Manchester United centre-half Charlie Roberts.

Billy's next three international matches would all take place in the following season, 1907/08, and again these were each to be played against the three '*Home nations*'. This meant fixtures against Ireland in Belfast on Saturday February 15th 1908, Wales at Wrexham on Monday March 16th, and Scotland at Hampden Park, Glasgow, on Saturday April 4th...

England started off by beating the Irish 3-1 at the Solitude Ground, Cliftonville, Belfast - in front of 22,600 fans, a new Irish record. Next up, they walloped an injury-hit Wales team by 7-1, this match taking place at the Racecourse Ground, Wrexham – Wedlock *finally* having some luck at this venue after having suffered two Cup Final defeats there whilst a player with Aberdare. But in reality, 7-1 as a score was a gross exaggeration of the 'difference' between the two sides, catastrophic injuries

ENGLAND EXPECTS...

and dire luck for the Welsh having completely ruined the game as a spectacle and a contest. The game had been 0-0 and an even match until a severe injury to the Welsh goalkeeper had occurred in the 15th minute. For Billy Wedlock *personally* however, it was to get better and better, as, celebrating the day with his fifth international cap, he was to mark the occasion with his first-ever goal for his country, it coming in the 30th minute to put England 3-0 up. John Rutherford had taken a shot which was saved, *"...but the ball came to the foot of Wedlock, and the Bristol centre-half, with a hard, straight drive, scored"*. England were *four goals* to the good as the half-time whistle approached, but then the Welshmen got a rare bit of luck with a penalty award. However, as if having their goalkeeper taken off injured, and then having to play the last twenty minutes of the first-half with only *nine men* was not enough, when Wales got their penalty in the dying moments of the first period, their superstar Billy Meredith promptly blasted it wide, adding to the many woes of the Welshmen. The England goals kept flowing in the second-half, and Spurs centre-forward Vivian Woodward (captain for the day) - whose heavy charge had caused the goalkeeping injury in the first place, claimed an eventual hat-trick as Wales were utterly destroyed. In amongst all the excitement though, the **Yorkshire Post** still found room to pay tribute to Wedlock, saying the little man had been *"...as active, clever, and untiring as ever at centre"*.

The Scotland match at Hampden Park in April drew an incredible crowd of 121,452, which upon its announcement, immediately became a new *world record.* It was certainly a higher attendance than the like of which Billy was used to at Ashton Gate! Amidst severe overcrowding though, 70 people were injured, with one taken to hospital. The main problem was crushing, resulting in crowds of people being forced to swarm down off the terraces and onto the *pitch-side* as a way of escape. On the field of play, the Scots took the lead via Andy Wilson in the 27th minute, with the English equalising through a Jimmy Windridge effort in the 74th minute – a 'Geoff Hurst-style' shot which hit the crossbar, and then bounced down onto the goal-line. The result meant that England 'topped' the final group of four as they possessed a slightly superior goal average over the Scots, but, as the teams shared equal records in every other department, such as number of wins, number of draws, and number of points, the two countries officially 'shared' the title of *'British Champions'*.

Scotland v England at Hampden Park, Glasgow – April 4th 1908

Fixture-wise, this was the pattern that would generally continue for a good number of seasons as far as Wedlock's international career was concerned. England would play their annual three

ENGLAND EXPECTS...

matches against the other 'Home nations', each country playing the other, once per season. These 'domestic' contests effectively comprised the old 'Home Internationals', or 'British Championships' tournament, which was to prove such a popular fixture in the national sporting calendar every year, much in the same way that Rugby Union's '*Six Nations*' is such a massive draw nowadays. In those days of course, there was no high-profile summer tournament to look forward to in the close-season, such as a World Cup or a 'Euro' Championship, these competitions were still a long way off, and as such, the winning of the 'Home Internationals' tournament was the very *height* of the FA's ambition. The only other matches ever played were perhaps the very occasional friendly game, every now and again there might be a summer tour on foreign soil, when two or three Exhibition or 'Test matches' would be played. And at the conclusion of the 1907/08 season, this is actually *exactly* what happened...

The FA decided to send a representative England team to the Austria-Hungarian Empire, for a two-week tour comprising of four friendly / exhibition matches. A squad of 13 professionals (with a smattering of amateurs) was selected, and the touring party departed from London on Wednesday June 3rd, returning to the UK on Tuesday June 16th. Wedlock, naturally, was one of the players selected, which was positive thing for his international *football* career, but not so good on another level, as it would have interfered with his usual summer (cricketing) activities somewhat! Football-wise, there were to be two matches played against Austria, at separate stadiums in Vienna, on June 6th and June 8th. Then there was to be a game against Hungary in Budapest on

WEDLOCK – THE FIRST HERO OF BRISTOL CITY

June 10th. The tour was then to reach its conclusion with a fourth match, against Bohemia in Prague, on June 13th. The *name* of the opponents in that final game was a bit of an oddity, as, strictly speaking, there was actually no such country by the name of 'Bohemia' at the time. (Prague would later be known as the capital city of the country destined to become '*Czechoslovakia*', but at this *particular* time however, in the pre-World War One-era, it was simply a part of the Austro-Hungarian Empire).

In the first game against Austria on June 6th, a 3,500 crowd at the *Cricketer Platz* Stadium in Vienna saw England win by a convincing 6-1 score-line. Two days later, the game dubbed the 'return match', featuring pretty much identical line-ups from the first contest, finished with an even wider margin of victory - 11-1 to England! Skipper Vivian Woodward scored *four times*, whilst his centre-forward partner Frank Bradshaw, of The Wednesday, grabbed *three*. Incredibly, Woodward was one of the *amateur* players in the England party, by virtue of his playing club football for Spurs, who were still in the Southern League at the time. The second match with the Austrians took place at the *Hohe Warte* Stadium, Vienna, with the attendance recorded as being 5,000. In the third match in Budapest, on June 10th, England destroyed Hungary by seven goals to nil, this time four goals going to George Hilsdon, with the crowd numbering 6,500. The tour concluded with a 4-0 win over Bohemia at the Letna Stadium, Prague, in front of the biggest crowd of the trip – 12,000. This game had also seen the inclusion of an English referee for the first time in the campaign, namely Mr John Lewis, of Burslem. Unfortunately, the natives took great exception to his decision to award England a penalty in the 50th minute (which gave them a

ENGLAND EXPECTS...

2-0 lead), also questioning a number of his *other* 'close calls', many of the Czechs believing he had generally shown far too much bias towards England during the course of the game. At the final whistle, although the England team was cheered and applauded, the referee was chased from the field, receiving a number of hard kicks and blows as he went. It was an ugly finish to a relatively successful tour. Wedlock played in all four matches, bringing his international appearance tally up to 10. Normal service was resumed in 1908/09, with England competing, as usual, in the *Home International* Championships. This year, they were to win all three games and would be crowned *outright champions*, becoming the first team to do so, without conceding a *single* goal. This meant that although Wedlock would finish the season as a disappointed FA Cup runner-up with Bristol City, he could at least claim a consolation prize, that of becoming a 'British Champion' with England.
The first game on February 13th against Ireland at Bradford Park Avenue resulted in a 4-0 win for England, when the sides had still been level-pegging at half-time. But second-half braces from Woodward and Hilsdon (one penalty) soon sorted out the men from *Erin's isle*. The match was watched by a very healthy crowd of 28,000. The big significance of *this* game though, at least, from a *Bristol City* point of view, was the inclusion of left-back Joe Cottle, for his first – and *only* – England cap. This occasion therefore also represented the only time in history that *two* current Bristol City players would be selected for the *same* England XI, in the *same match*. Cottle though, had a mixed game, and would not be picked again. The **London Daily News** meanwhile, in its Monday match report, gave a rather bizarre

verification of Wedlock's merits as a decent international footballer, seeming almost reluctant to admit his worthiness – these comments also going to show that, quite clearly, Wedlock was not *everyone's* cup of tea - *"fixtures in the team are Hardy, Crompton, Warren, the three inside forwards, and, <u>I suppose</u>, Wedlock. The Bristol midget was the most prominent man on the field; his tackling and his tirelessness were extremely valuable, but emphatically he is not so good an all round centre-half as either Veitch, of Newcastle, or Roberts, of Manchester United..."* Bristol City played at home to Sheffield Wednesday in the First Division on the same day, so Cottle and Wedlock's places had to be filled by Radford and Spear respectively.

Next up was Wales at the City Ground, Nottingham, on March 15th 1909. Watched by 11,500 spectators, the Englishmen won it by two goals to nil, the goals both coming in the first-half, from Sunderland's George Holley, in the 15th minute, and Everton's Bert Freeman, in the 42nd. Newspaper reviews were a little more complimentary for Billy this time round, with the **Sheffield Daily Telegraph** reporting that *"the half-backs proved a useful line without any of the three being particularly brilliant, though Wedlock's jack-in-the-box tricks, as usual, took immensely with the crowd".* The **Sporting Life** meanwhile added *"...the ubiquitous and irrepressible Wedlock, who was a sixth forward and an extra back. The Bristol City wonder is indeed a treasure, and so is Ben Warren, the right-half..."*

England completed their campaign, as usual, with the annual showpiece against the '*old enemy*', Scotland. This time, it was to be held at the Crystal Palace, London, on April 3rd 1909 – exactly three weeks before Wedlock would be returning to this venue to

ENGLAND EXPECTS...

play for Bristol City in the FA Cup Final against Manchester United. England team-mate George Wall however, who scored two goals against the Scots that day - *both inside the opening fifteen minutes* - would play for United *against* Wedlock in that very same Final, on April 24th. But in this clash of the *'old enemy'*, England defeated Scotland by 2-0, with the crowd at the Palace numbering 23,667, including the Prince of Wales - George Frederick Ernest Albert – who would go on to become King of England in little over a year. The attendance for the English FA Cup Final three weeks later however, would be significantly higher...

The **Yorkshire Post** meanwhile devoted a small section of its match report to offer a few words of praise to Wedlock, perhaps a reply of sorts to their rather critical colleagues at the **London Daily News** who had previously dubbed Billy *"the Bristol midget"*. The paper retorted *"Wedlock has his critics, but they must be prejudiced indeed if they could not see the immense amount of work he accomplished, either in worrying the opposing forwards – and he did much to put the redoubtable Quinn quite off his game – or in falling back for defensive purposes when Scottish attacks were being developed. Little Wedlock is a great player, let his critics say what they may"*...

With the domestic football season at an end, the England squad assembled once more for another foreign tour, the previous one a year earlier having presumably been deemed a considerable success. Geographically speaking, the trip would be a relatively similar one, albeit a little *briefer*, with the England team playing only three games instead of four – these matches also being squeezed into a mere four-day period.

WEDLOCK – THE FIRST HERO OF BRISTOL CITY

On the morning of Wednesday May 26th, the England party departed for Vienna via Charing Cross Station, London, arriving in the Austrian capital on the Thursday evening. They then spent the Friday travelling to Budapest in readiness for the first game, against Hungary, on Saturday May 29th. This was played before a crowd of 10,000 spectators, the tourists winning by four goals to two. The 'return game', two days later, featured an identical England team but a much-changed Hungarian side, England winning by the increased margin of 8-2 in front of a slightly bigger crowd, of 11,000. At half-time, the English players were each presented with *"handsome medals"* by the Burgomaster of Budapest, as a gesture of gratitude for honouring their country and city with a visit. Vivian Westward scored four goals that day, with George Holley and Harold Fleming contributing two goals each.

After this game, England crossed back over the Austrian border in order to face that country in Vienna on the following day, Tuesday June 1st. In this, the final game of the series, England achieved their best result of the tour, beating the hosts by eight goals to one at the *Hohe Warte Stadium*, in front of 3,000 fans. Prolific goalscorer Westward scored another hat-trick, bringing his total for the tour to an impressive eight goals in just four days. The other goals were scored by Ben Warren, George Holley (2) and Harold Halse (2), the latter of whom had played a prominent role in the Manchester United team that had recently defeated Bristol City in the FA Cup Final. Wedlock played in all three games, bringing his international tally up to a new figure of 16, these appearances having all come in successive games following on from his debut appearance against Ireland at

ENGLAND EXPECTS...

Goodison in February 1907. Billy had also been the *fourth most-capped player* in the England XI who had faced Austria in that final game. Skipper Bob Crompton meanwhile, who had now racked up 27 appearances, was the most capped England player in history – at this point in time.

In 1909/10, England resumed their *Home International* campaign with an opening game, as usual, against Ireland. The contest this year was played on February 12th 1910 at the Solitude Ground, Belfast, drawing an 8,000 crowd. It resulted in a rather disappointing 1-1 draw, with a 51st minute equaliser from Swindon Town's Harold Fleming saving English skins after they had been a goal down at half-time. This score-line did not appear to bode well for the rest of the tournament, and so it eventually proved. Although they narrowly beat the Welsh at Cardiff Arms Park in the next match, the English were beaten by Scotland in the showpiece finale at Hampden Park, leaving the team to share second place with Ireland. Scotland, despite having lost to the Irish in their second game, finished top of the group and won the title.

Strangely, Wedlock had been allowed to play for Bristol City against Liverpool at Anfield on Saturday March 12th, despite this match coming only 48 hours ahead of the Welsh game in Cardiff on the Monday. In the event, City won *their* contest 1-0, and England would get an identical result two days later. But because of the Scotland fixture on April 2nd, he missed a crucial game at Ashton Gate as City lost 1-0 at home to Woolwich Arsenal, to leave their First Division survival hopes hanging in the balance...

England's game with Wales at the Arms' Park on March 14th had been very tight and could have gone either way, with Wedlock's

WEDLOCK – THE FIRST HERO OF BRISTOL CITY

Scotland v England – April 2nd 1910. Wedlock appears to be the white-shirted England player on the right of the picture

half-back partner Andy Ducat, of Woolwich Arsenal, eventually scoring the only goal in the 66th minute. The crowd was 20,000. This subsequently left the Scotland v England tie as a '*winner-takes-all*' fixture, and another enormous crowd of 106,205 turned up on Saturday April 2nd to witness what would prove to be the taming of the 'Lions'. Two Celtic forwards, McMenemy and Quinn, scored the vital goals in the 20th and 32nd minutes respectively, to leave English hopes blown to smithereens.

A view of the Hampden Park crowd during the same match

ENGLAND EXPECTS...

Against the aforementioned Scottish duo, Wedlock endured a particularly torrid afternoon, this being probably the most difficult game of his entire international career. As previously hinted, it would be wrong to suggest that Wedlock's continued selection for the England team was being met with universal approval, and the knives would be out for Wedlock *again* in the Hampden Park fall-out, with members of the press looking for scapegoats. B. Bennison, of the **Faringdon Advertiser**, predicted *"I doubt whether Wedlock will be able to command the centre half-back position another season"* – yet Billy would certainly prove his critics wrong on *that* score...

If Wedlock had felt that his summer cricketing activities had been interrupted somewhat, due to the end-of-season England football tours that had taken place over Whitsuntide during 1908 and 1909, then there can be little doubt that his schedule would be positively *decimated* during the summer of 1910...

The English Football Association, perhaps looking to broaden its horizons somewhat with regards to the now-annual 'summer tour', had decided on a rather more ambitious destination this time around – South Africa. In short, Wedlock and friends were to spend no less than *ten weeks* (not including journey-time) in that country, during the close-season of 1910. Although this was to be an official English FA tour, the sizable group of players would *not* be travelling under the name of the England football team as such, therefore, no caps would be given out to participating footballers as the matches were not officially recognised as being 'full internationals'. Instead, the nineteen man squad would set out on its journey purely as representatives of the English

WEDLOCK – THE FIRST HERO OF BRISTOL CITY

Football Association, or perhaps more specifically, of its *Football League*.

Billy & his England team-mates, c. 1910. Wedlock is stood in the middle row, second from the right – slightly back from the rest of the team

Contained amongst this group though, was a sizeable chunk of established England players, Billy Wedlock being one of eight men who had previously represented that country as a full international. Over the course of the summer, a grand total of 23 matches would be tackled, the vast majority of these played against amateur and provincial sides. At the centre of things though, would be the three 'important' games, ie, three separate **Test matches** against the (new) national team of South Africa. This trilogy of games were seen as being the '*showpiece events*' of the tour, and they would be played on dates evenly spread out amongst the overall schedule of 23 engagements.

On the eve of departure, Wedlock was asked by a journalist what he thought on the prospects of the summer ahead – *"Fine"* he replied, *"a trip like this is as good as going to college..."*

Wedlock and his international colleagues, 1910.
Billy, stood on the back row, should not be too difficult to spot

On Saturday May 14th 1910, the English party departed Waterloo Station on the 11:35 Special '*Boat train*' for Southampton, where they later sailed on the *Kinfauns Castle*. Aboard this vessel for about ten days, the party finally arrived in South Africa on Tuesday May 24th, eventually setting sail for the return journey on Wednesday August 3rd. The FA's first game of the tour occurred in Cape Town on Thursday May 26th, a 7-1 win being secured against a team of Colonials *'born of Cape Town'*. The 23rd and final contest also took place in Cape Town, this being the final **'Test'** match of three played against the nation of South Africa. Across the summer, *other* venues visited by the touring party were to be Kimberley, Bloemfontein, Johannesburg, Krugersdorp, Pretoria, Ladysmith, Pietermaritzburg, Durban, East London, King

WEDLOCK – THE FIRST HERO OF BRISTOL CITY

William's Town, Port Elizabeth, Grahamstown and Vogelfontein. The FA XI's first **'Test match'** with South Africa took place in Durban on Wednesday June 29th, before a crowd of 5,000 spectators, Bury's Billy Hibbert scoring a hat-trick to give the English a 3-0 win. The **second** one was played at the Wanderers Ground, Johannesburg, before 13,000 fans, on Saturday July 23rd. England won this time by a score of 6-2, with Vivian Woodward and Harold Fleming scoring two goals apiece. The **third Test**, also being the final match of the tour, took place one week later in Cape Town, on Saturday 30th. A crowd of 5,000 people saw England win again, this time by a 6-3 score-line - Vivian Woodward and George Holley being the two men to score a brace each on *this occasion*.

Aside from his taking part in all three 'Test matches', Wedlock clearly played in a fair number of the 'provincial games' too. Records show that he scored five times (all 'single' goals) across five separate matches, and these occurred in a 13-0 win against Western Province (in Cape Town, May 28th), in a 4-1 success over Pretoria (in Pretoria, June 15th), in a 13-3 walkover against Klip River (in Ladysmith, Natal, June 20th), in a 6-0 victory over Pietermaritzburg (Pietermaritzburg, Natal, June 22nd) – and in a 9-0 win against Grahamstown (Cape Province, July 12th).

The touring party set sail for home four days after the final contest, having achieved a 100% win ratio across the 23 engagements, their full record being as follows:-

P 23, W 23, D 0, L 0 - GOALS (For) 143 (Against) 16.

When it came to meeting people, Billy was clearly the man with the *midas touch*, he, amongst the native South Africans, reportedly being the most popular member of the touring squad that summer. When it later became known that Wedlock was due to be given a testimonial match by Bristol City during the next domestic season, 1910/11, a contribution from the South African FA was accordingly arranged, and £86 subsequently sent to Billy's benefit fund in Bristol, with a note saying *"The money is some recognition of the value of your great services during the tour of the English team through South Africa by individual contributors, who have expressed a desire to add to your benefit fund as a personal appreciation"*. £86 was a whopping figure in those days, the Association having raised that amount through the circulation of subscription lists around all the various divisional associations of the *entire country*. A writer in the **Johannesburg Star**, commenting on Wedlock, elaborated further:- *"The wee chap came to this country with the English team, and right from the jump took the 'soccer' public by storm. They were attracted by his skill, his resource, his cheeriness, and good temper, but perhaps, most of all, by his tremendous sincerity on the football field. Instead of being a player on whom honours had fallen thickly, he might have been ENTERING on his career, so keen and enthusiastic was his play. Wedlock, on the field, was an irresistible magnet, Wedlock, off the field, was a modest, unassuming, happy little fellow, who said nothing about his prowess, and looked at things in a sane and sensible light. In brief, William Wedlock is one of the distinctive band of players, be the game what it may, who do not allow their success to spoil their personality"*.

If any proof was further required on Wedlock's ability to touch the lives of people wherever he went, then surely *this* was it...

In the following season, 1910/11, Billy Wedlock would defy the small percentage of England football critics who had predicted that his days as the national centre-half were as good as over. Once again, he was picked to play in all three *Home International* matches against Ireland, Wales and Scotland, this also being the case in fact for the *following* season, 1911/12.

Injury meant he was *not selected* however, for any of the three Championship matches in 1912/13, but was eventually recalled for the second match of the *following* season's tournament - away to Wales – in the early spring of 1914, this match proving to be his last-ever appearance.

In 1910/11 England beat Ireland 2-1 at the Baseball Ground, Derby, in front of 20,000 fans on February 11th. They next defeated Wales 3-0 at The Den, Millwall, on March 13th, in front of 22,000, with ace goal-scorer Vivan Woodward, now of Chelsea, scoring yet another brace. The Championship was clinched with a 1-1 draw against Scotland at Goodison Park, Everton, on April Fools' Day - the crowd of 38,000 creating a new English record for an international match. Although Wedlock became a 'British Champion' for a second time, the season on the whole was a desperately disappointing one, it marking Bristol City's relegation from the First Division after five years...

This fact alone made his continued selection for the England team in 1911/12 all the more surprising, given Billy's decision to remain with City in the Second Division - but selected he most certainly *was*...

Wedlock's final complete *Home International* campaign for England, in the late winter and early spring of 1912, ended with the team *sharing the Championship* title with Scotland, due to those countries finishing with identical wins and points records.

ENGLAND EXPECTS...

The official table though, would show England at the *top*, their goal average being slightly superior to that of Scotland's. On February 10th 1912, the team defeated Ireland 6-1 at Dalymount Park, Dublin, in front of a 15,000 crowd, Harold Fleming's hat-trick proving to be the highlight of the day from an English point of view. On March 11th, two first-half strikes sunk the nation of Wales at the Racecourse, Wrexham, in front of 10,000 spectators, this game ending as a 2-0 win for England. The deciding match, between Scotland and England, at Hampden Park, Glasgow, ended in a 1-1 draw – hence the 'tied' Championship, this match being watched by another new world record attendance, of 127,307.

A post-1913 cigarette card image of Wedlock.
The mini-biography on the reverse side (not shown here)
referred to his injury-interrupted England career

As has been mentioned, this *appeared* to be the end of Billy Wedlock's England career as, badly affected by injury, he was not picked for *any* matches during the following season, 1912/13, when the team won the British Championship in his absence. But he was surprisingly *recalled*, for one more match, in the second game of the 13/14 Championships – Wales away, at Ninian Park, Cardiff, on March 16th, in front of 17,586 fans.

WEDLOCK – THE FIRST HERO OF BRISTOL CITY

England won 2-0, with Wedlock signing off by scoring the crucial second goal in the 70th minute. There was an element of luck about his goal, the final shot *itself*, by all accounts, being somewhat wind-assisted – *"Wedlock back-heeled to Brittleton, and receiving the ball again, kicked high towards goal"*. The English team though, without Billy's services for the Scotland game, ended the campaign in a disappointing *third place*.

Billy in total would play 26 times for his country, and at the time of his final match against Wales in March 1914, he created a new record by becoming the oldest player – *33 years, 139 days* - to represent England, a feat that was later surpassed. Out of the 26 appearances, the first 25 had been made as an unbroken run of successive matches from the time of his debut, this also being a record at the time. Between March 1914 and May 1923, Wedlock's name was also in the record books as having been the oldest England goal-scorer, this being the aforementioned 33 years, 139 days.

ENGLAND EXPECTS...

Of the final total of 26 matches played, 19 had been made in 'competitive' matches via the British *Home International Championships*, the other seven being 'friendly' or 'exhibition' appearances (namely the seven games that had been played across the two Whitsun tours in the Austro-Hungarian Empire in 1908 and 1909).

Wedlock also scored two goals for his country, six years apart. Both goals were in the *Home International Championships, both* away to Wales, *and both* on the date of March 16th – these occurring in 1908, at the Racecourse, Wrexham, and in 1914, at Ninian Park, Cardiff – his final game.

The England team won *two* British Championships during the Wedlock era, in 1908/09 and 1910/11. The country *shared* the title on two other occasions, these being 1907/08 and 1911/12. The England team's full record over the 26 games that Wedlock represented them is as follows:-

BRITISH CHAMPIONSHIP –

P 19, W 12, D 6, L 1 - GOALS (For) 42 (Against) 12

FRIENDLIES -

P 7, W 7, D 0, L 0 - GOALS (For) 48 (Against) 7

TOTAL -

P 26, W 19, D 6, L 1 - GOALS (For) 90 (Against) 19

With Billy's legs not getting any younger, and a World War looming, Wedlock would never be selected for his country again...

WEDLOCK – THE FIRST HERO OF BRISTOL CITY

"I HAVE BEEN TOO LONG
ON THE FOOTBALL EARTH
TO BE SO UNWISE AS TO
UNDER-RATE ANY TEAM
IN A CUP-TIE...
...OFTEN IT IS A CASE OF
'ANYTHING MAY HAPPEN',
AND NOT INFREQUENTLY
ONE SIDE GETS ALL THE LUCK"

12] A Bridge too far...

Only two days before the death of his poor Rosina, Billy had played – and *scored* – for Bristol City in a friendly match against Southampton at Ashton Gate. The game in question had been watched by a crowd of only 2,000 people. Yet numerically speaking, this was fairly typical of the type of war-time attendance that Bristol City were attracting at the time...

As has been previously alluded to, City's match schedule from September 1915 until May 1919 was to mainly consist of friendlies, fund-raisers and exhibition games. Between January and April of the 1915/16 season, the club played twelve matches in the 'South-West Combination', consisting of fixtures against Portsmouth, Southampton, Cardiff City, Newport County, Swindon Town and Bristol Rovers. Of these contests, the biggest crowds came in the two matches against the Rovers – meaning at home *and* away – but these attendances, when *added together*, still only amounted to a rather modest figure of 8,000 spectators. The lowest turn-out was just *500*, against Newport County on New Year's Day 1916. On dates sprinkled throughout the rest of the regular season, between September and May, the club played a total of 25 friendly matches, 15 at home and 10 away, and the largest crowd among *these* fixtures appears to have been the 4,000 who attended the game against Southampton – *away from home!* The club therefore, was clearly not making any money and Wedlock, as one of only two professionals being retained by City during the war-time era, was consequently barely able to draw a regular wage. Bristol City *was* operating – *of sorts* – but in reality, it was eking out an existence, and merely *surviving,* rather than anything else.

The other player kept on by City was local defender Len Southway, a man who much later on was to become something of a club legend *himself,* as Southway would be connected with the club, in one way or another, for more than sixty years. As a *peace-time* player, *'Lemmo'* operated for City most often as a full-back, but during the war years, he played essentially anywhere he was needed, including centre-half and inside-forward. Southway had lost two fingers after an accident whilst working at Wills' Box factory, so instead of joining the army, he was sent to work at Avonmouth Docks.

And onto the shoulders of Southway and Wedlock – Bristol City's last *two remaining professionals* – a great deal of responsibility was then placed. For it now became down to Lemmo and Billy to keep a war-time public interest in Bristol City FC flowing.

They subsequently organised fixtures against teams from the docks, armament factories and the Services. But even as 'professionals', the pair were still only paid (*10 shillings!*) when City played Rovers, as local derbies were the only games that generated enough public interest, and – *henceforth* - worthwhile gate receipts. Not surprising then, that in two separate campaigns out of the four, City and Rovers met 12 times in each (seasons 1916/17 + 1918/19) - and there were to be 38 Bristol derbies in total across the war years. As most players were away, City made up the numbers with literally *anyone* who was available, but the rivalry with Rovers had grown very bitter and intense. After one City win at Eastville, Southway and Wedlock allegedly had to fight their way through an angry mob and eventually escaped – *rather hastily* - on a pony & trap!

A *BRIDGE* TOO FAR...

A major problem was that local derbies apart, hardly anyone was attending football matches during these testing times, and this had a knock-on effect so that pubs, like everything else, were being attended significantly less frequently than had been the case before. Yet Billy, of course, had seven *motherless* children at home, and was naturally desperate to keep a roof over their heads. In short, Wedlock sought a *third* source of income, and one that was perhaps a little more 'in keeping' with the '*war effort*'. For a considerable amount of time during the war years, he was accordingly employed as a labourer by *Charles Hill & Son (Shipbuilders)*, at the Albion Dockyard in Bristol – just a short stroll from the current location of the *SS Great Britain*. It was his work *here* therefore, and also his mere *presence* as a well-known footballer and personality in the city of Bristol – which probably prevented Wedlock from being sent to the battlefield in France. Apart from providing a salary, Wedlock's position at the dockyard was to prove quite useful in *other* ways, for it undoubtedly kept Billy in tip-top physical condition, and may even have accounted for more than 50% of his 'training' for Bristol City!

The war years then, kept Wedlock just as incredibly busy as ever. His day job was labouring at the dockyard with '*Charles Hill*', and then, when he got home he had a pub to run – the '*Star Inn*', of course – albeit a public house that probably wasn't doing much in the way of trade. In between all *this*, he was expected to keep match-fit, train with the City whenever he could, and turn out in football matches, *as and when* required. Quite a schedule! But Billy, as ever, just rolled up his sleeves and got on with it. Wedlock was always the same – whatever needed to be done, *he did it*.

WEDLOCK – THE FIRST HERO OF BRISTOL CITY

In 1915/16, Billy played in six out of the twelve 'South-West Combination' matches, including the two aforementioned games against Bristol Rovers – but he did not participate in any of the matches taking place outside the city of Bristol. He also took part in 17 of the 25 friendly encounters, and amongst these, as previously mentioned, he *scored* in the match at home to Southampton played on November 27th 1915.

Bristol City v the Third Officer Cadets Battalion (Bristol University), May 6th 1916. A unusual pre-match photo combining the two sets of teams and officials, but minus the referee. A smiling Wedlock can be seen (just) in the centre of the middle row. City won 6-3.

The 1916/17 campaign was exclusively made up of 35 friendly matches, many against teams consisting of either forces personel or dockers, and Wedlock played in 24 of these contests, scoring *once* – against the *Royal Garrison Artillery* at Ashton Gate, on January 13th 1917.

It has already been hinted at that City, at times, struggled to put out a complete XI, and Wedlock, flexible as ever, occasionally had reason to turn out in positions on the field of play that he was completely unaccustomed to. If a centre-forward failed to show up, then Wedlock would be there as a volunteer.....if the outside-left withdrew at the last minute, then - guess *who* – would be present to take his place! Yet on one incredible day at Ashton Gate, namely, December 23rd 1916 - spectators must have been rubbing their eyes with disbelief, when they discovered that Wedlock, running onto the field, was actually sporting the *goalkeeper's* jersey! Yes, Billy - for the only time in his City career – was indeed taking his place 'between the sticks'! Bristol's opponents, the Warminster-based *London Rifle Regiment* must have been just as startled as everyone else, yet the 'tactic' seemed to work quite well, as Wedlock got away with a 'clean sheet' and City ended up winning by a landslide. Billy of course, could not resist the temptation of coming out of his area on occasions, to join in with 'open play' – but in one incident his 'wanderings' were *nearly* punished, and the **Bristol Sports Times** reported that *"Wedlock wasn't much troubled, except when he was caught strolling in midfield"*. City though, were still far too strong for their opponents, and the Reds' won 7-0!

In 1917/18, Billy participated in eight of the eleven matches played in the '*Bristol County Combination'*, and he scored *one* goal – in a 4-0 home win over the *Royal Engineers of Portbury*, on February 23rd 1918. He also took part in 15 of the friendly games, adding four more goals as he did so. These strikes all arrived in home matches at Ashton Gate – via a 7-0 win over *Douglas Brothers* on September 15th 1917, in a 6-0 success against *Bristol Dockers* a week later, in a 3-2 victory over *Royal*

WEDLOCK – THE FIRST HERO OF BRISTOL CITY

Engineers (from the White City) on October 13th, and a rare penalty during a 13-0 walkover against the *Royal Flying Corps of Filton*, on November 10th.

In the final 'war-time season' of 1918/19, Wedlock played in only three of the eleven *'Bristol County Combination'* games, but in two of these contests he starred as an emergency centre-forward! He subsequently scored *one goal*, in a 3-2 home win over the *RAF (Filton)* on November 9th 1918 – two days before *Armistice Day*. Wedlock also participated in 11 of the 31 friendly matches during that campaign, scoring *once* – another penalty – during a 4-2 win over Ebbw Vale on March 29th 1919.

Wedlock's total recorded war-time appearances numbered 84 matches, and of these, 17 had been made in 'competitive games', and 67 in *'friendlies'*. The war had finally ended on November 11th 1918, but this had been too late in the season for the FA to re-start a full-blown League & Cup campaign, so 'proper' football would officially re-open the following year – in season 1919/20.

Every League club in the country would be affected by the horrors of the First World War, and Bristol City was certainly no exception, suffering *two casualties* – not including former players who had previously departed for other clubs. Tommy Ware was a Bristol-born goalkeeper who had made 51 Second Division appearances for the Reds' between 1911 and 1914. Prior to being bought out of the army to play professional football for City, he had served as a *musician* in the *Scottish Rifles*. Ware re-enlisted for the British Army upon the outbreak of the war in 1914 and joined the Royal Field Artillery...Geordie inside-forward Edmund Burton had signed for Bristol City – his *only league club*

A *BRIDGE* TOO FAR...

- in the year 1913, and then scored four goals in 18 league appearances spread over two seasons, before signing up for the Durham Light Infantry...

Ware and Burton are two of the players who gave up their City careers to enlist, and both ended up making the '*ultimate sacrifice';* Tommy Ware was killed in action on May 1st 1915, and Edmund Burton died during the *Battle of the Somme* on August 13th 1916.

George Hedley - City's manager for four years from 1913, was also called up in January 1917 – though he *survived*. City's legendary former goalkeeper Harry Clay, and Wedlock's long-time half-back partner Reuben Marr also signed up – and both came home to tell the tale...

But there was soon to be another '*war-time casualty'* which was to affect Wedlock very deeply, though *this* instance however, was not a case of an abrupt fatality that had taken place on the battlefields of northern France - it was rather 'closer to home' than that...

...Frank Bacon, Billy's long-time friend, influence, confidant and mentor, died at the age of 55 on Friday January 25th 1918, at his residence, the *'Masonic Arms',* North Street, Bedminster. Bacon of course, had been the one singular, *massive* influence which had resulted in Wedlock's 'coming home' from Aberdare to Bristol City, in May 1905. At times, Frank Bacon had been to Billy like a 'second father'. So far as Wedlock was concerned, Bacon was going to be sorely, sorely missed, and *Billy's* life - in particular his '*Bristol City life'* – would certainly never, ever be the same again... The funeral on January 31st at Arno's Vale was simply packed with the many admirers of the former Bristol City

WEDLOCK – THE FIRST HERO OF BRISTOL CITY

Chairman – not forgetting *Life President* of the Bristol Athletic Club - with people coming, of course, from many spheres within the local sporting world. The numerous mourners included, naturally, Wedlock *himself,* alongside his *Bristol-born* former City colleagues Joe Cottle and Arthur Spear, the current City 'war-time' manager 'Jock' Hamilton, Mr W. Pont, vice-chairman of the club - and the *father* of former Reds' striking superstar Billy Maxwell!

Wedlock never did end up getting sent to France, or any other part of the world connected with the war for that matter, although he must have come perilously close on one or two occasions. The most notable of these occurred in March 1918, when Billy engaged the services of a solicitor in order to make his case for an 'exemption'. An edition of the **Western Daily Press** dated March 7th, published the following story accordingly –
"Wedlock's Exemption - *The Bristol Local Tribunal heard yesterday the application of W.J. Wedlock, the veteran international half-back and City player, for exemption. He was represented by Mr W. Pepperell Pitt, solicitor, who stated that Wedlock is 37 years of age, and at present employed at the Albion Dock Yard. He has seven motherless children. A further period of exemption was granted until 7th July next, with no right to again appeal"*...
But as a high-profile sportsman, with the potential to raise the war-time spirits of many folk across the city of Bristol, Wedlock was still useful doing work in his home-town, and in the end, he 'got away with it' – the war was coming to an end, and Wedlock never went...

A *BRIDGE* TOO FAR...

There is however, a *slightly* amusing aspect connected to Wedlock's plea regarding 'motherless children'. Billy's hearing took place on Wednesday March 6th, by which time, he must *surely* have known full well that in less than six weeks, he was due to be getting married again – to Ada Owen, a 27 year-old former tobacco operative, of Bedminster. This was because Billy Wedlock, after two and a half years of widowhood, had found love again...

Ada Louisa Owen, the daughter of William J. Owen, a coal haulier, and Eliza (*nee* Merriweather), was born in Bristol on May 1st 1890. Hers had been a large family, for she was the eldest of *at least* eight children – five girls and three boys – although one her siblings died as a child. The Owen family had lived for many years in the vicinity of West Street, Bedminster, then later on after her father died - and when Ada had started work as an operative at the tobacco factory - she lived with her mother at No 8 Rowley Street, just off the main thoroughfare of the aforementioned West Street. By the time of her marriage, Ada was resident of the *Star Inn*, Bower Ashton Terrace – where Wedlock of course, was licensee...

The happy couple married at Wedlock's now-traditional church of Ashton Gate St Francis, on Tuesday April 16th 1918. In order to gain extra preparation for his big day, Wedlock had failed to turn out for Bristol City in their home match with *RAF (Filton)* at Ashton Gate on the previous Saturday, though as it turned out, the team didn't really need him anyway, as the Reds' won the contest by *fourteen goals to two!*

Ahead of the Wedlocks now lay 47 years of happy marriage,

nearly all of which would be famously spent at the *Star Inn*. Ada was just shy of being ten years Billy's junior, but at 27, she still faced a fairly onerous task ahead of her what with the running of the pub, and looking after Wedlock's seven children. Unlike Wedlock's poor Rosina however, his second wife Ada would live a full and lengthy life and reached a very respectable old age – outliving Billy, in fact, by 13 years. In time, she would also present the 'old guy' with three more children, meaning that Billy would eventually become the grand old *father of ten*...

Billy's three final children would be Ada Vera Wedlock, born on August 14th 1918, Ronald W.J. Wedlock, born on March 25th 1922, and Dennis J. Wedlock, born on November 8th 1925.

Billy had done well for himself, but he had also done well *by his kids*, because Wedlock had always been acutely aware that growing children – *no matter how loving the father* – all needed the feminine touch of a *mother* – something they had been missing for two and a half years.

The war years must have been somewhat frustrating for Wedlock the *sportsman*, having to endure a four-year period of what was, to all intents and purposes, *amateur* soccer. Football-wise, he had been getting a regular 'run-out', but little else – the opposition was invariably weak, and wins were not difficult to come by.

It is tempting to believe that *without* the interruption of war, Wedlock *may* have retired from the game two or three seasons earlier than he actually *did*, for it's extremely likely he would *still* have reached a landmark figure *of* 400 League appearances for Bristol City (when football closed down in April 1915, he had already reached 327). The temptation with *hindsight*, however, is to believe that he instead held out for *longer*, waiting for the day

A *BRIDGE* TOO FAR...

when League football *returned*, in order that he might add one last season or two to his credentials...

It must have been of great relief for Billy then, when normal service was finally resumed on August 30th 1919, the day that Bristol City at last kicked-off a new Second Division campaign, for the first time in five long years. For the record, City beat Bury 1-0 in front of 10,000 fans at Ashton Gate, with centre-forward Tommy Howarth netting the only goal against his home-town club. George Hedley, City's manager from 1913 until 1917, had of course moved on, as had his *replacement*, the Reds' end-of-war-boss 'Jock' Hamilton.

City's next manager, for two years starting in 1919, was Joe Palmer, a former army sergeant whom Hedley had previously brought to Ashton Gate as first-team trainer. Tough-guy Palmer was famously to incorporate his 'army-style' physical training methods into City's training programme. This may well have upset some of City's more 'cultural' players, but his ideas though, to some extent, seemed to work...

Joining Billy in the City line-up that year was Bristolian inside-forward Billy Pocock, a man who not only shared Wedlock's christian name, he had also gone to the *same school* as him, namely, Ashton Gate. At 35, Pocock was now a veteran *himself* even though he was actually several years Wedlock's junior.

The right inside-forward was Yorkshireman Bert Neesam, who had originally joined City well before the 1915 cut-off. During the war years however, he had been a free-scoring hero for the Ashton Gate club, netting 76 times in 104 matches, though many of these had been achieved against, as has been mentioned, significantly weak opposition. Tommy Howarth completed, what in theory *could* have been, City's main trio of striking hot-shots. Wedlock's eventual centre-half *replacement* meanwhile, Jack Wren, was now beginning life in the Reds' back line at No 4, watching and learning from the master himself. Although new-signing Wren was a local boy from St Werburghs', he had actually only been transferred to City in the summer after a spell in south London with Millwall.

The Bristol City squad is ready for football's return - Season 1919/20

The League season however, was not a classic one. To some of City's more cynical fans, it was as if football had never been away, as their inconsistent team stuttered and stumbled into a final position of eighth. This did appear to represent *progression* from the final two seasons before the war, but not much more. The *real improvement* however, was to come in the FA Cup... City's lengthy run in the competition was to naturally revive memories of what had happened in 1909, but there were actually a couple of striking differences this time around. Eleven years previous, City had needed nine matches to reach the Final,

A *BRIDGE* TOO FAR...

including *four replays* – it wasn't to happen this time, as in 1920, their run would be done and dusted in five matches, with *no* replays necessary. The most obvious difference however, was that this time round, ultimately - City would *not* make the Final... It all started at Grimsby Town in the First Round on January 10th 1920, when in front of a 7,000 crowd, Tommy Howarth netted two goals either side of half-time to put the Reds' of Bristol firmly into the driving seat for the last 32. Although Thompson later pulled a goal back for Grimsby, City held on for a hard-fought 2-1 win. The Second Round draw was greeted with much excitement when it revealed that The Arsenal would be coming to south Bristol on January 31st. No longer known as '*Woolwich Arsenal*' because they had relocated to Highbury in 1913, the now-North Londoners were a fairly glamorous and prominent First Division side, and City were not expected to win. But a new ground record attendance of 25,900 flocked to Ashton Gate and the vast majority were in for a big surprise. With Arsenal striker Fred Pagnam off the pitch injured, Tommy Howarth quickly took advantage and netted the game's only goal minutes before half-time. Pagnam returned to the field in the second-half and scored what most observers thought was an equaliser, but it was ruled out for offside. City fought like demons to hold onto their lead, and in the end were fully-deserved victors, the **Birmingham Daily Gazette** confirming that "*It was a triumph of tactics and understanding, and never was triumph more valiantly fought for*". The last sixteen brought another home tie, and this time it had a bit of a 'local derby' feel to it, as Cardiff City of the Southern League were to be the next visitors to Ashton Gate on February 21st. The scramble for ground places was subsequently even greater than it had been for the Arsenal game, and on the day itself an incredible 32,432 spectators packed into the stadium, yet another club record. It was the biggest Ashton Gate crowd that Billy Wedlock *had* ever, or *would* ever, play in front of. Although the Welshmen at this time were effectively *non-leaguers*, they were actually on the cusp of escaping this status, and in the following season would join Bristol in Division Two. On the big day, Cardiff shocked the enormous crowd by taking the lead through George Beare after half an hour, but against the run of play *that man* Howarth headed City level five minutes before half-time. In the second-half it was all City, and in the 50th minute, the Reds' Bert Neesam scored what turned out to be the decisive goal, and Bristol, in front of their ecstatic fans, had reached the quarter-finals.

Yet again, Wedlock's boys were to enjoy the luck of the draw, for in the last eight City found themselves at home once more, this time against First Division Bradford City. The Yorkshiremen though, were not enjoying a particularly spectacular season, and the result it seemed - at least to the *balanced observer* - could go either way. According to some sections of the popular press however, Bristol had next to *'no chance'*, for Bradford had only to *show up*, and victory would be theirs. These critics were to be left with egg on the faces, because when it came to March 6th, Bristol City played as if their lives had depended on it, scoring two goals to no reply, both coming from Scottish left-winger Jack Harris. The first, after 35 minutes came when Bradford goalkeeper Jock Ewart fumbled Harris' corner straight into the net, to gift the Reds' a half-time lead. The clinching goal came five minutes from time, when Harris latched onto a Howarth pass to make it 2-0 for a

A *BRIDGE* TOO FAR...

dominant City, who were now into the semi-finals. The crowd was another big one, 26,443. Wedlock, the old war-horse, had a vintage game that day, and the **Western Daily Press** would later sing his praises, claiming that Billy had been *"the generalissimo who led the City to victory. He was always giving his orders by word of mouth and action, and his squad obeyed his commands to his complete satisfaction..."*

For the penultimate round, City wanted to avoid Aston Villa and Chelsea, because these two First Division teams were now Cup favourites from the four clubs who were left. Bristol accordingly got their wish, drawing Huddersfield Town instead, but still knew a tricky match awaited them at Stamford Bridge in the semi, on March 27th 1920.

BRISTOL CITY, 1920: Standing—Treasure, Wren, Vallis, Banfield, Harris, Nicholson. Sitting—Reader, Neesam, Wedlock, Howarth, Pocock.

Bristol City's line-up versus Huddersfield Town in the FA Cup semi-final at Stamford Bridge

WEDLOCK – THE FIRST HERO OF BRISTOL CITY

Huddersfield, like City, were in Division Two, but pushing hard for promotion, and subsequently, would eventually find their way into the top-flight at the end of the season.

Wedlock photographed ahead of City's big FA Cup semi-final

A *BRIDGE* TOO FAR...

Unfortunately, this was to be where City's luck finally ran out, for on the big day in London, the Reds' would have to experience some of the most *wretched* misfortune that any semi-finalist would *ever* have to endure in the history of the FA Cup...

Yet in the face of adversity, the team played courageously well, and under any other circumstances, would probably have gone through to the Final. The team's problems began when Wedlock's half-back colleague Jack Wren injured his ankle after only ten minutes, he then being moved out to the right-wing where he could limp along and do no harm. But this meant the normal outside-right, Dickie Reader, had to switch to an *inside-forward* position, a role he was unaccustomed to, and Neesam went into the half-back line. With all the switching and swapping, City's whole line-up looked unbalanced, their rhythm was lost and the game plan went out of the window.

But it was to get worse than this...

After 21 minutes, an out-of-position Dickie Reader was clattered to the ground when he challenged Huddersfield goalkeeper Sandy Mutch, who, whilst attempting to punch the ball away, instead caught the Bristol man square in the ribs. Reader then fell awkwardly onto the ground and was seen to be writhing in agony, and after medical assistance was called for, he ended up being stretchered off – apparently *unconscious.* It was later found that he had sustained one broken rib, and had badly damaged *another.* It also meant that City effectively had to play the final 20 minutes or so of the first-half with only *ten men*, meaning nine men and one 'passenger' – Wren.

Incredibly though, this was still not the end of City's ill-luck, for they were almost immediately denied a clear goal when Tommy

WEDLOCK – THE FIRST HERO OF BRISTOL CITY

Howarth 'scored' with a header that most observers in the crowd and press box felt had gone a good foot over the goal-line before being kicked away. The referee and his linesmen though, being in poor positions, were unsighted and felt unable to allow the goal. City somehow struggled on until half-time with the score at 0-0. When the teams returned for the second period, spectators were astonished to see that Reader – *against* doctor's orders – had staggered back onto the field of play in a brave – or stupid – attempt to carry on. Unfortunately, Reader could hardly *walk*, let alone *play,* but City now continued the game with nine men, and two 'passengers' – Wren and Reader. The pressure on Bristol had to give eventually, and it *did* - Huddersfield quickly scored two killer goals within the space of three minutes, in the 65th and the 68th. This disaster however, appeared to spark the *nine men* into an unexpected fight-back as Wedlock's boys went charging forward in search of a goal. And to the astonishment and delight of the 35,863 crowd - 3,000 of whom had come from Bristol - Tommy Howarth soon pulled one back, running half the length of the field and unleashing a superb shot – incredibly, City *were back in it!* Wedlock rallied his troops for one last effort as the depleted Reds' bravely and pluckily poured forward in search of another, and Harris, Pocock and Howarth all had shots at goal, which were narrowly averted by Mutch. Huddersfield then spent the last ten minutes clinging on for dear life, and the neutrals in the crowd must have been positively *urging* the gallant Bristol boys to score a dramatic equaliser. Alas, it was simply not meant to be, and the Yorkshiremen clung on for a 2-1 victory. Heroic Bristol City, in the most desperate circumstances imaginable, had been knocked out of the FA Cup, and they would not be returning

A *BRIDGE* TOO FAR...

to Stamford Bridge for the Final on April 24th. Wedlock cut a *desperate* figure at the end. There was something of a *Shakespearean Tragedy* at the heart of the whole business, and it was, without doubt, one of the biggest disappointments of Billy's career. His last, remaining chance of gaining an FA Cup winners' medal had now gone for sure. The match had been played at the *same ground – on the 11th anniversary* – of City's 1909 semi-final with Derby, when Rippon had scored a penalty equaliser with the last kick of the game. But City's luck had certainly deserted them this time.

Sadly, this was also to prove Wedlock's *final* full-length season as a Bristol City first-teamer, as the years were really beginning to catch up on him now...

Football's post-war return had coincided with the extension of the Second Division, from 20 to 22 teams, which now meant that each club faced a programme of 42 matches, and of these, Wedlock played in 30, but he *didn't score,* because Billy's days as an occasional City goal-getter were well past him by now...

In the FA Cup however, Wedlock played in all five matches. The reason for his missing so many games in the league was partly down to a thigh injury he picked up away at Stoke City on November 17th 1919. This kept him out for five successive matches, meaning that he didn't play again until the Christmas Day contest at West Ham United. Occasional games were then sporadically missed during the second half of the season due to various niggles and minor injuries, that in previous years, Billy had been able to shake off *quickly*. He wasn't able to do that *anymore*. However, against Spurs at White Hart Lane on February 28th 1920, Wedlock reached his final big milestone for

WEDLOCK – THE FIRST HERO OF BRISTOL CITY

Bristol City, by making the 350th league appearance of his career. 38,000 people however, saw Spurs win 2-0 on the day, though Billy, even at the grand old age of 39 was, according to the **Western Daily Press** *"magnificent..."* and *"the most impressive player on the field".* Wedlock though, was now coming rapidly towards *the end...* In the summer of 1920, he actually signed up for yet another season, although behind the scenes, it is doubtful whether many expected him to *complete it* – the doubters probably including Wedlock *himself.*

In reality, the FA Cup run had been Wedlock's *last hurrah,* and Billy's legs were now finally starting to give up on him. At League level, he simply *could not go on any longer.* He would play in the first five games of the new (1920/21) season, and then after that – *it would be all over...*

The fourth match was at home to Blackpool on the Wednesday evening of September 8th, a 1-1 draw that attracted a very encouraging 20,000 fans to Ashton Gate – but not many present realised they were watching Billy play his final Football League match in City's colours at Ashton Gate.

Three days later, the team arrived in the East Riding of Yorkshire, for the fifth game of the season. The date was Saturday September 11th 1920. It was now 15 years and 10 days since Wedlock had played his first league match for Bristol City as a sprightly 24 year-old – but now however, he had reached the occasion of his *last...*

It was pretty much common knowledge by now that the current season was to be Wedlock's *last* – though there was nothing in the air to suggest that *this specific game* was to be his *swansong,* nothing to suspect that *this* day was to be anything out of the

A *BRIDGE* TOO FAR...

ordinary. City took to the field at Anlaby Road against Hull, and everything just appeared to be normal. There was a healthy crowd of 14,000 in the ground, and for forty minutes or so, everything for Bristol City went according to plan. Then, for the first time in his career, Billy suddenly, and without warning - *stopped running*... The old legs simply seemed to buckle and *pack up.* It must have been an incredible sight, astonishing, bizarre – and *desperately sad,* all at the same time. The **Hull Daily Mail**, in its subsequent match report, referenced Wedlock's sudden decline by observing; *"The first-half* (0-0) *was decidedly in favour of Bristol. The second half was the Tigers'. It did not need an expert to find out the reason...the solution can be summed up in one word – Wedlock. Yes, the veteran centre-half, who was probably playing his last game at Anlaby Road, thoroughly held up the home team for the biggest part of the first half. It was only when the game had been in progress some forty minutes that Wedlock began to show signs of distress, and once he had shot his bolt, the game was Hull City's..."*

"...After Wedlock's powers of defence and attack had given out however, the Bristol forwards seldom got the ball...so long as Wedlock could hold up the home forwards, Bristol did well. When he tired, the whole half-back line seemed to collapse, and I can foresee the Tigers' making their first away victory next Saturday if the same thing happens..."

For the record, Hull City scored two second-half goals and won the game 2-0. When Wedlock's name was *not* on the team-sheet for the return match between the same sides on the *following* Saturday, at Ashton Gate, the national papers were full of stories claiming that Wedlock had been 'dropped' – based on his *" lack of form"* - for the first time in his *"16 years at Bristol City".* They were *wrong,* of course, for Wedlock certainly hadn't been *'dropped'* as such. What seems absolutely clear however, is that between club and player, a mutual decision had been made that Billy's legs were simply no longer up to the rigours of League football. Not *anymore.* Wedlock had simply reached the *end of the line...*

It was a terribly sad way to end a glorious Bristol City career, but unfortunately, it *had* been coming. Although his first-class innings was now over – meaning that he was to take no further part in Second Division or FA Cup matches - it wasn't *quite* the end for Wedlock, who was still to participate in *three* further matches for Bristol City's first-team.

On Wednesday September 22nd, eleven days after the Hull City debacle, he played in fellow half-back Jock Nicholson's Benefit match against Cardiff City at Ashton Gate. (Although Jack Wren was to inherit Billy's famous No 5 shirt, it was *Nicholson* who had gone on to take over the captaincy. Nicholson though, was soon destined for Glasgow Rangers', and the baton was subsequently passed to Laurie Banfield, who would take over the duties in the following season). The benefit game ended in a 0-0 draw and attracted a crowd of 6,000, helping to raise a half-decent figure for Nicholson, which was 'topped-up' by City when he didn't quite get his 'guaranteed amount'. A week later, on September 29th, Wedlock played what turned out to be his final first-team game of any kind at Ashton Gate – at least, of a *competitive* nature – and this was in the annual Gloucestershire Cup match against Bristol Rovers. In the event, Wedlock's pal Laurie Banfield scored the only goal ten minutes from time, and City won the game 1-0, in front of a crowd that was only a whisker shy of 12,000. At the match's conclusion, the trophy was presented to Billy, back as captain once again, by Mr J A Tayler, President of the Gloucestershire Football Association.

On Wednesday December 15th 1920, it *really did* all come to the end of the line for Wedlock – and in the most low-key manner imaginable. His final game for the first-team was a friendly match against an Army XI at Portsmouth, played in front of a crowd of just 3,000 spectators. But City won the game 3-2, and Wedlock, just as he had done in his final England match, signed off in style with a fine goal. This game also represented the only occasion that Billy was to play a designated 'first-team' match having passed the age of 40.

Even then, it wasn't *quite* the end of the story just yet, because Wedlock had to keep himself as fit as he could, train as usual, and make himself available for the reserve team. He also needed to be on stand-by for the first-team in case of any injury emergencies, but the call never came and Wedlock subsequently played out the rest of the campaign in low-key fashion for the reserves. His absolute *final game* as a professional player for Bristol City was *supposed* to have been in a Western League fixture on Saturday May 7th 1921, away at Yeovil in a reserve game. Unfortunately, with a big crowd waiting, Wedlock unexpectedly failed to show up, and an apology was accordingly sent on to the Somerset club from the man *himself*. The reason for Billy's 'no-show' was said to have been injury, Wedlock apparently having knocked his thigh during his testimonial match three days earlier. Yes, that's right – *testimonial match!*...

Because Bristol City, as a final *'Thankyou'* to their departing son,

WEDLOCK – THE FIRST HERO OF BRISTOL CITY

had decided to award their veteran hero, for all his years of loyal and outstanding service, with an unprecedented *second benefit game* – ten and a half years after his first. This was played at Ashton Gate on Wednesday May 4th, and it consisted of a match played between a Bristol XI (*City & Rovers combined*) and a 'special' International XI. Members of the international line-up had been hand-picked by Wedlock himself, chiefly ex-England veterans whom Billy had played alongside in years gone by. They included Derby County and England goalscoring legend Steve Bloomer, plus Billy's other old friends Andy Ducat (then of Woolwich Arsenal, but *now* of Aston Villa) – and Vivian Woodward, formerly of Spurs and Chelsea. Interestingly, they also included Fred Milnes, whose speeding car had transported Wedlock across Sheffield in such manic fashion, prior to that legendary England trial match, all those years ago... Wedlock himself elected to play for the 'internationals', and he was joined by ex-City & England colleagues Joe Cottle and Billy Jones, with former City full-back Bob Young, a former Scottish *junior* international, also playing at short notice. The match ended in a 3-2 win for the Bristol XI, and Wedlock, the celebrated hero, was 'chaired' from the pitch afterwards, on the shoulders of Steve Sims and Ellis Crompton – two of the *Bristol Rovers* players! Because of a downpour an hour before kick-off, the attendance was a slightly disappointing one, consisting of 8,000 spectators, though Wedlock still received a sizeable cheque for his efforts. 'Gate' receipts amounted to £500, but as the attendance had been insured for £1000, Wedlock pocketed the latter amount, less expense.

Wedlock's final career statistics for City made remarkable

reading. He finished on a grand total of 17 goals in 362 league appearances, and when his FA Cup matches were also taken into account, this figure rose to 391 *first-class* appearances and *still* 17 goals, because surprisingly, Wedlock never once scored a Cup goal in his career.

The City MINUS Wedlock, a rare sight indeed.
Bristol City's typical line-up for season 1920/21 – but with Wedlock no longer a regular, and therefore, <u>missing</u>

A similar thing has been mentioned before, yet it is still worth saying *again*, because of its sheer relevance. The coming of the First World War made a very significant dent into Wedlock's League career, and assuming that he had remained relatively injury-free during that period, then it seems a safe enough thing to bet that had it not been for the war, he *would have* made 500 first-class appearances for the City.

WEDLOCK – THE FIRST HERO OF BRISTOL CITY

The final reward from the directors to their retiring skipper came in the form of a *job offer*, which from the following season onwards, would have constituted the joint roles of coach and 'advisor'. But Wedlock politely turned this down, apparently due to 'business reasons'. Billy of course already knew where his *next* calling was, as for the next 41 years of his life – he had a pub to run...
Full-time.
Just over the road, *'The Star'* was calling Wedlock home....

13] A Red Sky at Night

Wedlock's lengthy spell in the reserves at the end of his final season must have felt somewhat demoralising. In his absence, City had experienced a good season, and at the point in time when Billy had kicked off his testimonial on that emotional evening in early May, the first-team was reaching the climax of a genuine promotion battle. The top two teams in the Second Division eventually *achieved* their goal, unfortunately though, City weren't amongst them, as the Reds' finished in *third* place. Yet even though Wedlock was now a full-time licensee, it did not mean to say that he had washed his hands of Bristol City – in fact, *far from it*. Billy would retain a strong interest in all affairs at the club he loved for the rest of his life, and the 1920's and 1930's, in particular, were especially significant in this area.
At Bristol City, Wedlock was *still wanted*. He kept in touch with virtually everyone, from the players to the directors, and he would have known all the gossip and all the rumours. He must have watched from the doorway of the *Star Inn* as the players went coming and going, on their way in and out of training, with jokes and banter being exchanged between Billy and his ex-colleagues from over the road. Formally, Wedlock's opinion was always sought, and he was an attendee at all the shareholders' meetings for many years. There were also numerous charity games of course, mostly played at Ashton Gate, amateur matches designed to raise funds for various good causes across the city of Bristol. Here, Wedlock's presence was *always* required – and he was more than happy to help. Before any such game could kick-off, it was always made sure that

WEDLOCK – THE FIRST HERO OF BRISTOL CITY

Wedlock's name was on the team-sheet, that Wedlock was present and in his kit - and that Wedlock was fit, ready and able to play. And he usually *did* play. If Wedlock did not play, then more often than not, Wedlock would perform duties as the *referee*. And if he didn't referee, then he would act as a linesman. The very least he would do was to start a match by physically *kicking-off*. Or maybe present the medals at the end, or auction off the match ball for charity, or make a speech about what a good game it had been. But he would be doing *something*, he would be *involved*. Because Wedlock was still *wanted*. Wedlock was still in demand. As long as it could be worked around his daily duties in the pub, then Wedlock would be there...

In 1922, a year after his retirement, Billy arranged for a team of ex - Bristol City 'O*ld Pro's'* to take on an eleven *"selected from Bristol's unemployed"*. The match took place at Ashton Gate on the evening of April 26th 1922, with all proceeds going to good causes and areas generally connected with the needy. The **Western Daily Press** promoted the noble cause under the appropriate headline *"Wedlock's match for the unemployed"*. The '*Old Pro's'* charity match was to be become a recurring theme throughout the 1920's. On Wednesday January 24th 1923, there was another such encounter at Ashton Gate, played between Wedlock, Cottle, Annan, Young & company, and the 'B' Division of the Bristol Police; a contest which the '*Old Pro's'* won 4-0, and an occasion that saw Wedlock auction off the match ball for £2 during the interval. The attendance was 3,500. A second match between the '*Old Pro's'* and the Bristol Police took place at Stapleton Road, Eastville, on Wednesday March

A RED SKY AT NIGHT

21st 1923, with proceeds going to the *Lord Mayor's Unemployment Fund.* Messrs Annan, Cottle and Wedlock starred for the 'oldies' once again, and *this* game was kicked-off by the Lord Mayor himself, with the second-half being started by the Chief Constable. The final score was 4-1 to the *'Old Pro's'*. But in between the fun of the charity side of things, there was other *serious* business going on...

When Wedlock had retired, the City team had narrowly missed out on promotion, finishing in third. Yet inexplicably, the following year (1921/22) saw the team surprisingly relegated to the third tier of English Football (Division Three 'South') – for the first time in its history. In doing so, the team had also finished *bottom of the league*. Although the City were to bounce back at the first time of asking in May 1923, finishing as runaway *champions* - the team was promptly relegated *again* just twelve months later. A period of yo-yoing between the two Divisions was to continue for quite some time. In 1926, with the team having spent two further seasons back down in Division Three (South), there were strong signs that promotion to the Second Division could be achieved once again. Tommy *'Tot'* Walsh was to be the big striking sensation for City *that* season, scoring 32 goals in 39 matches. It then came to light meanwhile, that Wedlock was interested in making a return to City – via a place on the board. With the blessing of the club, he subsequently submitted a formal application, but the Football Association, it appears, had *different* ideas... the **Star Green 'Un** (of Sheffield) on Saturday October 30th 1926, reported what happened next in the following way; *"...Wedlock was refused permission to become a director of the club of which he was such a bright* *ornament for so many years. This savours somewhat of 'officialdom' carried to a ridiculous degree. This player was a great asset to his country, never gave the FA a moment's trouble, and is now anxious to continue his services to his old club as a director. Many old players have been allowed to renew their acquaintance with the game by means of joining the boards of different clubs. When one takes into serious consideration the fact that Wedlock has done so much for our football and is anxious to do still more, I think he ought to be offered every encouragement and assistance".* The reason for the FA's decision *against* Wedlock was generally touted as being '*Rule 37*', which was said to de-bar ex-professionals from a role within the governance of football in an amateur capacity. There were also whispers however, that Wedlock's keeping of a public house, just over the road and opposite the ground, was not looked upon favourably. Perhaps the FA could see the potential here for a clash of interests. But either way, Billy was *not* granted the clearance he wanted. The FA *had* tended to make occasional exceptions for 'special cases', as Billy's ex-England colleague Bob Crompton, for example, was now on the board of directors at Blackburn. But they did *not* make an exception for Wedlock. Interestingly, Mr J A Tayler of Bristol, President of the Gloucestershire Football Association, and the man who had presented Wedlock with the GFA Cup during his final season as a City professional, was allegedly *"one of the committee whose vote turned down the application"*. Newspapers such as the **Western Daily Press** and the **Star Green 'Un** publically displayed their anger over the decision of the FA, although the **Athletic News** apparently held slightly different views, writing *"...A man who has always looked at football as a business and formed his opinions on a monetary basis is not contributory to the attainment of the ideal. All games should be ruled by amateurs. There is no escape from that conclusion if there is any desire to keep sport in the foreground and thrust business in the background...we have no doubt the decision against Wedlock was given with great reluctance. The view of the FA may not be popular with everybody, but professionalism has to be rigidly controlled, even to the smallest details".* Yet could anyone have been truly surprised at the stance of the **Athletic News**, a *Manchester-based* newspaper, which had, on the whole, been a keen supporter of Charlie Roberts during the earlier era of the infernal *Wedlock / Roberts 'England No 5'* debates? On September 5th 1927, the same paper subsequently listed Billy as being No 12 on their list of *'Football's famous midgets'* !

Wedlock's consolation however, was in taking regular opportunities of simply *watching* his beloved team, whenever he could. The **Western Daily Press** accordingly reported that Billy had been amongst the 2,000 'excursionists' from Bristol, when City travelled to Merthyr Town, their fellow Third Division (South) members, in the first round of the FA Cup on November 27th 1926. City won the game easily, by two goals to nil, in front of a crowd of 6,000 spectators.

The 1926/27 season subsequently ended with City gaining promotion as the *champions* of Division Three (South) – for the second time in three years. Both title wins had been masterminded by latest manager Alex Raisbeck, a Scotsman and legendary former Liverpool defender. The Reds' then, were back in the Second Division. In celebration, the club threw a late-summer '*promotion dinner*' at Midsomer Norton, taking their entire playing staff and management with them to join in with the festivities. The event took place on Wednesday August 10th 1927, and Wedlock was made *guest-of-honour* for the occasion. Part of the day was dedicated to a cricket match, played in the afternoon between a Bristol City XI and members of the local village team. Photographic evidence appears to suggest that Wedlock *did not* take part in the cricket, what *is known* however, is that the game finished early so that the City party could travel back to Bristol and take in some greyhound racing at Knowle! But then Billy had already made his contribution *earlier on*. Lunch had been taken at the Greyhound Hotel, where 14 members of the City promotion squad were presented with gold watches for their efforts. Billy was then called on to say a few words to manager Alex Raisbeck, to skipper Walter Wadsworth – and to generally address the members of the promotion squad. And Billy, the famous 'man of few words', was as usual pretty amusing in the words he *did* use. He declared that although he had *"been referred to in the 'Sports News' as being 48 years of age * **(he was 46)**, he felt but 28 that day. All that was happening took him back to the days long ago..."* In its report, the **Western Daily Press** continued with the main points of Wedlock's speech, saying; *"He congratulated Mr Wadsworth, as captain of Bristol City last season, on the splendid display of his 'boys'. Wadsworth's brains and the play of the members of the side who had been recognised that day had carried them through to success. If the same spirit pervaded the camp as last season, then Bristol City would go a long way towards gaining* *promotion. If they did not succeed in this, he hoped they would win the Cup"...* The team however, would *not* get to enjoy a prolonged period of success. They spent five years in Division Two, before being relegated once again, in 1932.

In the meantime, Wedlock's part-time 'career' in the charity field, with his *'Old Pro's'* XI, continued in full flow. On Thursday December 6th 1928, he took a team of City 'old-timers' to Weston-Super-Mare for a benefit match against the local police force. The **Western Daily Press** would rather amusingly place their match report beneath the cheeky headline *"The Old Brigade"*. Played at the Recreation Ground, Weston, all proceeds went to the *Weston Poor Children's Christmas Tea Fund*. The City XI included Wedlock, Jack Wren, Laurie Banfield, Jock Nicholson, Lemmo Southway, and the current City manager Alex Raisbeck. Wedlock though, only played in his traditional centre-half position for a few minutes, before 'disappearing' out onto the left-wing for a rest! The *'Old Pro's'* won 2-0, and at the end of the game the match-ball was autographed by all the City stars, and auctioned off – it being purchased by Mr C J Hancock, the prospective Liberal Party candidate for the Division!

Another activity that gave Wedlock pleasure was meeting up with old football friends and rivals from far and wide *across the country*. In other words, Billy did not just save his reunions only for old *team-mates* – he reserved them for his *old rivals* as well. If Bristol City happened to be playing in Nottingham for example, then Wedlock would travel, see the game, and meet up with his old rival Enoch West, who had remained a great pal. Billy always kept his eye on the City fixture-list, with particular regards to the *away games*, and he made his reunion plans accordingly. In season 1929/30, Bristol City were struggling down near the foot of the Second Division, but the FA Cup third round draw presented them with the chance of a producing a shock at First Division high-fliers Derby County. The game was played at the Baseball Ground, Derby, on January 11th 1930. Unfortunately, there was certainly to be no 'cup shock' on the menu that day, as Derby trounced the Reds' 5-1. Wedlock though, will still have enjoyed his day out, as he sat in the stand and watched it all unfold with his ex-England pal Steve Bloomer, the former Derby County great.

Throughout the 1920's, and even into the early 1930's, Billy's charity commitments with the *'Old Pro's'* carried on in earnest. Wedlock would continue to play until he was simply *physically incapable* of doing so. But the match he participated in on Wednesday April 2nd 1930 must surely have been one of his last, for he was just six months short of his 50th birthday at the time, and local newspapers reported with some amusement that he had also 'piled on the pounds' somewhat. This particular match, against the *'Bristol Police'*, was actually played for the 'benefit' of Bristol City *themselves*, for the club were once again in financial difficulties at the time. The **Western Daily Press** reported that *"Three or four thousand people put in an appearance and they cheered their old favourites to the echo when they won by the only goal of the match, scored by Bert Neesam just before the end. Billy Wedlock captained the winners and summed up the game well when he said at the finish that he thought the Police had had the advantage in stamina and strength, but the old pros' still had the extra skill,* *which had turned the scales. The match naturally had its humorous phases and roars of laughter greeted Billy Wedlock's game efforts. He is now on the portly side and he found his extra weight a great handicap in endeavouring to reproduce his old brilliance. Many doubted whether he would last out the full period, but he stuck to his guns. At centre-half, the duties were a little too arduous, so he converted himself into an outside-right and made up for his lack of speed with some useful work with his head."* It was 1-0 to the *'old boys'* at full-time, and at the finish, skipper Wedlock and his exhausted team, including goalkeeper Frank Vallis, Jock Nicholson, Laurie Banfield, Lemmo Southway, Bert Neesam and Billy Pocock, were the proud receivers of a grand silver cup.

Wedlock had known tragedy, of course, in his family life, and unfortunately, he was to experience it again – *several times.* On December 19th 1930, his eldest daughter Rosina Ellen, who had never married, died at the tragically young age of 30, at home, the *Star Inn*, Bower Ashton Place. It was said that Rosina *"passed away, after much suffering, patiently borne"*...

It must have been a time of desperate sadness for Billy, however, poor Rosina would not be the *only* Wedlock child who was destined not to outlive her father. James Wedlock, usually known as '*Jim'*, would apparently show significant promise *himself* as a young footballer in the late 1920's and early 1930's, but he however, also died tragically young...

The Monday morning edition of the **Western Daily Press** dated September 4th 1933 had claimed that on the previous Saturday, *"F and J Wedlock, sons of Billy Wedlock, the famous ex-international, turned out for Bristol City 'A' in their Western*

WEDLOCK – THE FIRST HERO OF BRISTOL CITY

"F and J Wedlock" – two of Billy's sons – are pictured here sat next to each other in this team photo of Bedminster Wesleyan FC, season 1926/27. Jim is in the centre of the middle row, with the ball and trophy placed in front of him. Fred is dark-haired and smiling, sat on Jim's immediate right as we look....

A RED SKY AT NIGHT

League game against Bath City Reserves, at Douglas Ground...." The '*F and J Wedlock*' mentioned here *certainly* meant Fred and, presumably Jim, though the Bristol City 'A side' – otherwise known as '*Bristol City Colts*' - was technically City's *nursery team*, and so also in-effect, the third-choice XI. Either way, '*J. Wedlock*' was to make it no further in Bristol City's ranks, but Fred, a dashing left-winger, would actually make his debut for the reserves *that very evening*, on Monday September 4th, against Fulham at Ashton Gate. City won a sparkling game 5-2 in front of 1,000 spectators, and the **Western Daily Press** described Fred Wedlock's performance as being *"promising"* and said he *"put over several useful centres from the left-wing"*.

Longer term however, Fred's elder brother Jim Wedlock worked at the tobacco factory in Ashton Gate, which is probably where he met fellow employee Elsie May Wood, whom he married at All Saints Church, Long Ashton, in June 1940. The couple subsequently lived at 51 Hamilton Road, Southville, but in the duration of World War Two, he signed up for the army, and never came home. Bombardier James Wedlock, of the *Royal Artillery*, and 1st Bn. *The Royal Welch Fusiliers*, was killed in Burma on March 13th 1945. He was 11 days short of his 39th birthday, and was buried in Rangoon, Burma.

Thankfully, each of the other eight children of Wedlock were to be blessed with a full and lengthy life, because William, Thomas, Lilly, Ivy, Fred, Ada, Ronald and Dennis all lived to respectable old ages.

William James Thomas Wedlock, born at Aberdare on

WEDLOCK – THE FIRST HERO OF BRISTOL CITY

December 22nd 1902, worked with his father at the *Star Inn* for some years, and married Eleanor May Grimstead at Long Ashton in the year 1927. The couple lived at 34 Greville Street, Southville, but later relocated to Frampton Cotterell, where 'Billy Jr.' died, on March 17th 1981 – at the age of 78.

Thomas George Wedlock, born at Aberdare on September 11th 1904, was a storekeeper, who married Alice Hilda Ball in Bristol, in 1930. The couple lived at 13 Nelson Street, Bedminster, for some time – not far from the *Miners' Arms* pub, in Bedminster Down Road – but later moved away to Weston-Super-Mare, where Thomas died, around March 1980 – at the age of 75.

Lilly Wedlock, born in Bristol on October 21st 1907, married Harold John Lee just outside the city in the year 1938. The couple lived at 27 Dennyview Road, Abbots Leigh. She died around November 1985, at the age of 78.

Ivy Wedlock, born in Bristol on January 5th 1910, married Arthur E Veale circa 1954. She died in the district of Weston-Super-Mare, in November 1995, at the age of 85.

Frederick George Wedlock, born in Bristol on June 28th 1911, was on Bristol City's books as a young outside-left in the early 1930's, but he was released without playing a first-team game and joined Bath City in 1934. At Bath he would make a handful of appearances for the first-team, but never quite 'made it' as a professional footballer. He later became a licensee like his father, and ran the *York House* in Phippen Street, Redcliffe, Bristol. He also lived in Ilchester Crescent, Bedminster Down, and he married Vera Elizabeth Frost, in 1941. The couple had two children, but the son – and henceforth, Billy's *grandson* –

A RED SKY AT NIGHT

Peter '*Fred*' Wedlock, was to find fame as a very popular local folk singer. Frederick Sr. died in April 1985, at the age of 73.

Ada Vera Wedlock, born in Bristol on August 14th 1918, married Charles Hussey-Yeo at the tender age of 18, in Bristol, in 1936. The couple soon moved into No 4 Clift House Road, Ashton, where they spent the vast majority of their married lives. She died on September 10th 1992, aged 74.

Ronald William James Wedlock, born in Bristol on March 25th 1922, married Ena Blanche Chapman in the district of Weston, in 1944. He lived in the Bedminster and Ashton Gate areas, was the longest-lived of all Billy's children - and died in the year 2011, at the age of 89.

Dennis John Wedlock, born in Bristol on November 8th 1925, was an amateur footballer on Bristol City's books between 1945 and 1947, and also played as left-half for a Gloucestershire XI against Cornwall in a Southern Counties Amateur Championship match at St Austell on January 12th 1946. Soon after this, he played a first-team game for Bristol City in a 'war-time' fixture away at Cardiff City on March 16th 1946. It was in a Division Three (South) *South Region* Cup qualifying round at Ninian Park. City lost 3-2, and although Dennis was retained as an amateur for season 1946/47, he was later released after a spell in the reserves. He married Audrey R Shapcott in Bristol in the year 1948. The family later resided at 34 Greville Street, Southville – in the same house that his eldest brother William J T had previously lived with *his* wife Eleanor, before their move to Frampton Cotterell. Dennis died in January 1993, aged 67.

As has previously been indicated, Ada, Wedlock's second wife, would eventually outlive him by 13 years, and she died at No 4, Clift House Road, the home of her eldest daughter, on February 25th 1978 – at the age of 87.

But in the meantime, what of Billy *himself*?

By the early 1930's, even Wedlock the *charity sportsman* was starting to wind down his *'Old Pro's'* activities. He was now into his early 50's, and the old body simply couldn't take it anymore. The *'City old-boys'* could carry on playing their regular fundraisers if they wished – but Billy was no longer going to be able to make it with them. Even the continued talk about his one day becoming a director at Bristol City was now starting to ebb away. Rumours had persisted well into the club's 1926/27 promotion season, that Wedlock was going to 'have another go' in the close-season - that he was going to re-submit a new application. But nothing seemed to come of it. He simply appeared to change his mind. His priorities, it seemed, had since moved into other areas. For Wedlock was now becoming an established figure in the *licensing industry*. He was starting to make a name for himself in *this field*... He *still* attended all the top Ashton Gate meetings of course. And in early 1934, that *old* 'director' *chestnut* came back up – *again*. Bristol City by this time were back down in Division Three (South), and yet again, their financial struggles were the dominant topic of the day. The club simply had no money, and despite having made *"a profit of £3,649"*, it still owed the bank more than £10,000. There had been bickering in the boardroom, and now, fresh blood – and *money* – was being sought. Under these unhappy circumstances, the annual shareholders' meeting took place on Friday January 29th 1934,

at the *Provident Hall*, Prewett Street, Redcliffe. Chairman George Jenkins presided over the meeting, and Wedlock watched and listened carefully to every word that was said. The gathering had been a particularly stormy affair, with lots of people getting *a lot* of things off their chests – but it all ended on good terms. Towards the conclusion of the meeting, Jenkins made a speech and as he got towards the end, he began to look increasingly in Billy's direction – *"we (City) must have 12,000 to 14,000 gates if we want a team at all...we have an exceptionally good goalkeeper in view for the coming season, and also an outside-right. We will also try again to get William Wedlock on the board, if he would come forward..."*
In reply, Billy stood up, and politely made his feelings clear – that he did not think it *necessary* to have more *"football knowledge"* on the board, *"it's MONEY they want"* he quipped. And of course, he was *right*. And that *was it.* Wedlock's name would not be floated again, and he never got a place on the board. And everyone was satisfied with the situation, because everyone had *moved on*.
Wedlock's main interest in the game now became solely that of *interested spectator*. Anywhere in town there was a decent match in prospect, Billy would be *there* – even if that meant crossing divides and seeing a game in 'enemy territory'...
On January 11th 1936, Wedlock went to Stapleton Road to see Bristol Rovers play Arsenal in the third round of the FA Cup. He watched a very interesting game indeed, though Rovers, despite leading the Gunners' 1-0 at half-time, eventually lost 5-1. After the final whistle, he recognised an old familiar face, Sir Frederick Wall, formerly a high-ranking official at the

WEDLOCK – THE FIRST HERO OF BRISTOL CITY

Football Association, and now acting as a director at Arsenal. It is not actually known whether or not Wedlock's previously failed application for his Bristol City 'directorship' came up, or if they simply had a natter about Wedlock's old England days, but the two men *did* get talking, and for some considerable time. Wall no doubt left the happier of the two men, for Arsenal had done the job, and Wedlock was certainly not the type of man to bear any particular malice towards Bristol Rovers; indeed he'd probably gone to Eastville hoping to see them *win*. Some weeks later, on February 26th – Wedlock and the '*Star Inn*' played host to an important gathering of the '*Bristol Beer, Spirit and Wine Trade Protection & Benevolent Association'.* Billy was no doubt a proud proprietor that night *indeed,* but he had other reasons for hoping this particular event went smoothly – for he had his eye on gaining membership of the society *himself.* Subsequently, Wedlock was to get his reward for a very successive evening, because at the *next* meeting, held at the *Elephant Hotel,* St Nicholas Street, on May 27th, he *was* granted membership.

On very rare occasions, Wedlock was *still* active on the field of play, but these days, it was *not as a competitor*, but as a referee or linesman. If the occasion or charity was a *noble* one, then Billy would answer the call... On *Whit Monday,* June 1st 1936, Wedlock and his old Bristol Rovers mate Steve Sims acted as linesmen for a truly unique game of football - the England v France *Women's* international, held at Knowle Stadium, Bristol. The 70-minute contest proved a big success, attracting a crowd of 3,000 curious spectators, and England won by four goals to one.

A RED SKY AT NIGHT

It is highly unlikely that Wedlock had harboured any ill-feeling towards the '*suits*' of the Football Association since the turning down of his old 'directorship' application, for Billy was never a bitter person and certainly not a man to bear grudges. It is also clear that the feeling of respect was a *mutual* one, for in the autumn of 1938, Wedlock accepted an invitation to join in with the celebrations of the FA's 75th anniversary banquet, which was to be held at the Holborn restaurant in London on October 26th of that year. Wedlock, being one of 400 specially-picked guests, would have had an absolute *ball* on this occasion, being re-united with several of his friends and old England team-mates including Vivian Woodward, Bob Crompton, Jesse Pennington and Harold Fleming. According to the **Birmingham Daily Gazette**, the guest list included *"the most notable football personalities in Europe, and many of the finest players in Britain and on the continent..."* - it continued; *"...while the band played the National airs of 24 countries, all the flags were unfurled amid an enthusiastic demonstration. The scene culminated with the unfurling of the Union Jack and the whole of the guests joined in the singing of the National Anthem...at almost every table was one international player, and when the President* (Mr W Pickford) *desired to take wine with the international players, more than 20 whose names are known throughout Europe rose to their feet..."*

Unfortunately, it seemed that for every happy occasion, there was also a *sad one*, and only six days later, on November 2nd 1938, Wedlock and several of his old Bristol City team-mates, including Billy Jones and Arthur Spear, attended the funeral of Ashton Gate stalwart Dick Batten, who had been the club's

WEDLOCK – THE FIRST HERO OF BRISTOL CITY

trainer during the Reds' glory days in the 1900's. Batten, more recently assistant-groundsman, had died suddenly at the age of 72, whilst working behind the grandstand at Ashton Gate. The years 1939 to 1945 brought world war once again, and all League football subsequently came to a halt for six years. It was another desperately bad time for Wedlock, who lost his son James to this terrible conflict, in Burma, just before the end of the war in 1945.

But Wedlock *himself* was getting tired. Wedlock was now an *old man*. It was reported in the local papers that on October 9th 1947, Billy had gone into hospital for an unspecified eye operation. This however, would not be the last of his troubles in this area, as he would suffer from further eyesight problems for the rest of his life, and a subsequent photo taken of Billy meeting old football pal Fanny Walden three months later showed him wearing spectacles in public for the first time.

Left to right – Tom Smith (Northampton Town manager), Wedlock, Walden, and Bob Hewison (Bristol City manager)

A RED SKY AT NIGHT

The reunion with Walden took place at the County Ground, Northampton on January 24th 1948, this being the occasion of Bristol City beating Northampton Town 4-0 in a Division Three (South) fixture played on that day. Frederick *'Fanny'* Walden had been a diminutive right-winger for Tottenham Hotspur and England, and Wedlock had known him well from the many Bristol City / Spurs clashes that had taken place in the years immediately leading up to World War One. The pair had both played for their country *too,* though not quite *together*, for Walden's England career had begun in 1914 just weeks after Wedlock's had finished. Walden as a footballer was unusual to look at due to his lack of height, in fact at five feet two inches tall, he had been just about the *only player* in League football whom Wedlock could *look down* upon. Meeting Walden again was a nice moment, but arguably the biggest reunion of all was still on the horizon...

On April 24th 1948, on the 39th anniversary of Bristol City's only FA Cup Final, the 67 year-old Billy Wedlock went to Wembley to see Matt Busby's Manchester United play Blackpool. He didn't attend merely for the *occasion* however, big as it might have been. *Yes*, it was the *modern-day* FA Cup Wembley showpiece - *yes*, it was United's first Final since that far-off clash with Bristol City all those years ago. But Wedlock, as ever, wanted to see the *old* faces, the faces of *yesteryear*. And at Wembley's grand reunion, he met seven of the surviving members of the 1909 winning United team, unfortunately though, this group *did not include* skipper Charlie Roberts – who had died on August 7th 1939, at the age of 56. On the day, Wedlock was a fascinated spectator as United beat Blackpool by four goals to two, to clinch

their second victory in the Final of the competition. *It wouldn't be their last either...*
Still Wedlock continued to check his Bristol City fixture list, and *still* he travelled the country to meet up with old acquaintances, be they friend or foe... On Saturday October 15th 1949, he was in the city of Nottingham for more reunions, *and* to see Bristol City (lose 4-1) at Meadow Lane against Notts County, where the home centre-forward Tommy Lawton ran City's defence absolutely ragged. Wedlock discussed with a local journalist the subject of Lawton, and of how, in Billy's heyday, he *might* have been able to put the brake on the County man's progress. Billy afterwards however, admitted – *"This Notts' attack will want some holding".* And at the end of the season, County unsurprisingly finished as runaway champions, with Lawton the top scorer in the league, bagging 31 goals.

Wedlock was back at Ashton Gate on Tuesday April 25th 1950, for long-serving City stalwart Lemmo Southway's benefit game. A 23,000 crowd saw a combined City / Rovers XI defeat an International 'All-Star' XI by a goal to nil, and afterwards the players and guests were treated to dinner at the Grand Hotel. Southway, it will be remembered, had been one of only two *retained* professionals, alongside Wedlock, who had kept the City going across the dark years of the First World War.

The year 1950 also saw Wedlock planning another reunion for the Ashton Gate visit of Nottingham Forest on November 11th, a game that Forest duly won 3-0, in front of 32,878. Two days earlier, the **Nottingham Journal** had reported that *"Health permitting, a stand onlooker ...will be veteran England centre-half Billy Wedlock. Billy, licensee of a hotel a few yards from Bristol*

A RED SKY AT NIGHT

City's ground, has recently been suffering from failing eyesight. If ex-Forester (Enoch) *'Nocker' West makes the journey west, this pair will revive many memories of football battles..."*

At the Bristol City v Brighton match, on August 30th 1952, there was yet another reunion for Wedlock, this time meeting up with the former Liverpool and Aston Villa defender Jimmy Harrop, who back in the day had been in the running to challenge Wedlock for his England No 5 shirt - though Billy of course, had successfully held him off.

As Wedlock continued to serve up pints in the *'Star Inn'*, it was obvious to one and all that Billy still *loved* his football. Though the game had changed a great deal by now, Wedlock's fire and passion for the sport had clearly not diminished. He loved to talk of the game, and he enjoyed nothing more than a good old natter about the olden days... Yet Billy of course didn't simply *remember* – he was also *remembered* by *others*. Henceforth, visitors to *'The Star'* often came from far and wide – the length and breadth of the country...

In July 1953, the former Arsenal and England winger Joe Hulme, by then a successful journalist, paid Billy the ultimate compliment, by writing that Wedlock had been *"the Greatest Centre-half of them all"*. Hulme had been signed by Herbert Chapman in 1926, spending 12 years with the Gunners' and winning three League Championship medals and two FA Cups – so he *certainly* knew what he was talking about. During that summer of 1953, Hulme, on a visit to Bristol, decided on a whim to pop into *'The Star'* to see how Wedlock was doing. He subsequently wrote about his findings in a column for the Sunday paper **The People**, on July 12th. In his piece, Hulme described walking through the pub door and immediately noticing Wedlock's famous mahogany case, displaying 19 of his England caps. Looking over them with interest, Hulme suddenly heard a voice – *"I got 18 of 'em in succession, Joe – not bad, eh?"* After conversing for a while, Hulme decided to ask Wedlock the cheeky question *"How did a titch like you manage to make the grade as a centre-half?"..."They used to call me the india-rubber man",* Wedlock chuckled in reply – *"seems I used to bounce from attack to defence, and from defence to attack. They don't play the game like that these days, though..."* Hulme enjoyed his meeting with our Billy, though in his column he also reported the sad news that *"Fatty is 73 now, and blind in one eye – not that it prevents him enjoying a nice game of bowls..."*

The write-up ended with one of Wedlock's favourite stories – his recollection of the legendary 1906 England trial match, played between the *Professionals* and the *Amateurs*, when Billy had been driven through Sheffield at lightning speed in Fred Milnes' car. He then recalled running onto the field and immediately tripping *Amateur* centre-forward and future international team-mate Vivian Woodward, and Wedlock, with a further chuckle, then confirmed to Hulme - *"It was the only foul ever given against me in my career"..."No wonder they're proud of him down Bristol way",* concluded Hulme...

On January 2nd 1954, just over the road, Wedlock looked on as City's newest star John Atyeo notched the only goal in a 1-0 win over Southampton at Ashton Gate. After the game, Billy renewed acquaintances with Rotherham manager Andy Smailes, who had actually been *spying* on the Reds' that day, for the south Yorkshiremen were coming to Ashton Gate the following week in the third round of the FA Cup. Smailes and Wedlock had never been team-mates as such, yet Billy had got to know Andy when the latter had been a valuable member of the City side that had won the 1926/27 Third Division (South) title. Smailes accordingly marked down John Atyeo's name as being the 'danger-man' for the forthcoming cup-tie, and Atyeo subsequently *scored*, but Smailes' spying job had not been wasted, as Rotherham won 3-1.

In 1955, an Atyeo-inspired City were finally promoted to Division Two as *Champions*, after a 23 year absence, an event which would have cheered Billy's heart. But five years later, as had happened the *previous time* - they were back down again...

Yet Wedlock's Ashton Gate appearances were now becoming *less and less frequent*. He had constant trouble with his eyes, and crippling arthritis had set in. Billy was now a very old man. 1962 is the final year we see the license for *'The Star'* still containing Wedlock's name. It was nearly time to go...*nearly*...

But he had more than *served* his time – 1915 to 1962...

...47 long years of service to the good folk of Ashton Gate.

In November 1962, Bristol City were preparing for the visit of non-league Wimbledon to Ashton Gate, the team they were due to face in the second round of the FA Cup, on Saturday November 24th. And as the clock ticked down to the final three or four days before the day of the game, many newspapers across England communicated the important sporting news to all football fans around the country – namely, that *"Wedlock will be there..."* Because Wimbledon of course were *amateurs,* Wimbledon were *non-leaguers* – and if there was one thing which warmed the heart of Wedlock, the old romantic, it was the

lot of the *amateur footballer,* an affinity with whom had been forged during his long-gone days of playing for Aberdare.
"I remember many stirring games against amateur clubs..." he said, days after the event of his 82nd birthday - *"...and I shall be there to watch Wimbledon"*. For the record, a first-half brace from Brian Clark gave City the platform for a 2-1 victory, and in front of 13,778 spectators, Wimbledon were gallantly knocked out of the Cup. Henceforth, this was to become Wedlock's *last-ever* (recorded) visit for a match at Ashton Gate...

...and soon after this, Billy was to call *"Last Orders"* at '*The Star*' as well, and in May 1964, Wedlock left that pub for the final time, and the family quietly retreated round the corner to No 4 Clift House Road, the home of his youngest daughter, Ada, where the old veteran would spend his final months, weeks and days on this earth...For Billy now was weak and *getting weaker*, old and *getting older*...

Yet Wedlock, when he decided to slip away, had no need to worry over his *legacy*. Because Billy Wedlock, the boy from Bedminster, had done *good*. Billy the footballer had entertained the *millions* – and Billy the *human-being* had warmed the hearts of an equal number. And even his fiercest critics; the ones from all those years ago, who had so opposed his continued selection for the England team, *had* to admit that Wedlock had been *entertaining,* Wedlock had been *different* - Wedlock had been *unique*. Billy, the most sporting *gentleman ever* to walk onto a football field, had been admired across Bristol and the West Country and from *further afield*, he had made countless friends across the country *and beyond* – and he was *loved*.

From Cardiff to Cape Town, Wedlock had been *admired*, from

A RED SKY AT NIGHT

Nottingham to Natal, Wedlock had *made friends*, and from Jesmond to Johannesburg, Wedlock had been *loved*...
But *nowhere* had the man been more adored than at his beloved Ashton Gate.
On January 24th 1965, the British people received news that Sir Winston Churchill, former Prime-Minister, had died. The country had lost perhaps the greatest leader it *ever* had...
...and the following morning, at 4:30 on January 25th, Bristol City lost the greatest leader *it* ever had. Because on the 47th anniversary of the demise of his mentor - Mr Frank Bacon - Billy had *gone*. Wedlock was *no more* of this earth. Because Wedlock had gone to the top of the mountain, and he had been there a long, long time. But Wedlock was now tired...84 years old...Wedlock had *had enough*. He wanted to come back down. He wanted to rest. Wedlock had passed on the baton, because Wedlock could not go on *any longer*...
...Because Bristol City had reached the top of the mountain *too*. And on April 24th 1965, practically three months to the day after the passing of Billy Wedlock, and on the 56th anniversary of the 1909 FA Cup Final - the City beat Oldham Athletic 2-0 to reclaim a Second Division place *at last*. *Promotion*. It wasn't quite the 'promised land' of the First Division - *yet* – but they would get there in the end...
And on April 24th 1965, the sound of the celebrating Bristol City fans was *deafening*. And the patrons of that club witnessed the famous tears of joy from City's big number eight. The *modern-day* City captain. And the Reds' fanatics *responded*. For the supporters of Bristol City were no longer singing the names of Spear, Cottle and Wedlock – they were singing the names of

WEDLOCK – THE FIRST HERO OF BRISTOL CITY

Bush, Clark and Atyeo...
Because Billy had passed on the baton. To the *new generation*. And the noise was simply *deafening*. And maybe, just *maybe*, in some high-up heavenly place in the sky, Wedlock stirred. Maybe. *Perhaps*. And Wedlock awoke. Just for a few seconds. And he looked down. And when he saw what was going on below, at Ashton Gate, he settled back down again, and eased himself back to sleep, happy in his soul. Because it was all *good*. Everything was good and right in *his world*, the world he had departed, the world he had left behind.
And Bristol City would *go on*...and Bristol City *did* go on. It even survived a near-death experience in the year 1982, and *still* it went on...but Wedlock had now *gone*, Wedlock would *not* go on...
Yet the *legend* – the legend had barely *started*, the *legend* would continue...the legend would *run*. Just like those Wedlockian legs of old, in those far-off games of long ago, it would keep running and running – and it would never ever stop...
For it hadn't just been about the footballing genius, though a genius he most certainly *was*...
it had been about the way he had *conducted himself*.
And Billy had always done things *his* way – the only way – the noble way – the...

A RED SKY AT NIGHT

Wedlock Way, BS3

WEDLOCK – THE FIRST HERO OF BRISTOL CITY

W. WEDLOCK, BRISTOL CITY.

"IT IS GENERALLY ACCEPTED AMONG FOOTBALLERS THAT THE CENTRE-HALF HOLDS THE MOST PROMINENT PLACE IN THE TEAM…

…OTHER THINGS BEING EQUAL, THE *PIVOT* OF THE TEAM SHOULD ALSO BE THE *CAPTAIN*…"

'Triers', TRIBUTES AND TESTIMONIALS

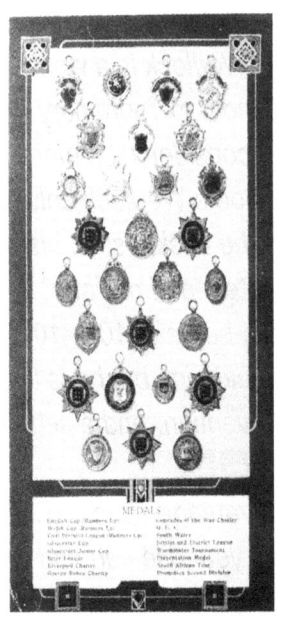

WEDLOCK – THE FIRST HERO OF BRISTOL CITY

"The Most Remarkable Player" -
Article written about Wedlock, published in the **Athletic News** on Monday February 24th, 1908.

"The Most Remarkable Player"

*We have been asked a quaint question – Who is the most remarkable football player of the day? No position is specified, and every nationality is included. We do not consider the interrogation ambiguous, and we do not intend to shelter ourselves behind any such response as "This is entirely a matter of individual opinion." Looking at his physique and the standard of his skill we shall without the least hesitation answer:
William Wedlock, of Bristol City. Wedlock is a wonder, a phenomenon, and one of the most extraordinary half-backs who ever lived. Readers should consider for a moment that before he draws on his football boots Wedlock only stands 5ft. 4 + a 1/2in. We shall not subtract the thickness of his socks. Again the breezy Bristolians have christened him "Fatty" Wedlock, but after all he merely pulls down the beam at 10st. 10lb. Thus he has neither height nor weight to aid him, but he is tireless, a parcel of pluck, un-erring in intervention, and a schemer who puts the ball out at compound interest.*
Never did he place with such advantage as in the 'North and South' match at Manchester this year. He can and DOES tackle giants, but some difficulty is experienced in charging Wedlock... It is far easier to tumble over him. William Foulke and William

'TRIERS', TRIBUTES AND TESTIMONIALS

Wedlock are as much alike as the Great Eastern and a ferryboat. Both have won their international caps, and the fact proves that football is for all sorts and conditions of men...

THE ENERGETIC WILLIE WEDLOCK.

Wedlock's Apprenticeship

Born at Bedminster on October 28 1887, **(sic)*** *Wedlock had three elder brothers, who all played forward with the Masonic Rovers. Their example fired the youngest with ambition and he joined Arlington Rovers when about fifteen.*** *Beginning as a centre half-back, he has never appeared in any other position. Possibly he was designed for the place. During an apprenticeship of four seasons with the Arlington Rovers Wedlock laid the foundation of his career. In one campaign the Rovers won the*

WEDLOCK – THE FIRST HERO OF BRISTOL CITY

Gloucestershire Junior Cup, the Bristol and District League, the Bristol and District Charity Cup, and a six-a-side competition known as the Warminster Tournament, all these honours accruing in Wedlock's third season.*** Thence he migrated to Aberdare, where he abandoned amateurism for what is known as a working-professional. The title means that he earned his livelihood, and was paid for his matches only. This should be the ideal of professionalism, with the motto: "No work, no pay". With Wedlock in their ranks, Aberdare carried off the South Wales Cup, ran second in the South Wales League, and in two finals for the Welsh Cup encountered the Druids and Wrexham. Harry Thickett, Bristol City's manager, saw Wedlock play against Wrexham, and signed him as a professional.

The Finished Workman

In League life his first match was against Manchester United at Manchester, and Wedlock quite remembers that Bristol City were beaten by 5-1. He declares that he is not likely to forget the game. Now in his third season with the Citizens, he has never been absent from duty in a league game except for the claims of international matches, or when given a rest by well-wishing directors in view of such a representative test. As an emergency man he last season came into the Trial Match on Sheffield Wednesday's ground between the Amateurs and the Professionals. Arriving in Sheffield about twenty minutes before the kick-off, he dressed in the train, was marvellously driven in a motor to Owlerton, played in great style, and has never been left out of any international encounter since.

'TRIERS', TRIBUTES AND TESTIMONIALS

<u>Grateful to his tutors</u>

Wedlock recalls that even as a centre half-back he scored twenty goals in one season for Aberdare, and he confesses that he has a hearty relish for the sport. Not unmindful of those who have lent him a helping hand, he recollects that he occasionally assisted Bedminster when Hugh Wilson, the famous Scotsman, was playing at left half-back. Hugh Wilson gave him many hints, for which he is still grateful, while he declares that he owes much to Annan, the Bristol back, who has helped him with advice and warm words of encouragement. It is nice to see a man who has climbed the ladder of fame mindful of those who have cheered him in his toil.

<u>The Opinions of Wedlock</u>

Wedlock has his opinions of the men he has encountered. All things considered, he holds that Andrew Wilson, of Sheffield Wednesday, is the best centre-forward he has ever met, although George Hilsdon, of Chelsea, runs him a close race for the honour. The most difficult man he has ever had to tackle has been George Wilson, now of Newcastle United. He regards Ben Warren, of Derby County, as the finest half-back he has ever seen. Without a moment's hesitation he asserted that Crompton, of Blackburn Rovers, was the cleverest full-back he had watched on any field, while Hardy was his embodiment of a goalkeeper. Although the battle between England and Scotland at Newcastle last April was the most exciting match he had ever taken part in, he never saw such splendid football as in the struggle between

WEDLOCK – THE FIRST HERO OF BRISTOL CITY

Everton and Bristol City at Goodison Park last season, when the home team prevailed by 2-0, for that day the ground was in superb condition, and both teams were on the top of their form. A modest man of few words, William Wedlock is immensely popular with his fellow professionals. There is no surer test of a man's worth.

* Wedlock was actually born on 28 October 1880.
** On joining Arlington Rovers, he would have been aged SIXTEEN.
*** This was season 1899/1900.

"William Wedlock – The Bristol Wonder" -
Article written about Wedlock, published in the
Belfast Telegraph on Wednesday June 7th, 1911.

"William Wedlock - The Bristol Wonder", by H. Slater Stone

There are some people who hold the belief that wooden legs run in families, but whilst that suggestion is open to question, it is an undisputable fact that since Bristol City renounced amateurism and the name of Bristol South End, in 1897-8, good half-backs have been perpetually in the employ of the club, and the greatest of these has been William Wedlock, their centre-half of today.

'TRIERS', TRIBUTES AND TESTIMONIALS

His connection to the club and his rise to fame read almost like a romance of sport, and if ever a player could attribute his greatness to the accident of circumstance, that player is William Wedlock, better known as 'Fatty' – a soubriquet that he never resents, and one that will forever be associated with him when he is no longer associated with active service on the football field.

BRISTOL BORN AND BRED

He is the first Bristol born player who has ever been capped for his country. He first saw the light of day at the Nursery, North-street, Bedminster, a matter of a thousand yards from Bristol City's present ground. That happened in – well, no matter – for a footballer is only as old as he feels, and Wedlock is a long way from feeling old. His first club was Melrose, a team formed by the lads of the Sunday School of which he was a member, and from thence he passed on to Arlington Rovers, one of the most promising of the junior clubs of that day. Whilst a member of that side he was recommended to the City, and they gave him a trial in a friendly match with Leicester Fosse at Ashton Gate **(sic)*** *in 1900/1. He made good, and so was played against Millwall in the Southern League and Queen's Park Rangers** in the Western League, but at that time the City appeared to have an adequate supply of half-backs, and so Wedlock went to Aberdare.*

A MONUMENT OF MODESTY

Even then he had taken the fancy of Mr Frank Bacon, the present vice-chairman of the City directors, and it is only paying tribute

WEDLOCK – THE FIRST HERO OF BRISTOL CITY

where it is due when it is said that it was owing to Director Bacon's pertinacity that Wedlock came to the City again.

He always had a warm corner in his heart for 'Fatty', and armed with the tongue of good report, he at length persuaded Wedlock to return. The City directors, too, agreed to it, and there are those who argue that Wedlock will remain with the club until Anno Domini insists that he shall play no longer.

It would be infinitely easier to stage "Hamlet" without a Prince of Denmark than to imagine Bristol City without Wedlock, and the way in which the wonderful little man has got 'right there' is a splendid rebuke for the players who feel it is necessary to beat the big drum to achieve fame. An epitome of energy, Wedlock is also a monument of modesty, and you would think his bête noire was HIMSELF, for about himself he never talks.

HELP FOR FRIEND OR FOE

Wedlock has been referred to by many writers with many phrases, but I like the simile of his being a little india-rubber man, for when he goes down he seems to come up again in one and the same action, and the way he scampers after the ball I have only seen equalled in the music hall by the terrier trained to head a big ball. In all truth, Wedlock is a terrier too, yet with none of the canine vices, and there is no kinder opponent playing to-day than Bristol City's captain. Directly a man is down, no matter which side he may be on, Wedlock is one of the first to help him up, and what he does on the football field in that respect is symbolical of what he does when he is OFF, for no old player down on his luck ever appeals to him in vain.

'TRIERS', TRIBUTES AND TESTIMONIALS

Another characteristic with Wedlock is that he always accepts the rulings of the referee with a good grace, Wedlock trusts the referees and the referees trust Wedlock. Small wonder that it should be so, for during the whole of his career he has only had one penalty given against him, and that is merely as it should be, for every rule has an exception.

<u>A BAD START AND A GOOD FINISH</u>

To hark back to the time when Wedlock returned to Bristol; I was at the match in Aberdare when that step was practically decided on, and I often smile at the innocence of old Job Jones, the Aberdare trainer, who had formerly been with Bristol clubs, when I sounded him as to the possibility of "Fatty" leaving Aberdare. Job not only told me of the clubs that wanted Wedlock, and what he might have made out of it if he had assisted them to that end, but ruefully he also told me what the pains and penalties to himself would be if the people of Aberdare found out that he had had a hand in it. For four seasons Wedlock was with Aberdare, and in one of the four campaigns scored no fewer than twenty goals from centre-half. And, by-the-by, his shooting has waned as his other excellences have developed. His return to Bristol City synchronised with the Bristol club gaining promotion. Yet goodness alone knows his first match argued nothing of that sort, for it was played at Clayton, where Manchester United won by five goals to one. It was the first and the only league match that the City lost away from home that season.

<u>HONOUR BY ACCIDENT</u> (Contd. over)

WEDLOCK – THE FIRST HERO OF BRISTOL CITY

It was not until the following season (the first season that the City were in the First League) that Wedlock received international recognition, and then it was the outcome of an accident in every sense of the word. Colin Veitch had been selected to play as centre-half for the Professionals against the Amateurs at Sheffield on the Monday, and no reserve had been chosen. On the Sunday it transpired that the Newcastle man had been injured the previous day, so, late on Sunday night, the football authorities got into touch with Mr Frank Bacon, and through him, with Wedlock. Next morning Wedlock, accompanied of course by Mr Bacon, went off to Sheffield, where a big motor-car met them at the station, and thus Wedlock was whisked off to football fame, for he did so well in that trial that he never lost favour with the Selection Committee, and in the next four seasons he gathered the full dozen of international caps against Scotland, Ireland, and Wales, besides others of lesser degree. He also toured in Austria and recently in South Africa. "Everywhere that Mary went, the lamb was sure to go", says the old nursery rhyme, and "Everywhere that Wedlock went, his friends were sure to grow". Unique testimony to that fact was found in the circumstance that after his recent return from South Africa, the South African FA made a special collection towards his benefit, which Bristol City this season gave him.

NEVER TIRED

Wedlock's presence is a tonic for any dejected side, and I have seen him many a time and oft, metaphorically pull up his sleeves and put in an extra ounce to save a game in which many a bigger

'TRIERS', TRIBUTES AND TESTIMONIALS

man would nonchalantly have decided that it was impossible to avoid defeat. Whole-hearted and big-hearted is William Wedlock as a player, and I have often thought what a benefit he would have had if he had linked his wagon to the star of one of the clubs in the North, where he would have been playing behind a front rank that did not want so much done for it as the Bristol City front rank has all often too often required. I have named the dozen International caps that Wedlock owns, and there have been six others and twenty-seven medals, to say nothing of a handsome silver cup presented to him on the occasion of his benefit, but I believe above all that he values the fact that he has been able to do so much for his beloved Bristol City. It has been said of Queen Mary that she protested the word Calais was written on her heart. I fully believe Bristol City is written on the heart of Wedlock. May he never suffer from 'Fatty degeneration!'

***Note from David Woods** – Several accounts (including H. Slater Stone's) – state that the Leicester Fosse game (which was actually Wedlock's SECOND match that season) WAS indeed played at Ashton Gate. But the Author - *earlier in the book* – went with St John's Lane, which was referenced in the '*Western Daily Press*' match report.   ****QPR was his first game.**

"My ideal teams from the Tests of England and Scotland" - Excerpts (concerning Wedlock) from a newspaper column, published in the ***Athletic News*** on
Monday November 3rd, 1924.

"My ideal teams from the Tests of England and Scotland", by Tityrus   (Contd. over)...

WEDLOCK – THE FIRST HERO OF BRISTOL CITY

"....Warren was, of course, famous as a charger, Wedlock as a phenomenon, and Lintott as a swift tackler and shrewd placer. William Wedlock, of Bristol City chose himself as the centre half-back of England in almost every match from 1907 to 1912 - and once afterwards. As I have said he was a phenomenon, as he stood the same height as Harry Davis, 5ft. 4in, but he only weighed 10st. 7lb. He was one of the world's wonders in getting the ball – whether it was in the air or on the turf. Here, there, and everywhere, intervening and doing his work with a contempt for fatigue, he dominated many a game. I have been told that he was tremendously popular during the South African tour, and that after one match Lord and Lady Methuen sent for him in order that he might be presented. At that time Lord Methuen was the Governor-General of Natal.

A RISKY RIDE

The Rev. J.W. Marsh, now the Vicar of Nelson, used to officiate, years ago, as a referee in League matches, and he declared to me that Wedlock was the finest gentleman he ever met on the football field. From a man of the cloth this was a great tribute. But it was deserved, for Wedlock was one of the free gifts of Nature, whether considered as a player or as a sportsman. Never shall I forget the debut of Wedlock in any representative match. He was chosen to play for the Professionals against the Amateurs in December, 1906 – the rendezvous being the ground of The Wednesday at Owlerton...."

(NOTE - the famous story of Wedlock's mad dash to get to Sheffield by train and car is recounted HERE)

'TRIERS', TRIBUTES AND TESTIMONIALS

THE PUCK OF FOOTBALL

"...After that unfortunate first step, Wedlock played like a man, and, as I have said, for the next five years he chose HIMSELF – much to the indignation of those who believed that Charles Roberts, of Manchester United, was the rightful heir to the throne. The night before Wedlock sailed for South Africa I asked him how he liked the prospect, and he answered "Fine; a trip like this is as good as going to college." Wedlock was the very Puck of football, for he annihilated space, and was never tired. He was the nearest approach to perpetual motion ever seen on the football field. Known at Bristol as "Fatty", Wedlock, in his way, was as much a phenomenon as William Foulke, who was twice his size. He has never had his superior for getting the ball and using it without waiting to see whether his purpose was fulfilled. And he was succeeded by almost as great a player in Joe McCall, of Preston North End..."

Note – in his England *"Team of all-time"* – consisting of the best England players that Tityrus had seen competing in the various England v Scotland matches over the years, Wedlock was subsequently selected as his centre-half.

"Famous midgets" (Has the Big Man an Advantage in Football?)
More excerpts (concerning Wedlock) – written by *Tityrus* - from his newspaper column, published in the **Athletic News** on Monday September 3rd 1923
(Contd. over)...

WEDLOCK – THE FIRST HERO OF BRISTOL CITY

"Bristol's Brightest Brilliant" (EDIT) - by Tityrus

*"...Throwing aside as almost mythological heroes "Daddy" Holt, "Bobby" Neil, of Hibernians, Glasgow Rangers and Liverpool; "Tommy" Morren, of Middlesbrough and Sheffield United, have all these upholders of the sons of Anak forgotten **William Wedlock**? Is popularity so fleeting that Wedlock is never thought of by the champions of length and breadth? Pish-tush! Can this be? Surely never.*

Wedlock, decorated with the nickname of 'Fatty', was precisely the same height as Holt, but he weighed 10st. 10lb. This bundle of human activity not only did honour to Bristol City, but to the game, and to his country. For some years he kept bigger men out of the national team. The International Selection Committee were firm in their faith concerning Wedlock. On the whole of the evidence their judgment was the best ever known.

Rarely indeed did Wedlock ever fall below a very high standard. His restless energy, bottomless stamina, and extraordinary capacity to get the ball and use it, were never better exemplified than in the international match against Ireland at Derby in 1911. At the time I said that this little man filled the field, and by a miracle, he did. Week in week out, Wedlock was the best centre half-back I ever saw, and his success was due to the fact that he forgot himself, as he was always thinking of the next move by the enemy, and how he could frustrate it and benefit his team....."

"......Saturday after Saturday, and on occasions when most was needed in big matches, Wedlock had as a rule no superior. Nor did he stoop to conquer. Wedlock played the game, for he

'TRIERS', TRIBUTES AND TESTIMONIALS

was by nature an honest man and had the high courtesy of a gentleman. During seven years he took part in 35 successive representative games. No-one could dethrone him until age and injuries gave McCall the preference.
When found make a note of – for Wedlock was 5ft. 4½ in. – not 6ft. 2½ in.

WILLIAM WEDLOCK'S VALUABLE HEAD.

WEDLOCK – THE FIRST HERO OF BRISTOL CITY

Quotes

In the summer of 1910, in South Africa, as the invited England (FA) team arrive at the residence of Lord and Lady Methuen -
"Have you brought Wedlock, as I am most anxious to be introduced to him!"
(Quote attributed to Lady Methuen)

December 29th 1906, at the
Manchester United (0) v Bristol City (0), First Division match –
"Why, that tom-tit of a fellow, Wedlock, is EVERYWHERE. See! He's there again!"
Quote attributed to Manchester's Welsh wing wizard Billy Meredith, watching the game from the stands.

Ashton Gate, Saturday October 8th 1910 -
"Shortly before Wedlock's Benefit match 'Fatty' presented Charlie Roberts with a bottle of 'something' and a box of cigars, with the hope that the Manchester United players would smoke and drink his health".
Observations made by the *Star Green 'un*, Saturday October 22nd 1910.

'TRIERS', TRIBUTES AND TESTIMONIALS

"He seems to be everywhere. Don't give me the ball, it's hopeless. I never played against such a confounded nuisance!"

Attributed to an ANONYMOUS footballer (centre-forward) – story recounted in *"The Football Who's Who"* **(Published 1935)...**

WORDS FROM WEDLOCK...

"How we keep in form during the summer" **(Edit)**
Article written by Wedlock -
published in various newspapers, including the **Lichfield Mercury** and the **Beverley and East Riding Recorder**,
during September 1911.

<u>**"How We Keep In Form During The Summer",**</u>
<u>**BY W. WEDLOCK (Captain of Bristol City)**</u>

"I am often asked how we football professionals manage to keep our form during the off-season, those four months from April to September, when there is a lull in the excitement of league-matches and fierce contests for the honour of figuring in the semi-finals or final of the English Cup.
Well, there are many ways by which we strive to retain our

activity, freedom of limbs and body, in readiness for the fray when it again commences with the day dedicated to St Partridge all over the British Isles. Yet do not imagine for a moment that those four months of non-football are altogether free from care, for the man whose very living depends on his fitness for the following season. You cannot make any bigger mistake than that in your study of the game and its conditions as played to-day. We must be ready, perfectly fit, and up to the mark, by that fateful September 1st. For the league match a club plays on that day, and those during the following week or two count just as much, and are just as important in reckoning points, as the matches it will play at the end of March. Indeed, I often think myself that the September period is the more important, for if a good club gets a really fine start, and so gains several points before its rivals get thoroughly going, it must be allowed that not only has it those valuable points in hand, but the encouragement and stimulus it acquires from such a beginning is of paramount value, an asset of striking importance towards making it more successful, and in bringing thousands of spectators to its ground.

Well then, how do we all manage to get ourselves ready for that critical September 1st, after a period of enforced rest from the strenuous life of footballing? The fact is that many of us have hardly had a rest, in the sense usually attached to that word. For no small number of great footballers are also famous cricketers, county-men or league professionals, who have to play the summer game all along, from the beginning of May to the end of August. Thus they are kept in form, kept fit, without any special trouble on their part, and at the same time they are enjoying a

'TRIERS', TRIBUTES AND TESTIMONIALS

thorough change from football. Such men are Ducat, of Woolwich Arsenal, who is in Surrey's team, Sharp, of Everton, who plays for Lancashire, with his friend Makepeace, then also there is Iremonger, of Nottingham; Leach, of Sussex; Wilkinson, of Yorkshire; Needham, of Derbyshire, the Sheffield United crack, and many others who contrive to combine cricket with keeping in form for football in such a pleasant way as to suggest that they have learned the art of both eating their cake and having it at the same time!

But not all the professionals at the winter game are thus blessed or favoured by the gods with a genius for cricket. Then how do these other good folk fare during the summer's rest?

I can best show the variety of things men do to retain their fitness, to employ the off-time, if I detail for you the doings of one or two whom I know more or less intimately, or of whose summer hobbies I have heard from mutual friends..."

(Here, Wedlock goes on to list GARDENING, FARM-WORK, "BULLET-THROWING" (!), BASEBALL (Steve Bloomer), JOBBING AS A BLACKSMITH, the TERRITORIAL ARMY – and TRAVELLING as among the favourite activities of his fellow professionals up and down the country, then he finishes his article in the following fashion)...

"But there is another way of keeping fit during the summer, a way likely to become more common as time goes on, though I am not sure just yet how far it will prove exactly beneficial for those who get too much of it. I refer to the summer teams now being sent out each year to the Colonies and other places where the game can be played when it is too warm here for it. I have myself been on such tours, and enjoyed them very much. But can a man play

first-class football for three or four seasons successfully, in fact, year in and year out, for many years? I should perhaps doubt it. For football is a terribly trying game when you have too much of it, and it needs strong stamina and sturdy frame to keep it going at one's best.

However, some men fancy this thing does for them, some that, and others find yet different hobbies or pursuits to serve their needs. After all, it is much a case of what one like and feels inclined to do during the summer".

"LONDON'S TIE - Wedlock replies to Bristol's critics"
Article written by Wedlock, one week ahead of Bristol City's FA Cup semi-final against Huddersfield Town at Stamford Bridge - published in the *Star Green 'Un* on Saturday March 20th 1920.

"Wedlock replies to Bristol's critics –
HUDDERSFIELD'S PROWESS"
(By W. Wedlock, Captain Bristol City)

"As so many of the critics have already been confounded by Bristol City in the results of the rounds they have so far played, it will scarcely rattle their nerves if they get another shock. The critics, or, at any rate, a majority of them, seem thus early agreed that Bristol City are bound to lose. But I am one of those searching for reasons why Huddersfield Town are bound to win, though no one has more respect for what Huddersfield have done

'TRIERS', TRIBUTES AND TESTIMONIALS

or can do than myself. I have been too long on the football earth to be so unwise as to underrate any team in a Cup-tie, for Cup-ties bring their own atmosphere. Often it is a case of anything may happen, and not infrequently one side gets all the luck. It is usually agreed that the side that scores the first goal in a Cup-tie is half way on the road to victory; but Cardiff City scored the first goal against us and we beat them, and Liverpool scored the first goal against Huddersfield, but Huddersfield won. The first goal means a tremendous lot, but not everything. Derby County possibly will remember they scored first against us the last time we reached the semi-final; but Rippon equalised for us with the last kick of the game from a penalty, and we won the replay with Derby County.

Huddersfield Overrated

It is urged by many of the critics that we have had an easier passage to the semi-final than Huddersfield, but I do not quite see how they reconcile that with the prophecies attending the draw for each round that threatened us each time with defeat, Huddersfield had a much easier first round task in receiving Brentford than we had in visiting Grimsby, for so many clubs with big reputations have lost on the latter ground. In the second round Huddersfield had a stiffer hurdle to mount in visiting Newcastle than we had in staying at home to the Arsenal, and I give them full credit for a fine performance.
In the third round we were supposed to have had more formidable foemen in Cardiff that Huddersfield had in Plymouth Argyle. In the fourth round I fancy we had fairly equal tasks, for it

WEDLOCK – THE FIRST HERO OF BRISTOL CITY

has to be remembered Bradford came to us flushed with success against Preston North End.

As regards our meetings with Huddersfield this season, which ended in a win for the home team each time, I cannot say much, for I was injured and not able to play in either game. But from information received I should say we have quite as good a chance of entering the final as we had last time, when we knocked out Derby County.

It is urged that Huddersfield have improved much, since we beat them last November, but so have Bristol City; they have confidence in themselves, and if luck is not dead against us I am hoping that the West will again be represented in the final.

I think it is a good idea that our semi-final is to be played at Chelsea, for it will give both Huddersfield and ourselves a chance to get to know something about the ground. What I am wondering is if Bristol City and Huddersfield fill the Stamford Bridge grounds for the semi-final, how will they manage to get the crowd in for the final that will want to get in with Aston Villa or Chelsea as one of the teams".

Note – Some of Wedlock's words were strangely prophetic – *"...if luck is not dead against us..."* In the semi-final, City endured an afternoon of appalling bad luck, and were highly unfortunate to get beaten by a 2-1 scoreline. Aston Villa won the Cup by defeating Huddersfield 1-0 in the Final at Stamford Bridge.

'TRIERS', TRIBUTES AND TESTIMONIALS

"My Methods at Centre-Half":
Points in the play of the pivot which are overlooked.
Article written by Wedlock,
just months after his retirement from the game.
Published in the **Nelson Leader** (Lancashire)
on September 2nd 1921.

"POINTS IN THE PLAY OF THE PIVOT"

By W. Wedlock
(The Famous English International Half-Back.)

"Among football enthusiasts one often hears the centre-forward of the team referred to as the pivot. Strictly speaking, though, this is not correct. The centre-forward is the pivot of the attacking line, but the pivot of the team is, in my opinion, the centre-half.
He is, or should be, the hub of the wheel around which the whole of the play revolves. To put the matter in another way, it is generally accepted among footballers that the centre-half holds the most prominent place in the team.
If we look for a minute into some of the things he is supposed to do, we shall see why the man in the middle of the half-backs is considered so important...
In the first place of course, he is the main connecting link between the attack and the defence. I have not the space to discuss the important question of whether it is more vital for the centre-half to be an attacker than a defender, but it is obvious, in passing, that the centre-half who is either one or the other EXCLUSIVELY, is not fulfilling the whole of the duties which,

WEDLOCK – THE FIRST HERO OF BRISTOL CITY

in the ordinary way, should fall to his lot.

I have suggested that the position of centre-half is the most important one in the team, yet I do not agree with the many people who consider that the centre-half is the hardest-worked player on the field. Possibly to the pivot the ball will come more frequently than to any other member of the side, but there are people with more running about to do than the centre-half.

The wing half-backs, for instance, probably cover a greater amount of ground in the course of the average game, while the inside wing men have more than an ordinary amount of running about to do.

But although, as I say, there may be players who cover more ground, of this we can rest assured - that the centre-half who means to do his whole duty will not have very many idle moments in the course of a match. When the forwards of his side are up and doing, he will be in their immediate vicinity, helping them to push home the attack. And when the pendulum of play swings back to the other goal, there the centre-half must also be, doing his level best to prevent the other fellows from getting through.

To me it has always seemed that the centre-half, more than any other player in the side, has it in his power to mould the play of the team as a whole. I have said the ball comes to him more than to other players: hence the vital importance of what the centre-half DOES with it. If the forwards of his team are playing too closely together, the centre-half can stop this by swinging the ball first to the left and then to the right – long, raking passes to the feet of one of the outside men.

Again, the centre-half is the man who must push the ball through

'TRIERS', TRIBUTES AND TESTIMONIALS

The old-style 2-3-5 "pyramid" formation – as used by ALL teams in Wedlock's day...

for the inside forwards to take up in their stride. The virtues of this through pass along the ground to the inside wing men can scarcely be over-estimated, and if done persistently and well, should bring a lot of goals to the side. And just as he moulds the

WEDLOCK – THE FIRST HERO OF BRISTOL CITY

play of the forwards, so should the centre-half marshall the defensive forces.
Because of these things, I am of opinion that other things being equal, the pivot of the team should also be the captain. From his place in the middle of the field he is able to pass the word along to his colleagues as to the best tactics to be pursued, as well as take a big part in the shaping of those tactics."

'TRIERS', TRIBUTES AND TESTIMONIALS

"The Cinderellas of Football – A Tribute to the Plodder".
Article written by Wedlock,
13 years after his retirement from the game –
published in various newspapers, including the **Mansfield Reporter,** the **Tamworth Herald,** the **Coventry Evening Telegraph** and the **Bedfordshire Times and Independent**,
during October and November 1924.

<u>"THE CINDERELLAS OF FOOTBALL –
A TRIBUTE TO THE PLODDER",</u>

<u>By William Wedlock (England and Bristol City)</u>

"This is an article in praise of the plodder, the plain workman, who in football, like in other walks of life, does not always get the honour he deserves. There are Cinderellas in professional, and amateur, football, just as there are in pantomimes. The difference is that in pantomimes the fairy godmother comes along at the right moment to cheer things up a bit. This doesn't happen so often in real life.
In practically every team there is the plodder. Very often he is given every sort of odd job there is going. He is the reliability man, the man who, when the club is in a hole, at short notice will turn out at outside right, centre forward, full back, or in goal if need be. On him the spot-light of publicity is seldom turned. He is rarely in the headlines of the newspapers. He does his job unobtrusively, but thoroughly. He doesn't know how to be spectacular, but he is always sound. Never very good, perhaps, but never very bad. If they gave medals for consistency he would

WEDLOCK – THE FIRST HERO OF BRISTOL CITY

be loaded with them.

Now and then, perhaps, some sturdy bit of tackling, or a daring save in the goalmouth, when the goalkeeper is at the other end of the goal, will earn him a modest round of applause. He is far too useful (and loyal) ever to get on the transfer list. He reads about so-and-so being transferred for £6,000 to Midchester United, but he knows that those sorts of plums are not for the likes of him. Sometimes he is even appreciated by directors, but that is not too often. As a rule he goes through life unhonoured and unsung. His colleagues generally know his true worth. They learn to lean on him for all the donkey work both in attack and defence. Where another player will stand still when he has been beaten, our plodder will wheel round and give chase. He never stands still; he is always looking for work – and it is never very hard to find work to do in a football match. Not often does he get on terms of affection with the crowd. They rarely hail him by his Christian name – the hall-mark of football popularity. To the "gallery" he remains plain Smith, Jones or Robinson. Like most of us he is only missed when he is not there. A casualty lays him aside – he gets more than his share of kicks because he is always in the thick of the fray – and then it is noticed there is something wrong with the team. Something seems to be missing.

All of you who watch professional football must be perfectly familiar with this type. Football couldn't do without him. It would never do to have eleven "flyers" in a team, and no plodder. Of course, there are super-plodders, and they occasionally get international caps. But this type is extremely rare. Ben Warren, for instance, was of the super-plodding type, and his value was

'TRIERS', TRIBUTES AND TESTIMONIALS

fully recognised. You couldn't play alongside Ben without catching something of his enthusiasm for his job, and his willingness to "pull out" to the uttermost. The fact is that the plodding type of footballer needs something distinctive about him, either in physique or appearance, to help him catch the eye. If he happens to be very big, or very little – like myself – he is half way to success. A good big fellow or a good little chap will catch the eye far more quickly on the football field than a player of exactly the same ability who is of ordinary build. A mass of vivid red hair has been known to be a useful asset for a player, whilst a bald head is another short cut to success. Have you ever stopped to reflect upon the number of successful bald-headed players there are in first-class football? Almost every-one I know is in high favour, both with his club and his public.

FASHIONS IN HAIR

Referring to hair; if some brave youth with ambitions to catch the eye were to turn up on the ground with, say, a heavy moustache or side whiskers, he would get all the publicity he seeks. It's quite instructive for us veterans to sit back and reflect how the football fashions in hair change. Gaze on the old football groups which adorn the walls in some famous club's directors' room and note the full sets of whiskers. By my day these had all vanished, but there were many fine sets of the brand of moustache generally known as "walrus". In due course these vanished too, and nowadays if a player turned out with even a "tooth brush" he would cause a mild sensation.

But this is digressing. I am not arguing that a young player should

WEDLOCK – THE FIRST HERO OF BRISTOL CITY

give up shaving as a necessary preliminary to winning international caps, but there have been cases of footballers of distinctive appearance winning fame denied to players of equal ability. There was once an Egyptian who kept his place in a first-class Midland team...

(Note, here Wedlock appears to be referring to Tawfik Abdullah, who played 11 matches for Derby County in the 1920/21 season).

...Had he been as ordinary in complexion as he was a footballer, I doubt if he would ever have risen beyond the ranks of reserves. I once knew a First Division club with a spectacular wing half-back, who was always cheered by the crowd, and who in due course was capped. He was of unusual stature.

I won't say whether he was a big or a little one, because you might guess at his identity.

On the other wing in the same half-back line was a plodder. There was no comparison in the merits of those two when it came to real value, but one got all the glory and the other - well, he just went on doing his job. In the course of time, in this case, the plodder became recognised for the sterling player he was – though he never soared to a cap – and the other player was relegated to the reserves. There is not so much "gallery play" in football of to-day as there used to be, but one sees quite a lot of it still, though of a more subtle variety. A clever footballer can play up for the plaudits of the crowd without it being apparent to any but his nearest colleagues or opponents.

I don't wish to be misunderstood. Genuine merit is more often than not recognised in the long run. What I wish to point out in this article is that I have seen many real good plodders passed

'TRIERS', TRIBUTES AND TESTIMONIALS

over when the honours have been handed around, and I felt I would like to say a word or two of encouragement to them.
I would rather have a team of genuine tryers to lead on to the field any day, than a side of brilliant stars, not all of whom were workers in the real sense of the word. It is the flyers who sometimes win matches, but they more often lose them.
To every young player going into the game I would say – cut out the fancy work and never forget that speed isn't everything".

(c. 1932)

'WEDLOCK THE ELDER'